The Transcontinental Maghreb

The Transcontinental Maghreb

FRANCOPHONE LITERATURE ACROSS THE MEDITERRANEAN

Edwige Tamalet Talbayev

FORDHAM UNIVERSITY PRESS *New York* 2017

the modern language initiative

THIS BOOK IS MADE POSSIBLE BY A COLLABORATIVE GRANT FROM THE ANDREW W. MELLON FOUNDATION.

Fordham University Press also publishes its books in a variety of electronic formats. Some content that appears in print may not be available in electronic books.

Visit us online at www.fordhampress.com.

Library of Congress Cataloging-in-Publication Data available online at http://catalog.loc.gov.

Printed in the United States of America

19 18 17 5 4 3 2 1

First edition

Pour Solan

CONTENTS

A NOTE ON TRANSLATION AND TRANSLITERATION

All unattributed translations from French, Spanish, and Arabic are mine. I used published English-language translations whenever they were available and listed them in the bibliography. I have followed a simplified version of the *International Journal of Middle East Studies* system for the transliteration of Arabic. The only diacritics used are ʿayn and hamza (the latter is dropped in initial position), respectively marked with an open and closed apostrophe. I have used French transliterations of Maghrebi proper names whenever they have become conventional in English (e.g., Mohammed Dib, Abdelkébir Khatibi, Nabile Farès). For book titles in Arabic, I have followed English capitalization rules.

The Transcontinental Maghreb

Introduction

The Transcontinental Maghreb

On El Boramar Square
Your eyes
The night filled with condor songs
Watch the crossing of silence
Pan flute, moon weighing anchor
It is a festival of moorings
A call from the Andes.

—Tahar Bekri, *Le Chant du roi errant* (The Song of the Errant King)

"On El Boramar Square." With this opaque Catalan moniker begins the twenty-seventh section of Tunisian Tahar Bekri's poetic paean to the legendary prince-poet of Arabic letters, Imru' al-Qais.[1] The phrase is accompanied by a footnote in which Bekri explains his choice of this specific Mediterranean locale: "El Boramar (Sea shore) is a small square in the Catalonian town of Collioure, where an ancient tower built by the Arabs can be found" (45).[2] This "ancient tower," renamed Torre de la Guardia, or Watchtower, after its incorporation into a sixteenth-century defensive fort on the French-Spanish border, was originally built during the Arab occupation of the town in ad 740.[3] Throughout its tumultuous history of belonging this tower embodies the dynamics of interactions and contestations underpinning the history of the Mediterranean. Collioure, a small French Catalan fishing community located a mere forty kilometers from the village where I grew up, has since gained international fame as the subject of renowned fauvist paintings by artists such as Henri Matisse and André Derain. Partaking in its own modest way in the romantic fascination exerted by the Mediterranean on artists and writers in search of rejuvenation, it has conjured a French Mediterranean redolent of Orientalism and exoticism. Dominant invocations of Collioure have situated it within a European context of humanism and artistic creativity, concurrently obscuring its trans-Mediterranean entanglements with the history of Arab incursions into Europe. It is to this past lying beyond European modernity's fascination with the primitive that Bekri's note lays claim, to a silenced past, in fact, since the official visitors' guide to the village lists conquests by the Phocaeans, the Romans, the Greeks, the Visigoths, the kings of Majorca, and the French, but never the Arabs. This legacy bears witness to the hybrid Mediterranean character of the region, revealing the multidirectional crossings of ideas, styles, religions, and thinkers that mapped out the ancient and medieval Mediterranean as a space of exchange and cross-pollination. Such a history, however, remains frustratingly peripheral, as the resistance of the Office du Tourisme of Collioure to acknowledge the Arab history of the town reveals.

This blind spot underscores the enduring authority of dominant historical framings of the Mediterranean as the cradle of civilization and the birthplace of philosophy and democracy—in a word, as the point of origin of a Europe "nationalist in form and imperialist in its reach" (Iain Chambers, *Mediterranean Crossings* 15). This disregard for the entangled origins of the Mediterranean contact zone underpins current-day definitions of Europe's southern boundaries. It has fractured the space of the sea into two supposedly incommensurable spaces and civilizational models: the northern Mediterranean, European and predominantly Christian, the object of Europe's exoticist imagination now reactivated in the lure of low-cost mass-tourism; and the southern shore, purportedly mired in Islam, backward cultural traditionalism, and gender oppression and, in the post–Arab Spring context, reluctant to implement democracy. Given the recent rekindling of age-old tensions through narratives such as Samuel Huntington's "clash of civilizations" theory or the European Union's exclusive definition of nationality and borders, this polarized reading of the Mediterranean seems promised to a prosperous future.[4]

Contrapuntally to these dichotomous narratives, other configurations have emerged that bring to light the infinite imbrications, translations, and overlaps that make the Mediterranean a key space for the study of transnational interactions and tensions. It is these alternative linkages, which stereotypical readings of the region typically obliterate, that this book is interested in retrieving. Against an embedded network of polarized reading grids (Global North vs. Global South, Europe vs. Africa, Christianity vs. Islam), the need to restore the liminal space of the Mediterranean to a place of critical prominence presses on with more urgency than ever. Critically building on early colonial framings of the Mediterranean as a "continent liquide," or "liquid continent" (Audisio), I examine what I call "the transcontinental Maghreb": the transnational deployment of the former North African colonies of Morocco, Algeria, and Tunisia within the millennia-old relation that has materially and culturally bound the region to a variety of sites throughout the broader Mediterranean. To a careful observer these connections will seem ubiquitous in the familiar material and symbolic landscapes of the Mediterranean. The traces of these exchanges are inscribed on the columns of the Punic temples in Carthage, Tunisia, and on the dilapidated façade of the Gran Teatro Cervantes in Tangier, Morocco. They infuse the Arab *muqarnas* (honeycomb ceilings) of the Cappella Palatina in the Palazzo dei Normanni in Palermo, Sicily, and the Arab architecture of the famed *mezquita* (mosque) in Cordoba, Spain. They are the product of displacement along trade routes and of waves of conquests predating European colonialism, which have made the Maghreb a key site of cultural and linguistic syncretism—the invasions led by the Phoenicians (eighth century bc), the Romans (ad 146), the Vandals (ad 429), the Byzantines (ad 533), the Arabs (ad 647), and the Ottomans (sixteenth century), as well as the various Jewish diasporas, starting with the destruction of the first Temple in Jerusalem in 586 bc and culminating in the expulsion of Andalusian Jews from Spain in the wake of the Reconquista in 1492. These material remains braid an alternative narrative anchored in cultural and artistic syncretic practices, which has left its imprimatur on Maghrebi self-perceptions and identifications. Indeed North African authors and critics have emphasized the plural, polyphonic quality of the region's past, revealing alternative, margin-to-margin itineraries that have displaced the cultural primacy of the French metropole.

I aim to retrieve literary engagements with these alternative histories of mobility and contact that map out the Mediterranean not only in terms of domination and antagonism (through patterns of European colonialism or contemporary labor migration) but also as a site of reciprocal exchanges and interconnections. I endeavor to reveal the ever-changing dynamics underpinning the Mediterranean, which has been perpetually reinvented as a space of mobility and creativity through its multiple human and cultural incarnations. My hypothesis is that this complex history has been appropriated throughout the corpus of Maghrebi literature since its early days in the late nineteenth century and that it has fostered the emergence of a transnational Mediterranean consciousness across ethnic and confessional lines. Both historically verified and powerfully mythicized, this ethos has been eager to lay claim to a sedimented identity stretching beyond the Arab, Amazigh, Jewish, and French cultures forced together by colonialism. Doing so, it has served to amend the parameters of the subject's engagement with the nation and with its restricted models of social agency and collectivity. In keeping with the plurilingualism induced by a Mediterranean framework, I rest my argument on an examination of the corpus of Maghrebi texts written in French from the late 1890s to the present, with incursions into texts composed in Arabic and Spanish (respectively, the language of Maghrebi nationalism and nation-building, and the second colonial language of the Maghreb). My focus is on texts that reach across the Mediterranean to more than one geographic or imagined site of contact—whether explicitly or implicitly, materially or symbolically—to shed light on the central role played by the space of the sea in the elaboration of cultural narratives before and after independence.

From its inception, the field of Francophone postcolonial studies has sought to bring to light the intrinsic plurality of the Maghrebi corpus that key writers such as Abdelkébir Khatibi had emphasized (see, chronologically, Sellin and Jaouad; Woodhull, *Transfigurations*; Donadey, *Recasting Postcolonialism*; Rosello, *France and the Maghreb*; Rice, *Time Signatures*; Graebner, *History's Place*, among others). In addition the constitutive significance of the twin concepts of exile and nomadism to Maghrebi criticism testifies to the discipline's early interest in unsettling national boundaries and linguistic canons (Lionnet and Scharfman; Orlando, *Nomadic Voices*; Laroussi and Miller; Bensmaïa, *Experimental Nations*). Such insights were extended by interventions into the field of Beur literature (the writing of second-generation North African immigrants to France), such as Alec Hargreaves's pioneering work, whose transnationalism shed light on national diversity and multiculturalism within the European metropole. In addition, recent work in Francophone studies has complicated the dominant idea that the literature of Morocco, Algeria, and Tunisia is to be primarily construed in relation to the former colonial metropole or to an imaginary Arab nation (Talbayev, "Between Nostalgia and Desire"; Abderrezak, "Burning the Sea"; Esposito et al.; Esposito; Segarra, "Migrant Literature"; Van der Poel, "Unlike[ly] Home[s]"). Building on this significant body of criticism, I show that the Mediterranean serves as a nuanced framework for sustained reflection on the Maghreb's multiple inscriptions into global modernity, both within the bounds of postcolonial nationalism and, beyond, in relation to the global. It is only by recovering these alternative, full histories that we can successfully uncouple the Maghreb from conventional North-South binary readings of the Mediterranean region. Destabilizing the polarized geographies of power embedded in those configurations, the Mediterranean approach delineated in these pages calls into question restrictive definitions of identity throughout Europe and the Arab world. It also excavates multiple North-South and South-South interactions, an essential adjustment in light of rising xenophobia in Europe and of Islamic fundamentalism globally.

This Mediterranean heritage is the undeniable product of the specific course of Maghrebi history. Yet it is also a strategically selective reading of the region's complex palimpsest of cultures. The choice to reclaim the Mediterranean substrate of Maghrebi culture rather than its Amazigh, African, or Jewish traditions is deliberate, and it certainly should not be downplayed as a natural development. At different times of crisis, when colonial power or models of postcolonial statehood showed their intrinsic limits, many writers delineated a Mediterranean frame of reference as a natural alternative. They often problematically neglected other affiliations to the benefit of a shared Mediterranean ethos that they considered to be sufficiently self-evident to exclude the need for argument. Most colonial mobilizations of a Mediterranean "race" or *pays* (country), such as those of Louis Bertrand, Gabriel Audisio, and Albert Camus discussed in chapter 1, but also the uncritical academic accounts that have accompanied them, sometimes to the present, are cases in point. This study, however, shuns such naturalizing readings and instead approaches the Mediterranean configurations that emerge in this corpus in their full idiosyncrasy and occasional incongruity. It reveals their undeniable partiality and rigorously probes their blind spots and inevitable entanglements with prevalent reading grids resting on more dominant histories, such as Arab nationalism or the ever-alluring postcolonial relation to France. Perpetually navigating the shifting sands of transnational interaction in the Mediterranean contact zone, the Mediterranean-infused Maghreb I propose helps us ponder the endless renegotiation of the fraught (and yet inescapable) relation between nation and transnation. Doing so also affords new insight into some of the most crucial critical perspectives undergirding the study of Maghrebi literature—most notably the issue of nomadism, the valence of myth in identity discourse, the role of utopia, and the potential and limits of critical melancholia in the wake of conflict and violence. These far-reaching amendments to the way we read both the Maghreb and the Mediterranean help us rethink not just the topographical space of the sea, the identities it produced, and the way it shaped historical dynamics (globalization, imperialism, decolonization, and nationalism) but also the very nature of postcolonial histories and identities along its shores.

One of the core insights of this book is that this mythicized Mediterranean identification ties in to broader social and political goals. It must be read across time in light of the underlying ideological stakes of marking the Maghreb with the seal of the sea. Providing a fully rounded perspective on this Mediterranean stance induces a number of interrogations: How does this transregional configuration interact (or conflict) with the imperatives of anticolonialism and nation-building? With the appropriation of an Arabo-Islamic heritage conceived as the path to authenticity? Or even with the issue of multiculturalism and ethnic plurality with which it overlaps so meaningfully?

TRANSCONTINENTAL HISTORIES AND OTHER-THOUGHT

With its long-standing history of contact and connectivity, the mediating surface of the sea forces us to rethink notions of reciprocity beyond the binary structures inherited from the past. The complex weave of embedded histories, encounters and conquests, ranging from peaceful cohabitation to brutal incursions and annexations, have left their trace on the Mediterranean region. They have fostered unique cultural experiences marked by interpenetration rather than mere superposition. Redefining the Maghreb along new routes and roots entails doing justice to the many forms of cultural imbrication and intermingling that have been a historical reality in the region, both before and during the years of French colonialism. Abdelkébir Khatibi's *Maghreb Pluriel* (Plural Maghreb) powerfully testifies to the intrinsic plurality of Maghrebi culture, rejecting the thrall of hegemonic metaphysical discourses on identity to the benefit of a "'third way' of thinking, speaking, and acting on a planetary scale" (Woodhull, "Postcolonial Thought" 213). As Woodhull convincingly argues, Khatibi's seminal text provides a compelling model for "the best recent works [on North African identity and culture that seek to] eschew the notion of a pre-colonial Maghrebian cultural essence at the same time as they chart a new historical course that carries reflection beyond the quest for national identity" (213). Jocelyne Dakhlia's illuminating work on the precolonial lingua franca used as a common language of communication among western Mediterranean communities gives the idea of a Mediterranean Maghreb historical density.[5] Revealing a history of contact that preceded the French conquest, Dakhlia hypothesizes a Mediterranean lingua franca mixing French, Spanish, Turkish, Italian, Arabic, Portuguese, and Amazigh languages that existed until the mid-nineteenth century. Stemming from the liminal space between two geopolitical entities, this lingua franca aspired to the condition of neutrality. It functioned as an enabler of contact but also as a marker of disjunction between two well-demarcated and eventually incommensurable idioms. If its very existence belied any real fusion of the two logics it connected, the lingua franca bespoke a certain degree of continuity or, in Dakhlia's words, a "continuum" (*Lingua Franca* 9) between cultural and structural systems on either side of the Mediterranean. It enacted interactions on multiple levels and fostered shared modes of expression and representation. Despite its ultimate demise, this dynamic persisted throughout most of the early modern and modern periods, and it ensured a modus vivendi between communities entangled in uneven, complex relationships. Yet equality was far from the norm, even on this linguistic level. Debating the issue of labels when studying mixed languages, Jean-Marie Klinkenberg points out that the structure of a lingua franca rarely displays equity between the two sources. Although created in response to the need for a third language that would give neither party the linguistic advantage, pidgins always lean toward one of the two linguistic logics (73). Unsurprisingly the lingua franca identified by Dakhlia heavily borrows from the Romance languages present on Maghrebi soil (Spanish, Italian, and French), an imbalance also suffusing its later incarnations under French colonialism, such as early twentieth-century *pataouète* in Algiers.[6] However, its pervasive presence, as well as the echo it found in Maghrebi imaginaries, testifies to the enduring attractiveness of moments of syncretism and interaction born of Mediterranean connectivity. Thus a cognate form of plurilingualism born of modern Mediterranean migrations still subsists in the corpus of Jewish Maghrebi writing in French, forming a "cosmopolitanism from below" (Watson 126), possibly the latest incarnation of Dakhlia's western Mediterranean lingua franca.[7]

Tracing this migratory dynamic to the contemporary period, recent work on diasporic Maghrebi literature has put a spotlight on the existence of a plurilingual body of texts linked to the Maghreb through their place of publication or the provenance of its authors. Its composition in various European languages defies the conventional breakdown of Maghrebi literature into two main linguistic traditions (French and Arabic) and disciplinary logics (Francophone studies and Arabic literature).[8] These texts illuminate other trajectories cross-cutting the usual hegemonic axes of empire and exploitation (the Maghreb in its conflicting relationship to the West) to deploy the Maghrebi text across a more capacious cultural and linguistic cartography. These new plurilingual constellations link together literary texts, theoretical paradigms, and critical traditions dispersed across continents and languages and afford a comparative reading of diverse literacies. Such texts include the Italian novels of the Algerian Amara Lakhous, often composed alongside Arabic versions (*Scontro di civiltà per un ascensore a Piazza Vittorio* [Clash of Civilizations over an Elevator in Piazza Vittorio] and *Divorzio all'islamica a Viale Marconi* [Divorce Islamic Style]), as well as other diasporic productions whose trajectory often exceeds the geographic confines of the Mediterranean: the Moroccan Fouad Laroui's recent Dutch collections of poems following his relocation to Amsterdam, *Verbannen Woorden* (Forbidden Words) and *Hollandse Woorden* (Dutch Words), and the Moroccan Spanish Najat El Hachmi's *L'Últim Patriarca* (The Last Patriarch), which won the prestigious Ramon Llull literary prize of Catalan letters.[9]

The uncanny transnational histories perceptible in these texts flag the Maghreb's deep imbrication in a globalized, transnational topography. From the early days of Maghrebi literature major writers such as Assia Djebar, Nabile Farès, and Tahar Ben Jelloun have deconstructed the France–North Africa dyad in their writings, striving to multiply connections between Maghrebi culture as a whole and other Mediterranean traditions (see Segarra, *Nouvelles romancières francophones*; Woodhull, "Postcolonial Thought"; Bensmaïa, "Media-terranean"). More recently pioneering works such as Jean-Pierre Lledo's film *Algérie: Histoires à ne pas dire* (Algeria: Stories Not to Be Told), Yahia Belaskri's novel *Une longue nuit d'absence* (A Long Night of Absence), and Cristián Ricci's research on Spanish-language Moroccan literature have gone a long way toward amending the Maghreb's linguistic map. They have engaged in a thorough and systematic study of the pockets of linguistic plurality that have historically survived the imposition of French: Spanish in northern Morocco and western Algeria, English in Tangier, Italian in Tunisia. Reaching outward to other translinguistic configurations of the Maghreb sheds light on new forms of subjectivities beyond the straitjacket of postcolonial identity politics and their reifying logic. In Woodhull's words, it also encourages "the cultivation of cosmopolitan forms of 'hospitality' that allow an array of languages, cultures and histories to intermingle and to speak through one another without any one of them silencing or effacing the other" ("Postcolonial Thought" 213).

It is with this meaningful history of contact in mind that Khatibi tackles the momentous task of decolonizing Maghrebi thought.[10] In its consideration of linguistic diversity in North Africa, his influential *Maghreb Pluriel* moves away from both colonial and Arab Islamic nationalist frameworks to emphasize the residual Mediterranean cultural elements underlying Maghrebi culture. Bringing to the fore the distinctive historical intermingling of influences in the area, Khatibi identifies "a mosaic of *interlangues* between the oral and the written, between the national and the extranational or the transnational" (qtd. in Woodhull, *Transfigurations* x). Through his concept of *bi-langue* (bilanguage) in *Amour bilingue* (Bilingual Love), Khatibi shifts the focus onto the sites of incommensurability—and therefore hospitality—intrinsic to every language, situating his bilingual linguistic practice in "the space between two exteriorities" (Khatibi, "Diglossia" 158). In his own words, to think through *bi-langue* is "to enter into the telling of forgetting and of anamnesis. Henceforth, 'I am an/other' i[s] an idiom that I owe it to myself to invent—a limit experience inherent in this situation" (158).

For Khatibi the rigid opposition between colonial Western influence and Arab Islamic tradition takes a backseat to the intrinsic instability of Maghrebi identity, which the critic locates in the intersection of several distinct traditions. Perceptible in the Maghreb's enduring linguistic diversity, this fluctuating principle also animates his perception of postcolonial subjectivity. Positing transnationalism as the prerequisite to any successful decolonizing practice, Khatibi confounds identity discourses resting on absolutes, such as normative theologies or ideological narratives. "An other-thought, maybe an unprecedented way of thinking difference": such is the avowed aim of Khatibi's reflection ("Pensée-Autre" 21).[11] Through it the thinker reaffirms the importance of an identitarian posture that would be both

character—here to be understood etymologically as the sea between the lands, the fluid site bordering two rooted, exiguous spaces and progressively eroding their integrity. It is an intermediate space restored to its historical relationality, "resonat[ing] in its plurality (linguistic, cultural, political)," a Maghreb "rethought, decentered, subverted" (26).[20] From this fertile soil sprouts the "intractable difference" postulated by Khatibi, a process mediating the radical critique of this double philosophical legacy but also the Maghreb's indispensable relation to alterity in all forms. Redefined along the lines of a fundamental coextensivity with the Mediterranean, Khatibi's Maghreb draws its connective power from its marginal centrality, gaining a point of entry into the great dynamic of global modernity in the process.

WHERE IS THE MEDITERRANEAN?

Dealing with the space of the Mediterranean involves positing a few fundamental difficulties and paradoxes. Posited as a hypothesis more than an assertive claim, the very notion of "the Mediterranean" is more akin to a speech act than a secure reality. Despite its resistance to fixed determination, the category remains remarkably persistent, which the recent resurgence of Braudel-inspired histories of the Mediterranean in the past decade can only verify. In spite of its de facto politicization as an identity marker by self-proclaimed "Mediterraneans" eager to distance themselves from other forms of identity politics, it nevertheless endures as a space marked by "intellectual fuzziness . . . [a] propensity to generate cultural stereotypes, and . . . roots in colonial history" (Dobie 389). Yet, for all intents and purposes, it remains a discursive space marked with fluid cadences and contested forms of belonging, a site in which conflicting visions of modernity and identity come to clash or be negotiated.

The Mediterranean construct born of the budding field of Mediterranean studies can be a theoretical model, a source of aesthetics, and a set of tools to dismantle some of the most entrenched misconceptions regarding local and global identities. The corpus of criticism it has generated has striven to shift critical attention from the localized space of the shore to the embracing site of the sea. A milestone in the development of historical and anthropological conceptions of the sea, the concept of Mediterraneanism has highlighted the existence of "distinctive characteristics which the cultures of the Mediterranean have, or have had, in common" (Harris 1). Encouraging comparison across vast swaths of space and time, critical configurations of the region in the disciplines of history and anthropology have fruitfully brought to light the presence of common denominators underlying the Mediterranean. These ubiquitous features, in turn, have warranted a regional diachronic reading of local history. Excavating millennia-old interactions at the micro level (what Peregrine Horden and Nicholas Purcell have dubbed "connectivity" [*The Corrupting Sea* 123]), this approach has striven to move the focus away from the myriad local histories unfolding across the Mediterranean's coastlands to bring the ever-shifting space of the sea as a principle of integration into relief.

The adjective *Mediterranean* can be found in French texts and dictionaries as early as the sixteenth century, but it is only in the eighteenth century that the lexeme appeared in nominal form in the *Encyclopedia* and the Trévoux dictionary (Fabre, "La France et la Méditerranée" 20). Ancient Mediterranean thought stopped short of reading the space of the sea as a united space. If a sense of unity pervaded early accounts of the Mediterranean (Plato's *Phaedo* comes to mind, with its vibrant "frogs around a pond" metaphor), the sea was primarily construed as a maritime site devoid of a regional identity (Horden and Purcell, "The Mediterranean" 735–36). Of greater importance to the ancient world was the examination of the societies that had settled on the shores. The conceptual recalibration of the Mediterranean from a maritime space to a cohesive object of study coincided with the rise of imperialism in the nineteenth century. Coined through historical, geographical, and political lexicons, the concept developed in lockstep with a complex web of geopolitical imperatives (how to extend European domination over the Arab world) and knowledge taxonomies (how to catalogue and discipline an expansive "Orient"). A semantic extension of boilerplate Orientalism, this new focus on the Mediterranean supplied a new reading grid for cultural enterprises subservient to the establishment of Europe's imperial power throughout the region (Yashin; Wick).

As Horden and Purcell have convincingly argued, "the connection between scientific knowledge and imperialism in the Mediterranean is . . . clearest in the French case" ("The Mediterranean" 728). Bringing his ancestor's 1798 conquest of Egypt to full geopolitical and theoretical fruition, Napoleon III toyed with the notion of a Mediterranean Arab empire centered on France. Its munificence was meant to draw the nations of the Middle East to the metropolitan center and to make France the leader of both the Christian and the

Islamic worlds (Ouerdane 32–33). In the wake of this openly civilizing politics, less abrasive intellectual projects pursued the subjugation of the Arab world through an indirect dynamics of "seduction" (Tageldin). Aiming to reduce the age-old tensions between Christianity and Islam dating from the Crusades, the Saint-Simonians' modernist utopia envisioned the relation between Orient and Occident as a mutually beneficial collaboration. The Saint-Simonians' humanistic vision championed an industrial, secular form of modernity based on a notion of progress that would develop through an East-West partnership. Purporting to downplay the superiority of Western civilization over the Orient, it emphasized the integration of both worlds into a Mediterranean civilization exceeding its Greco-Latin heritage (Temime; Figeac). Yet despite its seductive promise of egalitarian association (especially in the work of Émile Barrault) and its undeniable echo in the Arab world (particularly in Egypt under Muhammad Ali), this utopian concept of a common civilization ultimately gave in to the irresistible pull of Western supremacy. Much like the literary utopias that followed it in the colonial Maghreb in the 1930s, the project's inability to think modernity beyond the centrality of Europe spelled its eventual ineffectuality. With the polarizing dynamic of colonialism under way, the equal partnership of East and West in the Mediterranean remained an elusive hope.

The founding study at the source of Mediterranean studies, Fernand Braudel's 1949 *The Mediterranean and the Mediterranean World in the Age of Philip II*, identified a distinctive Mediterranean marked by ubiquitous traits on all shores and islands of the sea, the "local, permanent, unchanging and much repeated features which are the 'constants' of Mediterranean history. . . . [They express the region's] historical or rather timeless character" (1239). The influence of the *Annales* school on Braudel's work ensured that several layers of history would be taken into consideration to form a *histoire totale*—a *longue durée* history based on the consideration of environmental determinism ("a history in which all change is slow, a history of constant repetition, ever-recurring cycles" [20]), social history (the history of groups, including economic systems, societies, states, and warfare), and *histoire événementielle* (dates, historical trivia, and heroes), each layer the bedrock of the following one (20–21). In Braudel's reading the superimposition of all three facets of historical time delineates the Mediterranean as a space of unity and as a site of dissonance reverberating with the proverbial "many voices" of the sea, the latter necessarily subdued to the benefit of the former, since "the essential task before us is to measure the . . . coherence of [this] history, the extent to which the movement of boats, pack animals, vehicles and people themselves makes the Mediterranean a unit and gives it a certain uniformity in spite of local resistance" (277). While Braudel gives "local resistance," or, to put it more clearly, human agency, short shrift, his focus on ahistorical "constants" makes his *longue durée* narrative of imperceptible change look exceptionally close to a form of stasis. Because "the long run always wins in the end" (1244), individual influence fades, subsumed within wider impersonal dynamics. The subject remains "imprisoned within a destiny in which he himself has little hand, fixed in a landscape in which the infinite perspectives of the long term stretch into the distance both behind him and before" (1214).

Braudel's unified North African–southern European region exhibits the same "cultural unity of France's trans-Mediterranean empire" that colonial thinking emphasized (Dobie 391). If read in a colonial light, as Madeleine Dobie suggests, Braudel's paradigm offers disquieting parallels with colonial cultural constructs prevalent in French Algeria in the first half of the twentieth century.[21] Braudel's approach reverberates in significant ways with Algérianiste ruminations over a Latin bedrock of Maghrebi identity, as well as Audisio's concept of an eternal Mediterranean marked by conquests and colonialism. This comparative reading sheds more ambiguous light on his steadfast insistence on the many commonalities uniting the northern and southern shores of the sea into a single entity. Braudel's obsolete interest for the enduring persistence of Latin in Gafsa (Tunisia) until the mid-twelfth century could simply be construed as evidence of his "slow change" argument. Yet if read alongside his characterization of the unchanging way of life permeating the fiction of Audisio as a glorified, imagined antiquity of heroism and Greek myth, Braudel's profound investment in a certain form of colonial modernity is undeniable. This is only confirmed by his more reluctant engagement with Islam, presented as an antithesis to his Western-inspired Mediterranean (Armstrong; Liauzu, "La Méditerranée selon Fernand Braudel"). As Claudio Fogu explains in the wake of Jacques Rancière, Braudel's introduction of the "geographization of historical time" had the distinct effect of obviating the centrality of politics and historical agency in the rise of modern historiography (3). Attendant to this shift is the disdain for the subject's ability to change his circumstances or to lay claim to a more equitable form of governance. In the days of rising nationalist aspirations in Algeria and transnationally (the North African Star nationalist party was founded in Paris by Algerian exiles in 1926), Braudel's disregard is particularly striking, although not altogether surprising.[22] His vision was ultimately very much a product of its time.

More enlightening for present scholarship, Horden and Purcell's magisterial *The Corrupting Sea* offers a continuation of the Braudelian framework proposing to reach an "understanding of the whole environment" as "the product of a complex interaction of human and physical factors, not simply a material backdrop or a set of immutable constraints" (10). Setting out to restore the thwarted human dimension of the French historian's account, their argument defines the Mediterranean anew along the axes of reciprocal exchange and interrelations. In turn their focus on idiosyncrasies brings out the fractal nature of the Mediterranean, reconfiguring it as a key space of divergences, oppositions, and diffractions embedded in microregional specificities. With that gesture their model successfully fosters a different mode of representation based on local sociocultural elements, whose heterogeneity becomes a productive tenet of their Mediterranean approach. Their book takes as its focal point the "human geography" of the sea (2) in its dynamic aspect. Marked by countless crossings and invasions to the detriment of a stable, fixed geography, "the region's unity and distinctiveness must be conceived in relative, not absolute, terms: neat frontiers, enclosing blatant uniformities, are hardly to be expected" (487). Building from the notion of perpetual movement and instability rather than great historical breaks and dramatic evolutions, their book productively showcases inconspicuous small-scale dynamics over grandiose visions of historical unfolding. Their critique of a Mediterraneanist approach dispels the many forms of mystification suffusing the region. They propose to accomplish a "defamiliarization" of the locale through the use of two embedded concepts: microecologies and connectivity. Their "microecological investigations" (2) are interested in the history *of* the Mediterranean (the region's idiosyncratic history from a political, religious, social, and economic point of view), as opposed to histories *in* the Mediterranean (the local rendition of hegemonic global histories). *Connectivity* refers to "the various ways in which microregions cohere, both internally and also with one another, in aggregates that may range in size from small clusters to something approaching the entire

Mediterranean" (123). Their approach throws light on the fluidity and modularity of the multiple connections tying together the shores of the sea. Most of all it opens the door to a consideration of the Mediterranean "in terms of the unpredictable, the variable, and, above all, the local" (13).[23]

Offering a contrapuntal take on Horden and Purcell's concept of connectivity, recent criticism centered on bodies of water—what some, like Iain Chambers, have dubbed "maritime criticism" in the context of modernity's unfolding—has attempted to characterize the specificities of the Mediterranean in fruitful contrast to other aqueous logics.[24] In *Poetics of Relation*, Édouard Glissant proposes that "the Mediterranean . . . is an inner sea surrounded by lands, a sea that concentrates (in Greek, Hebrew, and Latin antiquity and later in the emergence of Islam, imposing the thought of the One) [while] the Caribbean is, in contrast, a sea that explodes the scattered lands into an arc. A sea that diffracts" (33). Used as a foil to set in relief the creolization intrinsic to the dispersed Caribbean space, Glissant's Mediterranean reverberates with Old World atavism. Construed as the cradle of civilizations and monotheism, his Mediterranean reigns supreme as a totalizing, homogeneous force uniting its shores. Yet, as Mireille Rosello has noted in recent reflections on seascapes, this vision is blatantly oblivious to the actual creolization that left its mark on Mediterranean cities ("Becoming UnDutch"), and the continuities between the two maritime bodies are in fact more prevalent than Glissant intimates. A consideration of some seminal reckonings of Caribbean identity proves Rosello's point further. Thus the Cuban novelist Alejo Carpentier coined the concept of a "New World Mediterranean" in relation to Haiti, referring to a long-lost time of Mediterranean existence whose reliance on the magical and the marvelous was to be resuscitated in the Caribbean in the form of *real maravilloso* (Dash 90).[25] In turn cradle of civilization, amniotic space, and "original womb" (Loichot 43), the Mediterranean crystallizes into a "matrix of values on which the identity of American otherness could be based" (Dash 90). In fact this transposability of the Mediterranean model stretches far beyond the transcolonial connection with the Caribbean. Recent proponents of "thalassology" (Horden and Purcell, "The Mediterranean") have capitalized on the comparatism intrinsic to the regional model, mostly on account of its rich trade networks. Chief among them, the Mediterranean historian David Abulafia reports that the connective quality of the sea makes it an appropriate model to apply to contexts as variegated as the Baltic "Mediterranean of the North," the "Atlantic Mediterranean" (the medieval period of explorations of the eastern Atlantic that predates the beginning of a properly Atlantic historiography), the eastern European "sub-Mediterranean" Adriatic, Aegean, and Black seas, but also the "Japanese Mediterranean" and the "Indian Ocean Mediterranean" (64–67).

In contrast with this sea-centered scholarship, my transcontinental model eschews an emphasis on the Mediterranean as a body of water to address the potential and limitations of Mediterranean models of critical localism anchored in the material specificities of postcolonial spaces. Ian Morris's concept of "Mediterraneization" provides a useful tool to think the shuttling between the local and wider-reaching paradigms. His focus on Mediterraneization as a process over static forms of Mediterraneanism does justice both to the perpetual fluctuation of the Mediterranean as method and to the specific set of challenges faced by the postcolonial Maghreb. Responding to Horden and Purcell's premise, Morris reads their interconnected paradigm as a productive shorthand to address the multiple forms of unevenness triggered by globalization. Considering Mediterranean belonging as a variable spectrum among other configurations implies "foregrounding change through time, different analytical scales, and tensions and conflicts" (Morris 33). Anchored in the general disciplinary shift toward globalization, this socially conscious take on connectivity accentuates fluidity and incompleteness. It also advocates for accrued attention to be paid to the human aftermath of globalism, which Morris defines as "conflict, inequality, and social dislocations . . . class [and] gender" (42). By emphasizing a subjective scale of action and a bounded temporal frame, Morris's model engages individual sites. He convincingly argues, "The Mediterranean may have been very open, but in other times and places large institutions and stable structures mattered more" (43). In light of these resilient structures it is crucial to attend simultaneously to the destabilizing potential of Mediterranean fluidity and the very real subordinating forces that this fluidity aims to confound—forces such as the persistence of global inequalities, racism, and neocolonialism that critical adjustments toward deterritorialization do not simply eliminate. As Woodhull insightfully remarks, if nomadic forms of meaning have introduced semantic variability at the core of key concepts, "the struggles over meanings, as well as struggles over the processes by which meanings are raveled and unraveled, are clearly situated within a national territory still deeply marked by the legacy of colonialism" (*Transfigurations* 122–23). A reflection on the subversive potential of the Mediterranean cannot sidestep the political imperatives pertaining to the context of the Maghrebi postcolonies and the strong need to advocate for more democratic politics.

On account of the contradictory nature of the Mediterranean concept on which it rests (the Mediterranean as a principle of dispersion *and* connectivity), the Maghreb that I invoke forms a sedimented site open onto the world, attentive to the fluid reroutings mediated by transnational paradigms and respectful of the region's historical specificity. Reading the Mediterranean transcontinentally—that is, in its intricate relation to the historically grounded, relatively bounded space of the Maghreb—provides the labile Mediterranean concept with new coordinates. Against the grain of Horden and Purcell's refusal to envision a distinct Mediterranean history past the end of the early modern world, I support Naor Ben-Yehoyada's plea for the theorization of a modern Mediterranean that would exist in its own right beyond the global narratives at work in the region. My historically situated model brings the Maghreb's vernacular specificity to bear on the diffuse paradigm of Mediterranean studies. It affords precise examinations of engagements with (and resistance to) the grand narrative of modernity, which has been negotiated transnationally in the postcolonial Maghreb in relation to questions of collective identity and the building of social consensus. If one is to follow Khatibi's admonitions, such an endeavor can only unfold from the recognition and durable negotiation of the Maghreb's colonial legacy.

THINKING TRANSCONTINENTALLY

The Mediterranean constitutes an "intermediate world between factual discourse and fictional discourse," the site of what Paul Ricoeur has identified as a "chiasmus between history and fiction" (qtd. in Fabre, "La France et la Méditerranée" 17). Reading the Maghreb in a transcontinental model implies considering transverse connections crisscrossing the Mediterranean alongside the more prominent North-South axes of integration and exclusion. In dialogue with recent works on a "Mediterranean alternative" confounding the exclusive epistemologies of Eurocentric modernity (Cassano, *Il Pensiero meridiano*; Iain Chambers, *Mediterranean Crossings*; Giaccaria and Minca), my book retrieves silenced histories contrapuntal to these inescapable geographies of power. Iain Chambers casts the Mediterranean as a site of "repressed alterity *within* modernity . . . a line of flight into another unauthorised critical space . . . a radical revaluation of the very processes and powers that have led to its contemporary subordination, marginalisation and definition" ("A Fluid Archive" 13). Building on Chambers's argument, Claudia Esposito reads the space of the sea as a pure literary trope exceeding the geographical limits of its historical realization. Beyond essentializing historical and anthropological constructions, her alternative cultural and aesthetic reading of the Mediterranean fruitfully delineates a space of infinite translations and hybridity, where rigid theoretical binaries deployed around aesthetic lines are contested. It is the domain of the "Mediterranean lyric," a "literary aesthetic of persistent deferral (translation) and referral (intertextuality), of untimeliness and anachronicity" (Elhariry). Whereas a focus on the colonial encounter and its postcolonial legacy encourages a reading marked by a dual logic of belonging and expression, the dissemination of the Maghrebi text across Mediterranean languages and sites forces us to rethink the very nature and limits of the corpus.

In light of the many unlikely encounters and indirect trajectories along which the Maghrebi corpus has developed, the need is pressing to identify more adequate ways to let the transnational world weigh in on our critical practices. Following more relational routes and suggesting reading protocols that can embrace the becoming global of this literature, the transcontinental Maghreb delineated in these pages is one such path. Anchoring my reflection in this trans-Mediterranean web of cultural and political struggle dismantles restrictive Maghrebi ideological outlines born of binary anticolonial and nationalist storylines. Tracing alternative readings and detours, I spell out their multiple points of engagement with (and rewriting of) modernity on various scales, from national through nation-building to regional and global. Recasting the space of the sea as *pontos*, in its fruitful polysemy as both sea and bridge, suggests an emphasis on connectivity, not just as direct connection between two localized spaces but as disorderly "criss-crossing . . . [a] multifarious, unscripted passage that fluidly brings disparate elements into contact along uncharted routes" (Talbayev, "Mediterranean Criss-Crossings" 70). This dispersion also calls for a reconsideration of the interpretive processes at the core of our critical practice. Implicitly such an approach touches on issues of comparatism in the layered context of global language politics (Apter, "Je ne crois pas beaucoup").

Beyond that it requires a more ethically engaged hermeneutic practice that would do justice to the stakes of transnational forms of writing and eschew the danger of a seductive globalist framework resting on homogenizing or differential logics. For considering the Maghreb transcontinentally implies looking beneath the surface of the plurality that these deterritorialized identitarian constructs invoke both within and against the framework of the nation. It highlights the need to problematize the reclaiming of "a right to difference" predicated on the assumption of romanticized, oppositional minoritarian positions supposedly immune from co-optations and hegemonic influences, a gesture that Khatibi himself calls "naïve" (qtd. in Esposito xiv). The challenge lies in envisioning a transcultural, relational, and intersectional critical practice attentive to the legacies of colonialism and dedicated to thinking its way beyond it.

This book's transnational, plurilingual methodology is intertwined with other long-established frameworks, whether they read the Maghreb locally (in relation to nationalism or the former metropole) or transnationally (in relation to pan-Arabism, diasporic Amazigh identity, or in an African perspective, for instance).[26] Among them the framework of Francophone postcolonial studies holds a central place for its continued usefulness as the linchpin for nuanced perspectives on the classification and interpretation of those texts. The transnationalism that it has fostered has brought along new literacies and margin-to-margin intersections undercutting vertical axes of postcolonial domination. It has enacted an indispensable *mise en relation* of the corpus of postcolonial literatures in French across geographic and contextual divides. Developing key connections along lateral axes in a transcolonial perspective, it has brought into contact disparate sites through comparative studies of empire.[27] For this reason the unity of the French colonial experience, like the use of Arabic in its many ramifications, remains a significant axis of analysis. Besides, its historical grounding in the aftermath of colonialism can be a fulcrum with which to pry open residual structures of hegemony and inequality born of this and other histories of domination. My transcontinental approach is therefore indebted to the Francophone and Arabic linguistic traditions and literary heritages that have substantially contributed to its establishment of a properly Maghrebi corpus of literature endowed with critical visibility.

Yet a careful critic should keep in mind that other configurations of power exist, both locally and transnationally, once one looks beyond the formalized hegemony of empire and its "infinite aftermath" (Ahmad 281). Speaking of the plurilingual Caribbean, Charles Forsdick and David Murphy offer cautionary words that find particular resonance in the context of the Maghreb: "Much scholarship on the Caribbean archipelago . . . has tended to be produced according to the dominant languages spoken within the region, with the result that a polyglossic, pan-Caribbean space is fragmented into smaller spaces still defined along transatlantic axes in relation to their former colonial occupiers" (12). Accordingly they warn against a practice where "parallelism might be suggested where in fact comparatism is essential" (12). Recent developments in Francophone studies have investigated possible global reconfigurations of critical methodologies that would open the concept of *francophonie* to insertion into a world literature system. It is only by showing sensitivity to the "multiplicity of possible meanings and idioms, each related to other local vernaculars that irrigate, destabilize, or complicate it," that *francophonie* can aspire to a truly global existence (Lionnet, "Universalism and Francophonie" 217–18). Recent efforts in both Francophone and Arabic studies to deploy the main paradigms of reference on a planetary scale have revealed a higher awareness of the global than was ever the case. The 2007 "Pour une 'littérature-monde' en français" manifesto, paralleled in Arabic studies by pressing calls to rethink the Arabic novel as global, are two prime attempts to further incorporate the local and the world beyond it.[28] Aiming to integrate the central corpus of French literature with its Francophone margins, the *littérature-monde* manifesto proposed to supplant Eurocentric models through an equalizing transnational gesture. Yet, as Christopher L. Miller has pointed out, the foundational monolingualism of their paradigm stands in sharp contradiction to their global aspirations, while their ambition to discount the relevance of the colonial experience does away with a crucial conceptual tool: "Declaring [*francophonie*] obsolete and replacing it with a universal *littérature-monde* will *not* provide us any new or more accurate way with which to describe the tensions between margin and center that will surely linger. . . . In fact, it could do the opposite by depriving us of an unpleasant but all too real analytical binarism" ("The Theory and Pedagogy" 38–39).

Lionnet and Shih's concept of "minor transnationalism" retains more potential. Fruitfully disentangling transnationalism from the hegemonic logic of globalization, the two critics redefine it as "a space of exchange and participation, wherever processes of hybridization occur and where it is still possible for cultures to be produced and performed without necessary mediation by the center" (5). This dynamic is freed from "the binary of the local and the global," which stretches over "national, local, or global spaces across different and multiple spatialities and temporalities" (6). Lionnet and Shih rightly uncouple their concept of the transnational from vertical models of opposition and assimilation, whereby identity is primarily a function of the group's ability to successfully engage with majority cultures. In addition they warn against the temptation to romanticize the local as a site of unadulterated, intractable resistance. Their refreshing accent on the "creative interventions that networks of minoritized cultures produce within and across national boundaries" recalibrates the local/global debate (7). They thus make room for the consideration of unscripted, scattered forms of diasporic identities exceeding models of opposition to a dominant structure. To echo Khatibi's prophetic judgment, theirs is an examination of difference that works on both active and reactive sites. These insights allow us to consider Maghrebi writing laterally, across national literature departments and in relation to all kinds of transnational contexts, such as Francophone and Arabophone Maghrebi literature, Afro-European literature in other languages (Thomas, *Afroeuropean Cartographies*), and other marginalized regionalist literatures from Europe in the case of the diasporic corpus. However, a transnational practice focused on nonhierarchical configurations runs the risk of undermining the potential of its concept for minority struggles in situ, which function within binary power logics. For, as Elleke Boehmer astutely suggests, "By downgrading the focus on empire and the nation-state, and increasing the emphasis on the . . . trans-border perspective, the theoretical purchase of resistance 'from below' is etiolated also" (n.p.). Reading transnationalism *also* in light of a politics of recognition requires a double anchorage in the relationality of marginal transnationalisms and the less enticing but nevertheless inescapable reality of enduring national paradigms and pervasive contemporary empires.

In a previous work I argued for a reconsideration of dominant monolingual approaches to Maghrebi literature constellated around French or Arabic as linguistic and disciplinary logics. By examining the diversity of the corpus of Maghrebi literature born of the diaspora to several southern European countries, I advocated instead for a translocal reading practice marked by plurilingualism and lateral trajectories between multiple sites across the Mediterranean

(Talbayev, "The Languages of Translocality"). In *Translocal Geographies: Spaces, Places, Connections*, Katherine Brickell and Ayona Datta bring to light a cogent definition of the concept of translocality, which they describe as "a simultaneous situatedness across different locales which provide ways of understanding the overlapping place-time(s) in migrants' everyday lives" (4). They continue, "These spaces and places need to be examined *both* through their situatedness and [through] their connectedness to a variety of other locales" (4, emphasis added). Revisiting ethnographic readings of place that restrict the local to a negotiation of global fluxes, they advocate a translocal methodology that would "understand the local as situated within a network of spaces, places and scales where identities are negotiated and transformed" (5). As a result of this outreaching form of groundedness, the translocal also fosters an agency-oriented approach because "grounding transnationalism within specific locales also mean[s] that scholars [can] move away from examining migrant subjectivities as overwhelmingly linked to structural limitations . . . and focus instead on social agencies of migrants in everyday spaces" (9). In other words, through translocality the emphasis lies equally on mobile spatial processes straddling multiple sites and on the situated contexts within which migrant subjects evolve—in relation to other contexts in lateral axes of connectivity, but also in contrast to vertical axes of hegemony.

As an aesthetic practice of other types of social and political activity, the concept of the transcontinental might be described as the attempt to link a number of local sites in a transnational gesture. It lends force to a form of the local that is traversed by connectivity and contact, nomadism and border crossing—in other words, a local appropriated by a translocal framework, with which it shares significant semantic space. Yet the transcontinental differs in that it is detached from the inflection of a diasporic frame of reference and recentered on the contiguous, connective space of the Mediterranean Maghreb through the consideration of centuries of common history. The transcontinental explores the ways subjects, ideas, and texts circulate in this continuum—how they form novel combinations and produce new cultural matrices and regimes of knowledge. Downplaying the hegemonizing effect of the global and the diffuse crisscrossing of the transnational, the transcontinental leaves room for consideration of the ways Maghrebi sites evolve in relation to other idiosyncratic Mediterranean spaces, whether marginal or hegemonic.

Returning to the sea as methodology, Iain Chambers suggests that to embrace a sea-centered configuration is "to unhook a particular language and its explanations from the chains of authority, allowing it to drift toward another shore, from where the locality and provincialism of its previous home can be registered" ("Maritime Criticism" 680). Chambers's judgment aligns with the displacement and rerouting of maritime models of theory, emphasizing the loss of coordinates experienced during the voyage at sea. However, it also points out the mutual, comparative process of recognition whereby each local comes to be defined; it is vis-à-vis each other and only in their reciprocity that the points of origin and destination of these cross-Mediterranean sites are configured. This constellation points to a plurilingual, multisite corpus of Maghrebi literature that calls attention to the material circumstances of each instance of connectivity. At the same time it encourages transverse connections between fundamentally unstable configurations of power, identity, and resistance. A transcontinental outlook thus suggests alternative reading protocols that affect our perception of aesthetic norms and political assumptions. Its consubstantial plurilingualism unearths alternative literary and poetic encounters that complicate well traveled critical routes, shedding light on novel transnational aesthetic and human matrices.

NATIONALISM, MELANCHOLIA, ALLEGORY

How might a sustained consideration of the Mediterranean throughout history color a critical reflection on the postcolonial present? Mediterranean tropes have often been cast as colonial-inspired utopias lacking political valence, and there is undeniable truth to this perspective. Several of the writers addressed in this study have developed their Mediterranean on a nostalgic mode against the rigid dominance of an authoritarian postcolonial nation-state. Colette Fellous's allegory of colonial Tunis and Nabil Farès's virtual Andalusia, examined in chapter 2, lay claim to utopian transnational networks, and their configurations significantly reshuffle the historical modes of affiliation that have emerged from national independence and decolonization. In a similar way Camus's use of a Mediterranean utopian identity common to all colonial subjects in Algeria serves to negate the irrepressible reality of anticolonial nationalism. His mythicized recuperation of the millennia-old history of contact between ancient cultures under the dominance of Greco-Roman civilization downplays the importance of the Arab conquest and subsequent Islamization of the Maghreb, two core elements of Algerian nationalist rhetoric. It also delegitimizes contemporaneous efforts to lay historical claim to Algerian independence and nationhood. In another distinctive example Boualem Sansal's exploration of a Mediterranean identity in his recent *Alger, poste restante* (Algiers General Delivery) denies historical relevance to the Arab Muslim past of Algeria, a move that gains full meaning and even some degree of justification in the context of the 1990s Black Decade of terrorism and repression. Yet, as Dobie has shown, his substitution of a French universalist worldview for authoritarian Algerian identity narratives remains problematic, and one could conclude with her that "Mediterraneanism seems . . . to be hard to disentangle from Eurocentrism and the forces of neocolonialism" pervading many contemporary Mediterranean invocations (403). Each of these accounts partakes in its idiosyncratic way of what Ben-Yehoyada has dubbed a "pluralistic cultural élitism" (117). Whether the product of late colonialism, as is the case with Camus, or of a "neocolonial" impulse, these openly cosmopolitan positionalities generate elegiac mobilizations of a Golden Age of plurality and exchange, an era that came to a brutal end with the ascent of nationalism. Born of the triumph of nationalism over cosmopolitanism in the former Ottoman Empire, this nostalgia effectively relegates the Mediterranean to the outskirts of a modernity of which it was to become the negation. Mediterranean or modern: the Maghreb could not be both, and, as Ben Yehoyada argues, it is often in the guise of a rejection of modernity that a literary Mediterranean has been articulated, in the lingering echo of the cosmopolitanism characteristic of late imperialism.[29]

The resilient influence of a nostalgic, colonialist ethos in Algerian literature might account for the central role played by the tutelary figure of Camus in Maghrebi studies' readings of the Mediterranean such as Esposito's groundbreaking *The Narrative Mediterranean*.[30] His Algerian texts from the 1930s typically serve as historical grounding for conceptualizations of a Maghrebi Mediterranean and as the intertextual ghostly voice underpinning the later Mediterranean elaborations (post-1980s) that critics routinely examine. And indeed many authors, such as Assia Djebar (most patently in *Algerian White* but also in other texts) and Maïssa Bey, have openly reclaimed the writer's inspirational tutelage in a context inimical to female writing.[31] What critics and later generations of Maghrebi writers retain from Camus's complex intellectual position generally falls under one of two readings: his lack of political support for Algerian independence, a fact met with bitterness and hostility by his many detractors, or, conversely, his refusal of the dichotomous identity models of colonialism and nationalism. I certainly have no quarrel with giving Camus's Mediterranean writings the recognition they deserve in the elaboration of Algerian and Maghrebi postcolonial literature. His intertextual influence can be credited with inspiring some of the most accomplished pages of Maghrebi writing. However, to effect this divorce from colonialist outlooks it is imperative to modulate Camus's influence to the benefit of alternative texts and, accordingly, to downplay his authority over our own critical narratives.

If the relevance of the Mediterranean trope during the days of empire goes a long way toward elucidating colonialism's inner workings, I find an examination of this ethos in the texts produced in the heyday of nationalism by militant nationalist authors to be even more conclusive, precisely because they effectively recalibrate the Mediterranean framework beyond the problematic colonial aura that still invalidates it in the eyes of many critics. Accordingly, in an effort to emphasize the political resonance of some of my Mediterranean readings, my book substitutes Kateb Yacine's *Nedjma* in place of Camus's writings as the founding narrative of my transcontinental Maghrebi corpus. Rather than considering it in isolation, I therefore approach Camus's work in the rich literary context of colonial literature: the early twentieth-century movement of Algérianisme, which served as a foil to his configurations, but also through his partnership with the subsequent literary school L'École d'Alger. I subordinate this analysis to Kateb's *Nedjma*, which fittingly serves as the foundational text in conventional literary histories of the postcolonial Maghreb and as the prevailing intertext coursing through my Mediterranean narrative in lieu of Camus. In the nationalist cycle of Kateb or in the budding corpus of clandestine migration narratives I examine in chapter 4, appropriations of the Mediterranean frontally lay claim to nationalist and anticolonial narratives, either in relation to a nation in the making, as in the context of Kateb's 1950s, or as a yet to be realized national ideal in our present dystopian context. These and other texts demonstrate that the Maghreb's Mediterranean can and does exceed its exiguous colonial origins. The move from Camus to Kateb performs the resemanticization of the concept of the Mediterranean in a Maghrebi context in the manner in which the notion of hybridity was recast, evolving through proper theorization from being a paean to the French colonial empire's racial and ethnic diversity to becoming one of the most widespread watchwords of postcolonial and transnational studies. For that reason this shift disengages the Mediterranean trope from its colonial nostalgic aura and redeploys it as a concept endowed with potential political valence in our postcolonial present.

This book thus poses an alternative Mediterranean genealogy in the corpus of Maghrebi literature—a lineage that would not find its point of origin in Camus's utopian colonialist vision of a "humanism of the sun" but would rather follow the intertextual trajectory of a transcontinental *Nedjma* as a Mediterranean reallegorization of the national myth. In an attempt to trace the evolution of this Mediterranean current throughout each stage of Maghrebi literature, I reread the tutelary figures of North African literature in French (Kateb, Camus, Khatibi, Ben Jelloun, Farès, Mokeddem) in light of less studied authors who have engaged similar issues (Fellous, al-Baqqash, Cruz, Bertrand, Audisio). The Mediterranean trope that I identify surges throughout this book as a heuristic tool to parse and engage the irrefutable material realities of the Maghrebi region. Recalibrating readings of Maghrebi national imaginaries, this enduring Mediterranean focus unsettles the dichotomy between the postcolonial nation and the deterritorialized space of the sea. Reading the Maghreb through the Mediterranean and the Mediterranean through the Maghreb, I showcase the deep imbrication of both spaces. This revised framework complicates dominant nationalist readings of Maghrebi identities but also postcolonial thought's core concept of nomadism as a form of pure deterritorialization oblivious to historical realities—here the Mediterranean as a postnational site of rootless liberation. Instead, through a sustained reflection on the potential and limitations of allegory and critical melancholia, and of their multiple points of convergence, I recast nomadism as a principle of intersubjective interaction that recalibrates deterritorialization as a form of politicized relationality. What distinguishes this argument is its sustained effort to relate the detours and transnational inscriptions afforded by the Mediterranean to subjective and collective engagements with historical instantiations of the national myth—to efforts to inflect it and to redefine the nation along more democratic lines through the melancholic anamnesis of inclusive narratives.

From this adjusted beginning allegory arises as the mode of expression most intrinsically entangled with the elusive fate of this amended postcolonial national ideal. By positing a national allegorical referent as the political hallmark of every Third World text, Fredric Jameson's model of "national allegory" relies on a reductive nationalist frame of reference that obscures heterogeneity within social formations. It downplays repressed identities kept on the margins of dominant narratives of nation-building and obliterates their own struggles with the forces of nationalism. In contrast postmodern takes on allegory have fruitfully emphasized the concept's resistance to cohesive expression and meaning. Springing from temporal incommensurability (Paul De Man construes the trope as "a distance in relation to its own origin . . . [that] establishes its language in the void of this temporal difference" [207]), allegory resonates with the potential to render the disjointed texture of the present. Etymologically derived from the Greek verb *agoreuein*, "to speak publicly," and the adverbial form for *allos* (other), allegory is literally what allows one to say things differently (Macey 8). Allegorical writing is by nature "elusive, its surface by turns mimetic and anti-mimetic, its procedures intricate and at times seemingly inconsistent, and its meaning or 'other' sense—how it is encoded, or what it refers to extrinsically—often indeterminate" (Copeland and Struck 2). Contrasting allegory to the romantic aesthetic of the symbol bearing the deceitful mark of unity and wholeness, Walter Benjamin emphasizes allegory's disconnect between the world of ideas and phenomena. In the context of Baudelaire's modern Paris allegory comes to mark the abrupt discontinuity intrinsic to the modern experience and the "sudden change of referentiality" that accompanies it (Cowan 120). A principle of demystification ("allegory should be shown as the antidote to myth" [Benjamin, "Central Park" 179]), allegory signals a crisis in representation, a "disjunction potentially inherent to all artistic media between the mode and meaning of an expression" (Mieszkowski 46).[32]

The constitutive flickering of allegorical representation makes it particularly well-suited to the rendering of alternative narrative threads forced out of the weave of history. It is the mode of expression most amenable to the multiple "discontinuous interruptions" prophesied by Gayatri Spivak—a "repeated tearing of time that cannot be sutured" (208). Allegory reverberates with the potential to commit to collective memory the marginalized identities that lie beyond monolithic official narratives and that undercut them. Running against the grain of monological history and its repression of difference, it captures the lingering traces of a diverse, unrecorded past "that disrupt[s] the efforts of the present to contain [its objects] within its categories or forms of narrative . . . [allowing for] the possibility that the reserve of the past will destroy aspects of the present and open it to the future" (Caygill 93). This "reserve of the past," or unrealized potential, contains its excess, its irreducibility to the narrative structures of the present. In no small measure it reminds us that the effacement of the past's complexity and fullness must be resisted, a duty partaking of the imperative of melancholic remembrance.

Post-Freudian engagements with the concept of melancholia have distanced themselves from interpretations that brought to the fore the pathological sense of incompletion imbuing its model of mourning (Brisley; Khanna; Gana, *Signifying Loss*). In their stead they have encouraged examination of the political and agential potential of melancholia as a foundation for political praxis. Lucy Brisley has defined melancholia as "a mechanism through which marginalized communities can recognize and safeguard their losses. Be it sufferers of AIDS, colonized peoples, or women, melancholia is posited as central to the subjectivity of their disenfranchised identities" (56). Bearing the mark of incompleteness, melancholic incorporation functions as a mode of "grief" susceptible to a political shift toward "grievance" as the subject appropriates the lost object and preserves it in its radical difference and singularity (Cheng 3). In this incommensurable reading of time, David Eng and David Kazanjian's "politics of mourning" clears the path for the articulation of an ethical framework where politically motivated testimony can take center stage and, through melancholia, attempt to mediate the reconciliation of subjective experience to an appeased form of collective history. Postulating the endorsement and advocacy of the imperfectly assimilated object of loss, melancholia locates in "impossible mourning" a turn toward alterity in "an ethics . . . [that] enable[s] us to recast widely the ties of identification, empathy, and epiphany, and to do so in an uncoerced and uncoercive fashion" (Gana, *Signifying Loss* 45).[33]

The stubborn residual presence of never-accepted loss ensures alertness to the forces of injustice underpinning it. In a complex argument on the question of rememoration, Ranjana Khanna has unearthed the residual topographies of nonmonumental modes of mourning. She locates in melancholia the affective commemoration of those bodies that bear the mark of utter disposability as a function of their exclusion from the structures of social life: "Modernity's injunction to mourn is exemplified in the monument, as if to construct a palliative in which disposability can be located once and for all and buried. A melancholic reading affectively resists this injunction" (20). Cutting through what she calls the "necropolitics" of monumentalization—the process whereby marginalized people are erased along with their aspirations to self-determination—melancholia insufflates new life into the ideal of political equality. A gaping wound of unresolved grief in the face of the modern nation's mechanisms of obliteration, melancholia's boundless rememoration safeguards diversity. Preserving the alterity of the inassimilable object of mourning (51), melancholia opens up the space of the self to its constitutive other. It embraces the fundamental duality at play within the self through the inassimilable echo of the voice of trauma. As Khanna argues, "critical melancholia, formulated through the ghosts with ideals, is the only answer for democracy to come" (27). In the conclusion to her discussion of melancholia in the "messy context of hybridized cultures muddled in . . . nationalism and colonialism and decolonization," Khanna pinpoints the origins of the melancholic condition in the prolonged, untraceable trauma induced by the epistemic violence of nation-state formation (169). Ernest Renan has argued that nations are constructed around the willful forgetting of discrepant experiences in the name of the national will. In this context melancholia needs to be invested in the perpetuation of the core of difference at the heart of the national body against the grain of professed assimilation. Kept out of the erasure performed by mourning, the latent trauma is susceptible to resurgence in the form of "moments of melancholia" that create a political countermemory openly defiant of national history's propensity to exclude difference. This is what Khanna has dubbed a "critical resistance to national forgetting." As she argues, "we do not simply remember to forget, but we take remembering seriously as an imaginative and political act" (166). At stake in this rememoration is the reactivation of notions of social justice and historical redress that lie at the root of any concept of citizenship that aims to successfully oppose institutionalized silencing.

Throughout this book the intertwined deployment of melancholia and allegory evinces a certain degree of instability. Sometimes the core of my analysis (as in chapters 1 and 3), sometimes the mirror images against which processes of nostalgia and subalternity are constructed (in chapters 2 and 4), their variable fortunes speak to the undecidability of the postcolonial present. If Mediterranean melancholia performs a productive form of estrangement from monological nationalist myths in the early stages of Algeria's national allegorization, its enactment in the wake of trauma in the tail end of the Black Decade negotiates national belonging in more pressing terms than ever before. Mediterranean-infused melancholia, as it manifests in this book, reconceptualizes nomadism not as a pure principle of deterritorialization but as intersubjective interaction in the geographical space of the Mediterranean. As my analysis of Mokeddem's *N'zid* will show, this is a connectivity that performs the "working through" of trauma and reintroduces heterogeneity to the national construct. For such is the power of the Mediterranean: to "work through" the lingering trauma of past marginalization with the felicitous result of writing diversity back into the nation. Through its melancholic take on relationality, the Mediterranean successfully mediates the nomadic subject's reinsertion into a revised national collective attentive to its intrinsic heterogeneity.

Thus in chapter 1 I recast Kateb's canonical *Nedjma* in light of the plurilingual, multiconfessional space of Djerba mobilized in little studied ancillary texts from the "Nedjma cycle" published in journals in the 1950s and 1960s. I tease out the ways *Nedjma* resists the cohesive power of the Algerian myth of origins elaborated ahead of independence to reveal an investment in Mediterranean transnationalism. Those ancillary texts show that the quest for Algeria's identity cannot be completed without spatial deployment in the Mediterranean island of Djerba. The intertextual tutelage of the Homeric episode of the Lotus-Eaters, situated on the same island, places this relocation under the mark of willful amnesia. It is exemplified by the local myth of the exiled Djerbian Jews who refused to return to Jerusalem, favoring Djerba's hospitality over ancestry. Djerba supplies a model of felicitous mixing among strata of Mediterranean migrations. It provides late colonial Algeria with a mythical space wherein to hone the very workings of its nation-building aspirations in a plural context evocative of Algeria's own diversity. On this Djerbian detour Kateb's text reveals a Mediterranean ethos at the core of Algeria's founding narrative, performing what the writer Nabile Farès later dubbed the "re-allegorization of national myth" in a Mediterranean mode—a reallegorization hinging on hybridity and estrangement, the two pillars of Kateb's Algerian identity in the making.

While chapter 1 traces the arc of the allegorical realization of national myth in the utopian context of early nationalism, chapter 2 engages what Réda Bensmaïa has dubbed "the interruption of myth"

(*Experimental Nations* 25). Through a study of the resurgence of the nostalgic trope of Andalusian coexistence (a period recurrently mobilized throughout my book as the Golden Age of Arab civilization) in Nabile Farès's and Colette Fellous's fiction, chapter 2 explores the multiple and conflicting reappropriations of al-Andalus in the Maghreb and Spain—as a historical moment stretching from 711 to 1492 and as a mythopoetic trope of intellectual collaboration among Jews, Muslims, and Christians in medieval Iberia. Assessing Khatibi's hypothesis of an Arab "traumatic chiasmus" that followed the Spanish Reconquista, I argue that this entwined yet symmetrical bond between Orient and Occident is colored by reflective nostalgia (Boym) for an imagined transnational, transconfessional, and multilingual community. In light of Juan Goytisolo's notion of an "Andalusian legacy," I start with a thorough examination of cultural and literary representations of al-Andalus produced in Spain and the Arab world as a product of historical truncation and traumatic memorialization. I show how Khatibi's restoration of contemporary Spain to its privileged position in the Arab imaginary appropriates the Andalusian shared past to rethink Morocco's claim to historical agency beyond the frameworks of French and Spanish colonialisms. I also reveal how Farès' dystopian "virtual" Andalusia (Deleuze) gives in to the influence of politically unconvincing *tristesse*, silently acquiescing to the irreparable rift forever separating the self from his constitutive other. To conclude I show how the Jewish Tunisian writer Fellous obliquely appropriates the Andalusian model of coexistence in *Avenue de France* to articulate claims about Jewish-Muslim relations in Tunisia. Willfully deserting the political arena, Farès and Fellous embody a fundamental sense of belatedness that casts the Mediterranean as a mythical refuge averse to historical realization. In this respect they offer a powerful counterpoint to the kind of allegorization performed by Kateb at the apex of nationalism.

Chapter 3, the contemporary counterpart of the reflections developed in chapter 1, brings the discussion of allegory and melancholia to bear on the post-traumatic aftermath of the Algerian Black Decade. In a critique of dominant readings of Mokeddem's transnational framework in light of Deleuzian deterritorialization, I argue that the fluctuations of the allegorical mode of expression developed in her novel *N'zid* functions to uncover and work through past trauma on the subjective and collective levels. Tearing apart the seemingly clear-cut opposition between rooted and nomadic subjectivities, Mokeddem's allegory reveals more complex forms of identity that, if they do not sacrifice the singular in the name of the collective, do not for all that sacrifice the collective in the name of the singular. Both exceeding the nation and actively laying claim to it, the model of mobility developed in the novel elaborates a politicized Mediterranean framework of social interactions intent on reclaiming and preserving the diversity of the Algerian collective in a melancholic mode. I demonstrate how this empowered form of "plural singularity" (Nancy, *Being Singular Plural*) navigates the meanders of collective and individual memory to undo many years of forced oblivion. A remodeling of her well-known Deleuze-inspired desert nomadism, Mokeddem's Mediterranean trope emerges as a strategic transnational channel of opposition to narrow definitions of collective identity and spawns a new social compact in the wake of a decade of terrorism and civil strife.

In a Moroccan context redefined along the routes of trans-Mediterranean clandestine crossings, chapter 4 combines the embedded frame of reference of the postcolonial nation resting on the legacy of Francophone decolonial thinkers such as Fanon with the imaginary of Arab nationalism's *watan*. It sheds light on the conflicting incarnations of the national ideal in the context of clandestine migration to Europe and substitutes dystopian visions of the sea for the romanticized topos of happy Mediterranean hybridity. Reflecting on these pressing realities, I address literary engagements with the phenomenon of *hijra* (illegal migration from Africa to Europe) produced on either side of the Strait in French, Spanish, and Arabic. I read Mediterranean *hijra* and its concluding shipwreck as the negative mirror image of the illustrious tradition of *rihla*, the knowledge-seeking journey underpinning the development of Arab modernity from the days of al-Andalus. In contrast to the accumulation paradigm of *rihla*, *hijra* emerges as a journey of loss, often ending in shipwreck and death. I start with Tahar Ben Jelloun's configuration of Tangier as the realm of subversive poetic *parole* in *Harrouda*, the lingering intertext for my two subsequent readings of the Strait zone: Muhammad al-Baqqash's *Al-Hijra al-Sirriyya* (Clandestine Migration) and Trino Cruz's *Rihla*. I demonstrate how al-Baqqash's deconstruction of *rihla*, a model entangled with the Arab Renaissance and Arab nationalism, reframes his Mediterranean crossing as an extension of subaltern resistance to the postcolonial *watan* (the national construct of Arab nationalism). I then show how Cruz shifts the focus from national space to the deadly maritime plane of the crossings. As the hope for inclusion into alternative networks through emigration to Europe founders, only physical disintegration awaits the migrant. I conclude by showing how this form of mobility delineates a new dystopian Mediterranean. This recalibration of the sea as abyss brings to light the epistemic violence intrinsic to the region, complicating readings of the space of the Mediterranean as a site of cultural mediation and *convivencia.*

As they perform their own kind of inclusivity, regional frameworks are also enmeshed in idiosyncratic brands of epistemic violence. They bring together spaces that under certain circumstances may fare better if left to their own configurations. Likewise they exclude other groupings with the same deleterious short-sightedness as more expansive forms of globalism. Even within the transcontinental context of my analysis choices had to be made, languages ignored, connections downplayed. In a Mediterranean space in which full plurilingualism would require thorough knowledge of Semitic, Slavic, Romance, Turkic, Amazigh, and Hellenic languages, the prospect of absolute Mediterranean comparatism remains elusive. Of necessity my focus thus lies principally on the western Mediterranean rim in geographic contiguity with the space of the Maghreb, the literal "West" of the Arab world. Additional studies are needed to take the Mediterranean paradigm into a variety of directions, embracing through this dissemination the fluid structure of the Mediterranean trope. This book is thus not an exhaustive foray into the rich corpus of Maghrebi-Mediterranean literature but an explorative venture loosening the straitjacket of dichotomous reading methodologies. Other Mediterranean connections must be made outside the European Union–Maghreb axis. One such connective space is Turkey, which remains excluded from teleological visions of European destiny, as the tumultuous negotiations for its accession to the European Union remind us, and from the imaginary of the Arab Nation—but which still partakes in the experience of Mediterranean empire, albeit from a reversed perspective. The task ahead is to chart new investigative routes for research that will extend and rectify the map suggested in these pages. As the predictable failure of the so-called Union for the Mediterranean to change patterns of distrust and antagonism between the northern and southern shores of the sea demonstrates, margin-to-margin contrapuntal alignments are truly indispensable to promote a more equitable vision of the region and to develop forms of southern solidarity across continents (Cassano, *Il Pensiero meridiano*). Returning the Maghreb to the layered, multifarious context of the Mediterranean region, the transcontinental reanchors it in its historical position on the interface of Europe and Africa. This restored positionality makes it a key space to call attention to the political relevance of locally grounded, margin-to-margin constellations to convincingly remap our world through less polarized, uneven perspectives.

CHAPTER 1

Hybridizing the Myth, Allegorizing Algeria

Allegory should be shown as the antidote to myth.

—Walter Benjamin, *The Origin of German Tragic Drama*

The emergence of a properly Algerian body of literature engaging Algeria's national aspirations coalesced around the search for a narrative of origins that would not be restricted to a binary, oppositional model of writing. Although the first novels published in French by Algerian authors can be traced back to the interwar period and the ascent of the *roman indigène* (indigenous novel), the current critical canon generally locates the birth of Algerian literature in the polarized, confrontational 1950s and the war of independence.[1] In an imbrication of literary writing, anticolonial violence, and resistance to oppression, the founding figures of the Algerian novelistic tradition have been typically memorialized in literary history as *la génération de 52* (Déjeux, "Bibliographie"; Sayeh). Generative of a narrative of origins endowed with the aura of all foundational myths, the fiction of Mohammed Dib, Mouloud Feraoun, Mouloud Mammeri, and Kateb Yacine bears the imprint of heightened political awareness and anticolonial activism. While elaborating a sustained inquiry into the nature of Algerian identity, this budding, self-proclaimed Algerian corpus refused all forms of alienation. It thematized resistance to colonial domination and its attendant obliteration of native cultures before turning its deconstructive insights to the increasingly totalitarian views of the triumphant Front de Libération Nationale (FLN), the nationalist movement at the root of the 1954 insurrection, which soon appropriated as its credo Sheikh Abdelhamid Ben Badis's militant identitarian formula "Islam is my religion, Arabic is my language, and Algeria is my country." Born of the contestation following the brutal repression by French troops of the 1945 Setif and Guelma riots, these texts refused the easy refuge of fixed monological identity narratives. Instead they produced a counterdiscourse to the totalizing rhetoric of institutionalized nationalism. Braiding together complex historical references with disparate collective memories and popular myths, they delineated a more capacious history of the Maghreb and set out to elucidate the increasingly pernicious question of what shape the future Algerian nation was to don.

Réda Bensmaïa's classification of the relation between this Algerian corpus of literature and the process of nation formation sheds light on the intricacies of mythical narratives in the early days of nationalism. In contrast to the earlier period of *roman indigène*, Bensmaïa reads the self-affirming model of writing developed in the 1950s in light of Jean-Luc Nancy's *pensée mythique*, a form of myth representing "multiple existences as immanent to its own unique fiction, which gathers them together and gives them their common figure in its speech and as its speech. . . . It means that myth and myth's force and foundation are essential to community" (*The Inoperative Community* 57). Nancy construes myth as the guiding force behind community formation: "Myth works out the shares and divisions that distribute a community and distinguish it for itself, articulating it within itself" (50). It is a site of communion and communication through which community gains self-consciousness. It is coextensive with "the thought of a founding fiction, or a foundation by fiction" (53) that reveals community to itself in its idiosyncrasy and acquiescent communion. Myth is indicative of the "*will* of community: the desire to operate, through the power of myth, the communion that myth represents and that it represents as a communion or communication of wills" (57). In Bensmaïa's analysis community's accession to itself through myth (what Nancy calls "mythation" [45]) is deeply embroiled in the reality of postcolonial nation formation. Reverberating with Fanonian nationalist militantism, this mythical elaboration rejects "all compromise, all reconciliation with colonial France. . . . Writing was contemporary and synonymous with the *laying of the foundation of the nation to come*" (Bensmaïa, *Experimental Nations* 23). In other words, only through the production of myth can a community come into being, a perspective that injects myth with the truth value necessary to the possible actualization of a national collective. Bensmaïa reads this necessary foundation of myth as truth in terms of the promotion of a "single, unified Algeria" (23). In his perspective authors such as Kateb Yacine, Mouloud Feraoun, Jean Amrouche, Malek Haddad, and Assia Djebar promote a converging narrative recalcitrant to acknowledge the multiple forms of violence perpetrated by myth itself (22). In contrast Bensmaïa construes Nabile Farès as the earliest "discordant voice . . . a radical questioning of the transparency and the validity of the myth" (23–24). Farès is recast as the first to "interrupt the myth" and denounce the "forgetfulness" of nation-building that Ernest Renan has solidly erected into one of the fundamentals of the process—a movement imbued with distortion and manipulation since the existence of a cohesive nation requires the denial of its very mythical nature.[2]

Farès's interruption is linked to the FLN's increasing authoritarianism and its attendant regime of monological truth, which rested on the twin pillars of reified state-mandated nationalism and ossified Islamic identity. Yet his debunking of national myth must also be read in light of another myth: the colonial allegory born of Camus's "amorous drama of Algeria," which Farès himself takes as the starting point for his discussion of national allegory in *Un passager de l'Occident* (A Passenger from the West; 35).[3] In the context of a dialogue between the narrator and an attractive, melancholy young man claiming European Algerian origins, *Un passager de l'Occident* stages a contrapuntal reading of the two founding fathers of Algerian literature. Rejecting the young man's claim that they share "the same land" (34),[4] the narrator opposes a cynical outlook to his companion's concept of origins predicated on a common geographical territory: "I then thought that being 'from the same land' referred to splendid coastlines and open landscapes. . . . I then realized that the accounts of the rifts and disasters and historical struggles of Algeria were all bogged down with great forgetting" (34).[5] The polysyndetic repetition of *and* in relation to the cataclysmic historical dynamics that have politically affected Algeria indicts the sense of attachment born of the subject's affective rapport with the landscape. It forms a caustic rebuttal of the type of subjectivity suggested in Camus's early Algerian texts, such as *L'Envers et l'endroit* (The Wrong Side and the Right Side) and *Noces* (Nuptials). Predicating identity on the immediate sensory (and sensual) experience of the sea and the sun, in an echo of Paul Valéry's "Inspirations méditerranéennes,"[6] Camus's texts forge a Mediterranean kinship between Algerians and other Mediterranean subjects in a renewed form of humanism. As Farès suggests a few lines later, "only some of Camus' texts have expressed . . . this great forgetting," a forgetting evocative of the kind of erasure performed by Renan's process of nation formation (34).[7]

To the affect captured by Camus's realist mode of expression (a realism denounced as a purveyor of "reactionary" politics), Farès's text opposes the exegetic impulse of Kateb's *poétique*, a heuristic quest into the nature of Algeria's allegorical reality.[8] Farès argues that a realist aesthetic runs the risk of flattening out the intricacies of Algeria's dense allegorical representation and of instrumentalizing it to mystifying ends. In its stead he advocates restoring allegory's power—"fighting the right allegorical fight" (Bensmaïa, *Experimental Nations* 25)—that is, refusing to let a mythicized, purposefully distorted realism co-opt allegory's community-defining potential. Such deep reallegorization of national myth is the only way to implement "the passage from an allegorical reality to an allegory turned reality" (Farès, *Un passager* 37), that is, the move from a coercive vision of reality draping itself in legitimizing allegorical garb to a socially operative, realized form of allegory effectively transforming reality.[9] Bensmaïa has identified this shift as a "revolution in mentality," the avowed aim of a true Algerian poetics. For Farès such is the potential and onus of Kateb's *Nedjma*, whose task lies in enacting this transformation to restore the density of a genuine foundational myth to Algerian literature. Bensmaïa remarks that Farès's reflections acknowledge the elusiveness of this task, investigating its dynamic at the same time as it takes note of the difficulty of its actualization. Signaling both an "interruption" of the national myth and a cognizance of allegory's intangibility, the voice of literature undertakes the "demystification or, rather, the demythification of a country that had been reduced to nothing more than the stooge of a State that would never rise to the task with which its people had entrusted it" (Bensmaïa, *Experimental Nations* 26). In this context the poetic restoration of Algeria's allegorical destiny against the corrosive influence of politically conservative realism is imbued with the aura of a political act.

Writing in the context of the Black Decade of terrorism and social strife in 1990s Algeria, Emily Apter has cogently put to the fore strategic Algerian reappropriations of Camus as "a code-name for the promulgation of an international democracy movement that would heal the breach between the Islamic world and the West" ("Out of Character" 501). Her commentary places emphasis on the political potential of reinserting the much maligned *pied noir* European author, who conspicuously failed to speak in favor of independence in the 1950s, into the national literary lineage. In the context of the 1990s about which she writes, this symbolic gesture is a meaningful effort to loosen the grip of totalizing discursive formations on either side of the FLN-Islamists divide in the context of the Black Decade (Algeria as the product of FLN nationalism or Islam). Yet its significance extends further as it concurrently strives to identify and secure a space within the Algerian nation for an alternative identitarian middle ground that could complicate all too clear dichotomous delineations of difference. Epitomized by Camus's complex origins, this "cosmopolitan . . . bloodline" (502) is respectful of a certain historical form of hybridity and acts as a token of society's resilience to conflicting monological mystifications. Apter is careful not to absolve Camus of historical responsibility when assessing his role during the Algerian War, and her analysis of the cosmopolitanism he embodies should not be construed as an endorsement of his apolitical reading of Algeria's identity and future. Yet secular Algerian intellectuals' gesture of bringing Camus back into the genealogy of Algerian literature is significant. In the interruption of nationalist myth, the national community is revealed as incomplete, the "communication of wills" at the heart of its collective existence long suspended. For Bensmaïa this incommensurability spells the emergence of a productive discordance: "The part that would remain . . . would not be a single, unified nation, nor the communion . . . 'but the division [*partage*] itself'" (*Experimental Nations* 26). In this dissonant coexistence discrepant forms of national consciousness emerge, reestablishing the intrinsic heterogeneity of Algeria at the core of community building. In this context literature comes to inhabit the caesura of national consciousness that follows the interruption of the myth of national unity. It concurrently negotiates new spaces of expression for the multiple viewpoints and idioms of an Algerian community marked with the possibly felicitous seal of social disunion.

Under the weave of this appropriation of the power and limitations of Algeria's "demythification" lurks a cognate dimension of the country's social segmentation: the long-standing debates and instrumentalizations of Algeria's fundamental hybridity, which has been endowed historically with significant political clout. Of crucial relevance to the 1990s evoked by Apter, Algeria's long-standing history of contact and hybridity has in fact accompanied the coming of age of Algerian literature, from the Algérianiste literary movement starting in the 1890s to anticolonial musings on the nature of the nation to be formed in the 1950s and extending, in this respect, far beyond the late colonial era of Camus. This chapter builds on Farès's fertile conceptual quest for an adequate mythical rendition of national consciousness—one cognizant and respectful of Algeria's intrinsic diversity as the basis for a full reallegorization. I interrogate the legacy of colonial visions of hybridity in their complex and at times paradoxical relation to the concept of an Algerian nation in the making. I assess the interplay among multiple, evolving instantiations of a Mediterranean consciousness that was mythically mobilized as a principle of pluralism through history. To that end and as a counterpoint to the usual dominance of the figure of Camus in this debate, I consider Kateb's *Nedjma*, the founding text of the Algerian literary tradition, through a Mediterranean lens, reading it against the grain of the Algérianistes' Latin Mediterranean and L'École d'Alger's Mediterranean "consummate oxymoron" (Apter, "Out of Character" 506) that preceded it. This detour through European Algerian writing contextualizes the complexities of Kateb's fiction in the *longue durée* of a century-long corpus of Algerian literature, illuminating his own dealings with colonial legacies that have left their mark on Algerian society and culture. It also delineates a diachronic genealogy of Mediterranean-inspired Algerian writing that cuts across the usual readings of national culture in terms of colonial versus Algerian authorship by revealing its centrality at different times and on different sides of the struggle for decolonization.[10] Supplementary excerpts from little-known ancillary texts from the "Nedjma cycle" ("Djerba, l'île de l'étrangère" [Djerba, the Stranger's Island]; "Le Lotos"; and "Les Poissons sautent" [The Jumping Fish]) delve deeper into the Mediterranean density of Kateb's identitarian configurations. They shed new light on the writer's own engagements with Mediterranean hybridity in their complex relationship to the rhetoric and demands of rising nationalism. Placing an irreducible kernel of *étrangeté* bearing the mark of exile and hybridity at the heart of Algerian identity, Kateb's mythical Mediterranean cycle operates a transnational deployment of national consciousness and reorients the allegorization of Algeria beyond its postindependence confines. Thus through its recuperation of hybridity I argue that Kateb's foundational oeuvre performs a first interruption of the nascent myth of independent Algeria, precociously revealing the fictitiousness of its exiguous narratives of origins. Instead the cycle of Nedjma enacts the reallegorization of national myth in a Mediterranean mode, inserting the Algerian nation that Kateb's writing helped form into a transnational, more historically capacious map.

THE ANXIETIES OF UNCONTAINABILITY

Christopher L. Miller has argued that the concept of hybridity is indelibly marked by its connection to "the French colonial empire . . . [which] promoted a multicultural 'Greater France' of all colors" (*Nationalists* 4). Homi Bhabha's familiar reflections on the stakes of the concept highlight the myriad ways in which hybridity, situated in the unpredictable Third Space of enunciation, is embedded in the hegemonic logic of colonial rule. Emphasizing its contiguity with the slippage and excess born of the repetition of "discriminatory [identity] effects," hybridity generates a form of disruption that reveals the ambivalence and ultimate vacuity of colonial power—a lacuna propping it up as fertile ground for a form of "uncontainab[ility]" of the hybrid, "break[ing] down the symmetry and duality of self/other, inside/outside . . . the boundaries of authority" (Bhabha 160, 165–66). In an Algerian colonial context the multiple echoes of Bhabha's hybridity expose the insecure position of a settlers' community looking to reinforce its legitimacy on Algerian soil while forging its own discrete identity in opposition to metropolitan models of Frenchness. As the all-out opposition between a settler's community invested in its own continuance and a rising nationalist faction determined to put an end to colonization escalated, a semantic struggle over the designation *Algerian* gained traction. The term was reclaimed by both the *colons*, then the only legitimate Algériens, eager to crystallize their unique colonial identity, and by those whom they indiscriminately called "les musulmans" (the Muslims), a term coextensive with the whole of native society, whether Muslim or not. Entangled with these centripetal identity constructs, a mythical, proteiform, and evolving Mediterranean transnational identity emerged. It was increasingly reclaimed over time as a third, if utopian way out of the late colonial bind that found its eventual resolution in the torments of the Algerian War of Independence.

With the definitive capitulation of Emir Abdelkader's forces in 1847 and the subsequent departmentalization of Algeria the following year, France's colonial reign of conquests became virtually uncontested, paving the way for a period of expansion and invigorating population influx from France and the neighboring Mediterranean and European countries. Well ahead of the hyperbolic celebrations of the colony's centenary in 1930, the deep colonizing of Algeria had been under way. It prolonged the phase of military conquest with the enactment of colonial policies meant to establish the discriminatory order of colonialism at all levels of Algerian society, a dynamic particularly visible in the distinctive space of the colonial city (Graebner, *History's Place*; Prochaska, *Making Algeria French*; Çelik). Yet despite having established a strong economic and political hold over the colony, the *colons* were in many ways an embattled group. A community internally divided by diverse ethnic segments as well as a numerical minority in the face of the native population, they were equally disdained by metropolitans, who had a caricatured image of their long-lost, far-removed countrymen. Despite the massive naturalization of the Jews following the 1870 Décret Crémieux, Algerian-born French citizens remained far less numerous than their foreign-born European counterparts until 1896 (Abun-Nasr 32), which reinforced the sense of beleaguerment of an otherwise hegemonic colonial community. Economic and social disparities reigned supreme over the microcosm of the colony, with wealthy landowners such as Sénateur Duroux, the richest man in Algeria, topping the pyramid, whereas the overall standard of life among Europeans reached only 80 percent of that of the metropole (Evans 26).

Colonial society remained "a racially structured social formation in a state of overt flux, where socio-economic boundaries (and associated taboos) were still permeable" (Dunwoodie, *Writing* 99). At hand was the task of forging an Algerian identity that would vindicate and reinforce the many forms of privilege granted by the colonial order while stabilizing the potential "uncontainability" of Algeria's substantial ethnic and religious diversity—on either side of the staunchly enforced racial divide. The settlers occupied an apprehensive intermediary position at the juncture between two opposed imperatives, demarcating themselves from the nefarious influence of an incommensurable France on the wane and ensuring their continued dominance over the native majority. In this context the mastery of Algeria's powerful (and potentially dangerous) hybridity—between colonizer and colonized but also, in the context of French Algeria, between the contrastive segments within each construct—amounted to nothing short of survival.

In this struggle over symbolic and social capital, literature emerged as a key forum of self-affirmation, and the Algérianiste movement at the turn of the twentieth century reclaimed the literary medium to construct and convey the colony's first major attempt at constructing Algeria's identity. While rejecting the previous Orientalist *littérature d'escale* on account of its exoticized foreign perspective, the movement emphasized for the first time the mixed Mediterranean character of the land. It reconfigured Algeria as the crossroads of disparate Western (Latin) and Oriental cultural influences. Capitalizing on the devalorizing perception of metropolitan Frenchmen and on the territory's marginality, these early authors mapped out Algeria as a self-sufficient regional space. In a metropolitan context regionalist sentiments were on the ascendant as a means of opposing the perceived deliquescence of France's international dominance. Following the 1870 defeat to the Prussians and the loss of Alsace and Lorraine handed over as reparation, conservative regionalisms were regarded as the only legitimate form of resistance to a Republicanism of universalist humanist ideals, which purportedly effected the *déracinement* (uprooting) of the country's youth to the benefit of morally suspect civic values. Algeria's insularity from the rest of the national territory made it a particularly suitable space to develop the kind of hyperlocalized, backward-looking model of identity that conservative intellectual figures such as the Lorraine native Maurice Barrès had spawned (*Les Déracinés*).

Significantly Barrès's seat in the Académie Française went in 1925 to another regionalist *lorrain* writer, Louis Bertrand, who was based in Algeria and whose 1899 novel *Le Sang des races* (The Blood of the Races) has often been considered the literary manifesto of the Algérianiste movement (Lorcin, *Imperial Identities* 198). Based on the writings of Bertrand (1866–1941) and Robert Randau (1873–1950), the Algérianiste school probed the density of Algeria's diverse social fabric from the dual standpoint of racial mixing and *latinité*—a form of Algerian genealogy harkening back to the history of Roman colonization in the Maghreb, which Algérianistes considered to be the determining influence over North Africa's identity.[11] As Bertrand emphasizes in his preface to *Les Villes d'or* (The Cities of Gold), "North Africa is simply . . . the ancient Roman province of Africa" (5).[12] Whether rediscovery of a substantial heritage or wishful symbolic reconstruction of the ruins of a vanished past, the ideological benefits of this distorted vision of the region's history were multiple.

What they had in common was the affirmation of the legitimacy of the French colonial presence in North Africa, which the *latinité* paradigm construed as the latest incarnation of a transhistorical *pax romana*: "In other words, French Africa today is an enduring Roman Africa that never stopped existing even in the most troubled, barbaric times. Archaeologists know this ancient Africa very well" (Bertrand, *Les Villes* 6).[13] The passing mention of Roman archaeology in Algeria harkens back to the pervasive impact of colonial historians and archaeologists whose findings partook of the imperial effort and were a direct source of inspiration for Bertrand—most notably the works of Gustave Boissière (*L'Algérie romaine*), Gaston Boissier (*L'Afrique romaine: Promenades archéologiques en Algérie et en Tunisie*), and the immensely influential colonial historian Stéphane Gsell, who published nearly fifty works on Ancient Algeria (*L'Algérie dans l'Antiquité* and *Histoire ancienne de l'Afrique du Nord* among them).

This genealogical narrative construed the French *colons* as the direct descendants of the Romans, while the native populations were considered only insofar as they exhibited residual signs of Romanization. In a significant conflation of *latinité* and Amazigh identity, Bertrand reconciled these new Algerians in a general movement of *rebarbarisation*. As he argues in *Les Villes d'or*, "what matters is the old legacy of Romanized Berber North Africa" (8), and elsewhere: "The Berber, who was once Christian and Latin, can be converted" (qtd. in Dunwoodie, "Colonizing Space" 1013).[14] Capitalizing on the paronomasia between *berbère* (Berber) and *barbare* (barbarian, that is, a noble savage), Bertrand perceived in the condition of the Berber a model for "barbarian" Latin Mediterraneans to emulate: "I thought . . . that after centuries of exhausting civilization, France could rejuvenate itself through contact with this patent, vigorous primitiveness" (qtd. in Merdaci 25).[15] Taking their cue from Randau, the Algérianistes predicated a mythical "Grande Berbérie" (Great Berber North Africa). The model for the necessary rebarbarization of the French Algerian race promoted by Bertrand, this construct was yet another instance of the modern fascination with the primitive (Dunwoodie, *Writing* 204)—in this case a safe, containable primitive, since Orientalist anthropologists had postulated elements of kinship tying the groups then called Berbers to other Indo-European groups (see Zhiri, *L'Afrique au Miroir de l'Europe*; Anselin; Michel). All these supposed affiliations worked toward the establishment of "the Berber myth" already present in the 1860s—the

Berbers' supposed preeminence in relation to Semitic groups (the Arabs), which functions as a biological justification of the divisive legal measures enacted by the colonial power, such as the 1930 Berber *dahir* in Morocco (Maghraoui; Lorcin, *Historicizing*). The connection to these so-called Berbers as representative of a pristine state of nature also functions on the cultural level, as the focus on "native" Maghrebi populations downplays the importance of successive waves of Muslim conquests, whether Arab or Turkish. Unsurprisingly it is a southern Frenchman descended from Kabyles that Randau chooses as the hero of the eponymous novel *Cassard le Berbère*. Randau's protagonist conjoins pristine Indo-European origins with the vigorous energy of the supposedly true Algerians—the ones whose ancestry can be traced beyond the Arab invasion back to Roman colonization, in a move legitimizing the French conquest of Algeria as the repossession of a long-lost land and echoing the Spanish Reconquista's ambition to reclaim North Africa from the Muslims.

What the Algérianistes found in the most prosperous French colony was a land full of promise and renewed vigor, the ideal setting for the emergence of the new "race" that was robustly taking hold through the (variously successful) integration of the European communities brought together by France's triumphant colonialism. It was a site bursting "with energy, and sometimes heroism, with rejuvenation—physical, intellectual, national, and social" (Bertrand, *Les Villes* 10).[16] Valorizing the building efforts undertaken by the French as part of their civilizing mission (*Le Sang des races* opens with the sentence "They were building modern Algiers"), Bertrand saw in the colonists' determination to leave their mark on the Algerian territory a materialization of the dynamism and energy animating the colonial effort.[17] Although mostly a myth (the vast majority of settlers were urban dwellers), the cult of farming and the cultivation of an unwelcoming, virgin land nevertheless had traction for a colonial *province* determined to invent itself as France's most energetic and promising region. Wresting the Maghreb away from the strictures of an exoticist perspective, it is a Mediterranean Algeria that Bertrand delineates for the first time: "I discarded the Islamic, pseudo-Arab scenery that mesmerized superficial gazes, and I showed . . . an energetic Africa that is barely different from the other Latin Mediterranean countries" (*Les Villes* 6).[18]

This restoration is envisioned in racial terms through the creation of a new bloodline, a bold, hybrid people formed in the image of

Cagayous, Musette's colorful literary figure characterized by his epicurean ruffianness, his Spanish-inspired *espadrilles*, and its humorous use of *pataouète*, a hybrid Mediterranean lingua franca supposed to reverberate with the youthful vitality (and irreverence) of this new race in the making.[19] Along with his truculent male chauvinism, Latin pride, and picaresque adventures, Cagayous's high regard for his Algerian identity became his most recognizable characteristic. To the question "Are you French?" he would always respond with a sonorous "We are Algerian!" Bertrand's fictional world hinges on Cagayous's native Bab-El-Oued, one of Algiers's most distinctive working-class neighborhoods pictured as a Mediterranean melting pot. In this Algerian Babel, Spaniards, Catalans, Piedmontese, Marseillais, Genovese, and other immigrants were united through their physical strength, unbridled sexuality, and epicurean uncouthness, fostering a sense of energy and ebullience born of hybridization and mixing. They converged in an "eternal Mediterranean" figure, an ideal that ultimately espoused the contours of the most rebarbative form of conservatism reminiscent of the "Travail, Famille, Patrie" (Work, Family, Fatherland) slogan of Vichy France (Belamri). Bertrand benevolently emphasizes the cohesion and brotherhood uniting his "African Latin" characters. Yet, as indicated by the fracture separating this new race from its abhorred others—the Muslims as well as the Jews, whom Bertrand's Cardinal Puig urges to exterminate (*La Cina* 262)—Mediterranean unity seemed a flimsy construct when faced with the threat of commingling with native communities. Thus, speaking of the Maltese, Bertrand writes, "Yet, in the end, the rest of them despised them on account of their mixed blood and of their resemblance to the Moors and the Jews" (*Le Sang* 8).[20] A paradigmatic example of Bertrand's rhetoric, this judgment interestingly emphasizes the centrality of blood mixing as the main factor to assess closeness to the natives. Yet the decisiveness of genetic hybridity as a marker of differentiation yields to other considerations. If Malta was indeed under Arab domination from ad 870 to 1090, so was the Iberian peninsula for seven centuries, making the Spanish settler community even more likely to be the product of a racially mixed bloodline. In a dynamic oblivious to the interconnected history of Spain, Rafael, the hero of *Le Sang des races*, nevertheless boasts a Spanish background, and it is in terms of fundamentally Spanish pride that his machismo is emulated by all men in the novel. The disquiet elicited by the Maltese community's proximity to the natives is therefore not merely a matter of long-standing blood mixing; it is also a matter of "resemblance," as Bertrand himself admits. For what set the Maltese apart in colonial society was the ease with which they adapted to colonial life among natives, mostly on account of the Semitic origin of their own language, a mix of North African Arabic and Italian dialects. As the 1879 Keenan Report on Maltese education and language reform argued, "the Maltese had, in fact, become Arabs in language" (qtd. in Mallette 115).[21] As lack of differentiation from an uncontainable native community stands out as the real object of Bertrand's concern, the purported inclusive nature of his Mediterranean ideal is called into question. For if, as expected, the Jews and Moors are bundled together in a position of otherness, the anxiety surrounding the hybridity of other groups ultimately seeps into the very fabric of the community that his writing postulates, revealing the dark underbelly of his Mediterranean construct.[22]

Bertrand's Latin construct thus remains woefully discriminating, restricting the privilege of inclusion to those Mediterraneans who can boast a Latin ascendency, which is mostly demonstrated through affiliation with a Romance language. His "eternal Mediterranean" is in fact little more than an extension of his concept of Latinity, whose failure to take account of the existing permeability between southern Europeans and North Africans indexes the concept to the variable fortunes of the order of segregation on which it rests. Later Algérianiste literary output attempted to detach itself from the glorification of Algeria's Latin past, preferring instead to propel the literature of Algeria forward through the theorization of a more inclusive Mediterranean ideal. Sensitive to the evolutions of the social situation (namely the rise of Algerian nationalism in the interwar period), this new moment went as far as to advocate "the fusion of the races" (Randau, *Les Colons*; Pomier). These later works nevertheless presented the same fixation on the recording of the birth of a new race, in a move reminiscent of Bertrand and in contradiction to its professed inclusive perspective. For all intents and purposes these texts were still European in culture and ardently colonialist (and segregationist) in their outlook. Randau's novels directly tackled the growing peril of budding nationalist claims for more equality, remedying Bertrand's erasure of the natives. Yet the relative assimilation that his writings postulated was no more than a feeble attempt to curtail the explosive potential of nationalist radicalization; docile and always containable within the order of colonial power, the newly represented natives nevertheless remained restricted to the boundaries of their segregated social position.[23]

AN ODYSSEY OF NO RETURN: L'ÉCOLE D'ALGER'S MEDITERRANEAN PAYS

Later generations of self-proclaimed Mediterraneans followed the Algérianistes, taking their predication of Mediterranean identity further in the direction of inclusiveness through assimilation into the French nation—a first, if insufficient, step toward the recognition of the shortfalls of colonial segregation and the need for a sustained engagement with Algeria's wide-reaching hybridity in an egalitarian perspective. During the late 1930s, at the apex of colonial modernity, a group of writers descended from various Mediterranean cultures formed a movement that was to be known as L'École d'Alger (hereafter, L'École).[24] Writers such as Gabriel Audisio, Camus, Emmanuel Roblès, Jules Roy, Jean Amrouche, René Jean-Clot, and Claude de Fréminville coalesced around the figure of Edmond Charlot, the founder of the Editions Charlot, whose series "Méditerranéennes" served as a locus of dialogue for authors with otherwise diverse interests (Dugas, *La Méditerranée*; Rencontres Méditerranéennes Albert Camus; Puche). It is in the small bookshop owned by Charlot on rue Charras that Camus met Audisio in 1937. The shop soon became a fertile site of literary activity in a colony resolutely averse to high culture (Jaffeux; Puche). Journals and literary reviews abounded—among them, *Terrasses, Simoun*, Max-Pol Fouchet's *Fontaine*, and the influential *Forge*, a bilingual French-Arabic journal launched by Emmanuel Roblès, Louis Julia, and El Boudali-Safir, in which Mohammed Dib and Kateb Yacine published some of their earliest texts (Ellis-House, "Hybridity").[25] In addition L'École developed transnational ties with other Mediterraneanist journals, such as Armand Guibert and Jean Amrouche's *Cahiers de Barbarie*, published in Tunis; Henri Bosco's *Aguedal* in Morocco; and Jean Ballard's Marseille-based *Cahiers du sud*.

In the days of L'École, Gabriel Audisio was Algeria's only writer to be published in the metropole by the prestigious NRF. The son of a Piedmontese father and a Niçoise mother, born in Marseille before relocating to Algiers as a child, Audisio evinced a strong interest in historical figures of the Mediterranean, such as Hannibal and Harun al-Rashid, the eighth-century Abbasid caliph who led many expeditions against the Roman Empire in the eastern Mediterranean and the subjects of two books published with Gallimard. The son of a Frenchman who died young, Camus was raised by his mother's Balearic family and nurtured a passion for Spanish culture. In his book written in homage to their friendship, Emmanuel Roblès, a descendant of Andalusians himself, fondly reports their evenings in Andalusian cafés, where both drew inspiration from the hybrid vocal genre of *canto jondo* (Roblès 29). In his veneration of Iberian culture Camus acknowledged and cultivated another layer of identity irreducible to *pied-noir* identity or metropolitan Frenchness. Endowed with the civil and social privilege of French citizenship since 1889 (unlike most Muslim natives), Spanish, Italians, Maltese, and other southern Mediterranean groups were nevertheless considered second-class citizens, in part on account of their working-class status. From their intermediary position between the two main communities (they were dubbed "fifty percenters" [Depierris 19]), the authors relayed a vision of the colonial situation that confounded the dominant discursive framing of French colonial society in binary terms. The mythical pan-Mediterranean identity they elaborated was both cosmopolitan in nature and generative of regional awareness, and it downplayed racial and religious differences between communities.

Audisio was chronologically the first of the group to develop an interest in the cultural interaction brought about by the colonial encounter. An early contributor to *Afrique* and the editor of an anthology of Cagayous stories for Gallimard in 1931, Audisio was no stranger to Algérianiste interpretations of Algeria's heritage. His reappropriation of the potential of Mediterranean hybridity can be read as a direct debunking of the movement's instrumentalization of the concept. Refusing the Algérianistes' very impulse to theorize the existence of a specifically Algerian entity in the making, Audisio dilutes the space of Algeria into a transcolonial Mediterranean paradigm straddling French, Spanish, and Italian colonial borders. Deployed on a wide-reaching geographical scope, his Mediterranean transnational *pays* undermines all nationalistic doctrines, whether European fascism, colonialism, or nascent Algerian nationalism. In the opening pages of *Jeunesse de la Méditerranée* (Youth of the Mediterranean), Audisio delineates his Mediterranean as a "liquid continent with solidified contours," unexpectedly associating the construct to the concept of a "fatherland": "For the people of the sea, there is but one true fatherland—the sea itself. . . . I speak of the 'Mediterranean' as a fatherland, restoring the centripetal force that has completely deserted this 'Mediterranean' concept" (15).[26] The emotionally colored pendant to the concept of *pays*, the transnational *patrie* that Audisio reclaims is said to operate "its own integration" (11).[27] Centrifugal in its perpetual movement, the sea nevertheless unites the diverse groups produced by the region's long history of conquests into a North African mosaic, or "amalgam": "I do not believe in pure races. . . . 'My people' has multiple faces, just like everything that's alive, and its authenticity rests on an amalgam of suspicious antecedents, as do all truths" (13).[28] Adding biological assimilation to cultural mixing (Audisio speaks of "natural blood mixing" [11]), the argument goes as far as to establish the existence of a Mediterranean race, a "cauldron where 'the blood of the races' simmers in a very spicy sauce indeed" (12), in a derisive allusion to Bertrand's magnum opus and its restricted racial genealogy.[29] For Audisio's "eternal Mediterranean" (12) extends inclusion to racial components typically ostracized in the Algerian colonial context ("this Jewish and even African *je ne sais quoi*" [13], even though the specter of Africa is soon to recede into the hazy distance of its trans-Saharan location [18]).[30] If the Mediterranean people (Muslims and non-Muslims alike) constitute a different race, it is one that presents itself as rejuvenating for old northern Europe. Yet this historical eternal youth is not connoted as immaturity or cultural primitivism. A new semantics ties youth to regeneration and vitality, and indeed the slogan of Charlot's bookstore, "Young people for young people by young people," capitalizes on this youthful energy (Jaffeux 19), far from the conservative undertones of Bertrand's regionalist paradigm.[31]

Linking together vitality, nostalgia-inspired mobility, and the paganism inherent in Oriental (i.e., non-Christian) cultural traditions, the recurrent figure of Odysseus the wanderer epitomizes such hybrid Mediterranean forms of being, incarnating what Audisio dubs an enduring "Mediterranean unity" ("unité méditerranéenne" [16, 17]). A common disposition appropriated from the residue of successive civilizations, it joins all the people of the sea in loving kinship. Concurrently shifting the focus from the primacy of Roman history to the ascendency of other Mediterranean civilizations, Audisio's Greek paradigm figures an inclusive Mediterranean stretching beyond the Greco-Latin tradition that northern European colonial modernity has reclaimed as its foundation. Resting on the primacy of paganism and the culture of epics, Audisio's selective appropriation of Greece paves the way for his subsequent discussion of Semitism in *Sel de la mer* (Salt of the Sea). The book downplays the reading of Carthaginian history conveyed by Roman historiography, revealing that it was anti-Semitic sentiments rooted in the fear of cultural and racial contamination that led to the city's repudiation. Rid of its threatening aura, Carthage is reconfigured as the complement to Rome, a locus of fruitful collaboration between Orient and Occident. Through his consideration of Carthage, Audisio thus extends the genealogy of the Mediterranean to include a Semitic element—Jewish rather than Arab, although both branches are inseparable for Audisio. Under the double influence of Greek creativity and Jewish mysticism ("the Semitic Orient . . . of Jewish mysticism" [52]), which should in fact be understood as a form of unreason rather than a purely religious principle, Audisio's Mediterranean surges from the perpetual conflicting encounter between East and West through "horizontal" waves of eastern migrations to the West.[32] In this fluid Mediterranean geography, Tunisia operates as a symbolic heartland, encompassing in its embrace Carthaginian Semitism and Roman Christian domination, a contrast necessary to "faire des étincelles," that is, for the sparks of cultural hybridity to fly (51). A space of conciliation and fusion between Orient and Occident, Audisio's Mediterranean stands the test of time and defies appropriation by any one wave of colonization: "Under Roman rule, Latinity changed almost nothing" (55), a concept that could possibly include the French colonial presence.[33] The "constants . . . of Mediterranean man" ("Homère à Alger" [Homer in Algiers] 358) thus resist dissolution into the transitory rule of empire, aligning Audisio's Mediterranean race with Amrouche's "eternal Jugurtha" as the epitome of an amalgamated North African character (Talbayev, "Berber Poetry").[34] Restoring the mediating impulse intrinsic to the space of the sea, Audisio reinforces its centripetal, desegregating power. As the only true *patrie* the Mediterranean thus becomes a space of reconciliation and synergy, a crucible of otherwise disparate energies generative of balance and measure among its differentiated segments.

Audisio's writing thus performs two shifts. In terms of scales, it mediates the passage to a transnational, hybrid Mediterranean from the self-enclosed Algeria of the Algérianistes, whose model of local hybridity—a result of contemporary migratory patterns rather than a long-standing history of mixing—collapsed under the weight of racial discriminations. On the level of Mediterranean genealogy, it shifts from the proclamation of an exclusive Latin heritage to a strategic reclaiming of Greek Semitic ancestry. The emphasis on the pre-Roman past relativizes the watershed of the Roman conquest, an important political gesture in the heyday of Italian fascism in eastern Africa in the name of a renewed *pax romana*. Concomitantly the absorption of the Semitic element into his Mediterranean genealogy further displaces the very workings of Algérianisme and its putrid anti-Semitic propaganda (*Sel de la mer* 59). In the context of the 1930s, as European nations were increasingly leaning toward fascism, Audisio's focus on a hybrid North Africa transgresses its local boundaries to make it a key locus in the struggle against fascism in all its forms and, beyond it, a restrictive idea of modernity (Dunwoodie, *Writing* 209–11). An analogous positioning against the talons of French colonialism never quite materialized, however, even though fervent nationalist activism marked Algeria for most of the 1930s. Audisio's mistrust of nationalism, an extension of his distaste for fascism, rings hollow when read in the light of Algerian claims, and it could be argued that the predominance of his *pays* concept, a geopolitically inept categorization, was a deliberate denial of the very real and increasingly pressing reality of nationalist claims that had been on the rise throughout the 1930s. In his 1957 *Algérie Méditerranée: Feux vivants* (Mediterranean Algeria: Live Fires), Audisio reasserts the nonexistence of Algeria, positing his mythical Mediterranean hybridity as a suitable substitute for independent national existence. Speaking of a Mediterranean mind-set, he writes, "North Africa, and Algeria more specifically, reveals itself to be a small-scale image—a microcosm—of the whole Mediterranean world" (22).[35] His refusal to engage the category of the nation only leads to aporia as he finally concedes that his vision is doomed to failure: "The amalgam of these diverse elements remained superficial, more apparent than real. . . . There is no such thing as the Algerian community" (25–26), an admission that his shift from "natural blood mixing" in his 1935 text to the concept of "cohabit[ation]" in 1957 amply demonstrates.[36] Inaugurating a pattern that would become all too pervasive in L'École's corpus, Audisio's benevolent transnational Mediterranean thus founders on the colonial question, endlessly oscillating between "the Algeria that was *conquered* . . . and the Algeria that has been *colonized*" (*Jeunesse* 11), his only two possible readings of Mediterranean Algeria.[37]

Camus's approach to the Mediterranean evinces the same distrust of racial and ethnic dichotomies as Audisio's, as well as a similar interest in a transnational paradigm. Camus shares Audisio's belief in the "eternal Mediterranean" and makes use of the same strategic deployment of the transnational *pays* paradigm. His analysis nevertheless attempts to reconcile his belief in the nonhierarchical nature of Mediterranean culture with the realities of colonial rule in Algeria. On account of his failure to embrace the cause of Algerian independence as the ultimate step of his denunciation of colonial inequity, Camus's commitment to social justice within the colony, which his journalistic work for *Alger Républicain* had epitomized from an early date, eventually gained little traction. His position during the war of independence that was to tear Algeria asunder a couple of decades after the publication of his Mediterranean texts has often been construed as little more than a reassertion of irrepressible *pied-noir* colonialist entitlement.[38] Reflecting the inability to maintain a putative, untenable claim to the country of his birth, a sense of affective exile and estrangement waxed large in Camus's texts (his 1942 novel, *The Stranger*, is a case in point), exuding a sense of belatedness that will be echoed in Kateb's appropriation of the concept of *ghorba* (exile). Camus's reflections on the Mediterranean suffuse his speech on the inauguration of the Maison de la Culture in Belcourt in February 1937, an address generally considered to be the founding text of L'École d'Alger (Foxlee). Despite the rise of organized nationalism, which the nearly concomitant founding of Messali Hadj's Algerian People's Party exemplifies, Camus rejects nationalism as the chief principle of identification, favoring instead the same nebulous *pays* ubiquitous in Audisio's texts. Alternately linked to the Mediterranean (Camus, "La Culture indigène" [Indigenous Culture] 567, 569) and North Africa (569), this *pays* dilutes any sense of nationhood into the "edification of a [Mediterranean] culture in a regional frame" (565).[39] The epiphenomena of debilitating decadence (Camus gives the example of the disintegration of the Roman Empire), nations emerge as the residue of unnecessary mediation through abstractions. Desiccating "life" (the essence of Mediterranean culture for Camus), abstraction also petrifies it in "dead thought" ("pensée morte"). Both are categories that eventually shape realities that man, the subject of Camus's humanistic reading of Marxism, should control. Camus's text thus advocates a return to an ancestral Mediterranean "living culture" as an alternative to malicious Germanic and northern European "dead civilization," also to be understood as the nationalistic phase of culture.

Pursuing Audisio's critique of Latinity as the bedrock of a Mediterranean paradigm, Camus restores the predominance of Greece invoked as a principle of irrationality in the face of Roman order and measure. However, his analysis implicitly disunites it from its Semitic pendant. Refusing to postulate a "nationalism of the sun," Camus advocates a Mediterranean humanism in the shape of a "new Mediterranean culture" rid of historicist narratives of progress and producing its own form of connectivity between Mediterranean men communing in the universalized experience of Mediterranean subjectivity: "No need to express this scent or this fragrance through words: we all can sense it with our skin" ("La Culture indigène" 567).[40] A text annunciatory of *la pensée de midi*, which he was to develop in *The Rebel*, the address situates the specificity of Mediterranean modernity in its immediate, intuitive perception through identification with the land in an original experience of the senses. To wit, the lyricism of Camus's contemplation of the Roman ruins in "Noces à Tipasa" (Nuptials at Tipasa), one of the canonical texts in which his hedonistic engagement with a disincarnate Algeria is revealed: "Here, I leave order and measure to others. It is the libertine love of nature and the sea that absorbs me fully. In this blend of ruins and spring time, the ruins have turned back to stone and, losing the polished quality imposed by man, they are reunited with nature. . . . Today, finally, their past deserts them and nothing keeps them from this deep force that brings them back to the crumbling center of things" (15).[41] If "order and measure" harkens back to the notorious discipline of the Roman armies whose conquests the ruins have come to epitomize, Camus immerses his text in sensuality, in an instinctive connection to his environment in which the subject finds its own brand of measure away from distorting ideologies. An anti-intellectual dynamic resting on the primacy of sensations surfaces, recalling the Algérianiste concept of felicitous primitiveness to which Camus himself had laid claim in "*Rivages*: Revue de culture méditerranéenne": "Nothing barbarian can be foreign to us" (870).[42] The exact nature of this barbarian quality is left undetermined, as is the impressionistic Mediterraneanness reclaimed throughout Camus's corpus, the very "amorous drama of Algeria" that Farès denounced so vigorously in *Un passager de l'Occident*. This primitiveness lies close to the "indigenous" character of the new Mediterranean culture that the title "La Culture indigène" postulates, possibly extending the concept to include the healthy primitiveness characteristic of Audisio's early heroes (*Héliotrope*). Camus therefore presents the concept of a Mediterranean identity predicated on subjective experience as the most adequate safeguard against possibly harmful abstractions, for the hybrid quality of the culture with which it is connected is *felt* without mediation by every Mediterranean subject in a renewed (although utopian) solidarity. His analysis endows it with both historical and geographical relevance as it becomes a substitute for nationalistic paradigms, which have historically led to iniquitous colonial situations: "The Mediterranean may be of all countries the only one that truly connects with great oriental thoughts. For it is not classical or orderly, but rather diffuse and turbulent. . . . And, in this space of confluence, there is no difference between the lifestyle of a Spaniard or an Italian from Algiers' docks and that of the Arabs that surround them. The essence of this Mediterranean spirit may spring from this unique encounter in history and geography between Orient and Occident" ("La Culture indigène," 569).[43] In this uncertain *pays* Algeria remains unnamed, partaking in the Mediterranean identitarian maelstrom uniting all subjects in its ahistorical embrace. The Mediterranean "race" inhabiting it, "the curious and strong race living on our shores" (566–67), is a function of this diffused geography.[44] The only acceptable metonymy for the absent nation, the liminal space of the shore glistens. It casts Algeria as the matrix of Camus's "insular spaces . . . independent . . . spaces inhabited by 'happy people that have no history' . . . spaces that seem to be out of time . . . almost like mythical spaces" (Rufat 35).

This indeterminate nature will be transposed to Camus's later work as a principle of belatedness and dissonance (Gonzales), a pervasive silence accompanying the silencing performed by his writing—the mark of the subject's inadequacy to his *pays* once the shroud of the legitimizing Mediterranean myth has been lifted. Centered on the space of Algeria, Camus's posthumous novel *Le Premier homme* cloaks the land in its etymological insularity (the Arabic name for Algeria, al-Jaza'ir, means "the islands") as a space unaffected by the course of history. It is "[some] kind of vast island, protected to the North by the moving sea and to the South by the sands' petrified waves . . . a nameless country" (11) that echoes the "diffuse and turbulent" Mediterranean as a point of confluence that his early works postulated.[45] Camus's late colonial iteration of his *pays* eventually inhabits the differential space between an untenable colony soon to be dissolved and an impossible claim to nationhood. In an echo of Farès's prescient judgment, Camus proclaims that "the great forgetting . . . was the final fatherland for the men of his race" (212), consecrating the failure of Mediterranean hybridity to mitigate the unbridgeable material differences between communities in a colonial context.[46] Adumbrating this late admission of incommensurability, the recourse to the principle of cohabitation ("cohabitent") in his 1937 address ("La Culture indigène" 569) echoes Audisio's avowal of the failings of Algerian hybridity, making true integration an even more elusive prospect. Citing "an encounter" (569) and "a contact" (570) between Orient and Occident, Camus never quite advocates the fusion of races underpinning Audisio's utopia. The previously cited enumeration on the docks of Algiers is a case in point. While the Spanish and Italian subjects are endowed with the privilege of individuality and associated agency, the natives are presented as an indistinct group ("the Arabs"). Moreover the focus is on the central two characters, the European subjects, while the natives who surround them hold their habitual peripheral, marginal position. Likewise, when reconstructing the prestigious genealogy of this "Mediterranean truth" (569), from Romance languages to medieval feudal orders, Camus deliberately excludes Arab, Muslim, and Amazigh elements, relaying the restrictive vision of a purely southern European origin of Mediterranean history.

Even Camus's early argument appears to be at odds with colonial reality, and his efforts to promote the equality of all subjects (his denunciatory chronicles of inequality under colonial rule in Kabylia are well known) seem to eventually fall prey to the same colonial dynamics of segregation. His strategic move toward a small-scale, culturally specific geography of revolt within an internationalist framework does not in any way promote the end of colonialism or Algerian independence. Nationalistic thinking, even the anticolonial kind, is dismissed, further limiting the practical impact of Camus's proposition since the natives' position within colonial society excludes them from any nonnationalist configuration of revolt. Apter reads this blindness in the face of ineluctable historical change in the governance of Algeria as a "consummate oxymoron; a cosmopolitan hallucination of hybridity hatched in full view of decolonization . . . [that] illustrates the conflict . . . between worldly hybridities and nationalist ethnic and religious particularisms" ("Out of Character" 506). The myth of origins Camus attempts with his Mediterranean ideal never quite finds its way to actualization, and his meditations on the Mediterranean evolve toward a quest for a truth that would make the European Algerians' presence (those he calls "les Algériens") legitimate. From this failed effort Camus's notorious silence will emerge late in his life. It will leave its mark on his conflicting legacy throughout Algerian literature.[47]

OF CITIES, RUINS, AND BLOOD

Kateb's *Nedjma* follows the peregrinations of four young Algerian men in the wake of the French colonial regime's repression of the 1945 Sétif riots. At the core of this group is Nedjma, a striking beauty born of a southern French Jewish mother and an Algerian father of the Keblout tribe, whose exact identity remains unknown. The object of the four protagonists' desire, Nedjma mediates their quest for origins, which will perpetually interrogate the contours of the independent Algeria that she allegorizes. A "refuge of values" for Khatibi (qtd. in Woodhull, *Transfigurations* 26), Nedjma embodies the tumultuous connection to the men's Keblout tribal origins, which the novel deploys along an unnostalgic, forward-reaching trajectory intertwined with the development of the protagonists' nationalist leanings. Bensmaïa's trifurcate model of Algerian literary history (divided in successive colonial, mythical, and interruptive moments) reads Kateb's work as partaking of the second moment of "mything fiction," that is, the affirmation of a "single, unified Algeria . . . [a truth that] would continue to be reinforced during the first decade following independence" (*Experimental Nations* 23). In a reading slightly closer to Farès's text, I tease out *Nedjma*'s resistance to the cohesive power of the myth of origins elaborated in the days of anticolonialism. Starting from the reading of Nedjma as "an emblem of the contradictory forces at work in Algeria's search for national identity" (Woodhull, *Transfigurations* 1), I trace the multiple, irreducible tensions that permeate a text more invested in the denunciation of any myth of pure origins (Bensmaïa's "demystification") than in the definition of a strictly contoured form of nationhood.[48]

The national consciousness perceptible in the novel hinges precisely on the very concept of Mediterranean hybridity that presided over colonial limnings of Algerian identity. The novel's fragments set in Constantine provide a particularly auspicious context for the examination of this sedimented form of Algerian heritage. Interspersed with Rachid's hashish-tinged meditations in the *fondouk* in Constantine, an evocation of Algeria's variegated past surges, coalescing around the material rubble of ancient Numidian ruins. Constantine-Cirta and Bône-Hippone form a twofold metaphorical urban nexus stretching over illustrious historical episodes and crystallizing distinguished genealogies. Constantine, the seat of the Association of Algerian Muslim Ulama led by Sheikh Abdelhamid Ben Badis, the Arabo-Islamic faction of Algerian nationalism, is also Kateb's birth city. Underlying the politically influential modern city of Islamic revival, the ruins of Cirta, the epitome of Numidian resistance to Roman rule, captivate the narrative. Capitalizing on its near-unassailable geographical position on a rocky flat-topped hill surrounded by the labyrinthine gorges of the Rummel River, the city is known locally as "ad-dahma" (the crushing one). Nestled in a terrain naturally hostile to colonial expansion, "the Rock" fostered a history of staunch resistance to invasions across centuries.[49] The palimpsestic urban markers evoked throughout the novel (Rachid's Turkish house, the Roman bridge, the casbah, the palace, the catacombs where the bey's enemies were entombed) delineate a convoluted, layered topography, which the dereliction and disrepair following the French conquest cannot mask. The last major Algerian city to succumb to France's military onslaughts, Constantine is cast as the realm of origins and historical ruins, fostering a sense of disorientation generated by the difficulty of finding one's place within the surfeit of available historical references. In contrast Bône, as it was known in Kateb's day, materializes as a modern city built from the ground up by a government eager to lay claim to its favorable coastal location. By 1945 the rectilinear city had become the city of colonial modernity (Graebner, *History's Place* 266). Lying at the end of the train line, the mechanical synecdoche of colonial progress, the cityscape was dominated by the clock atop its fabled neo-Moorish train station; geographically and teleologically Bône was colonial modernity's ultimate enactment.[50]

In the topography of colonial Algeria, Bône figured as a space of interaction and exogamy, a Mediterranean microcosm that might have been endowed with the potential to bring to life a refreshing mixing of bloodlines. Yet the new abundance spilling over the city bears the stigma of opprobrium and ill omen. Whereas the meeting point of the local river and the Mediterranean sea is painted as a "mirage," echoing Audisio's disillusion with a genuine form of biological hybridity among Algeria's populations, the eventual outpouring of the river into the sea evokes a decomposition of cataclysmic proportions: "Drowning in the slaver of a lamentably wallowing sea, that low, cold-blooded mother who spreads through the city an odor of sorcery and torpor . . . '*A nation of beggars and parasites, fatherland of invaders*,' Mustafa thinks, '*a country of hooded women, of femmes fatales*'" (*Nedjma* trans. 88).[51] The femme fatale of highest symbolic capital, Nedjma reigns supreme in the landscape of Bône's undecidable terrain. Tied to the urban site enshrining her, she embodies its predicted annihilation, infecting the city with the lascivious accents of her seduction: a "woman-city" for Jacqueline Arnaud, "she is a courtesan. . . . She devours conquerors, like Nedjma the ogress, the soul of the city" ("Les Villes mythiques" 14). Herself an irresistible mirage appearing at one of the windows of the Villa Nedjma, the family residence nestled in an unkempt, luxuriant, verdant patch suggestively blocking the tram's route, Nedjma is defined by indomitable fluctuation—now characterized by "auburn hair" (*Nedjma* trans. 89) and "native pallor" (104), her throat evocative of "the white gleams of a foundry" (105), now "very dark, almost black" (104).[52] She nevertheless remains "Mediterranean" ("Méditerranéenne" [104/73]), possibly precisely on account of this fickleness. Although Nedjma draws irresistible power from this unpredictability, her eventual captivity at the hands of Si Mabrouk makes her "a final gleam of autumn, a besieged city fending off disaster" (244).[53] Circulating endlessly in a concealed carriage on the road between Constantine and Bône, she consecrates the two cities' ruin, their sepulchral alienation. As the unfolding of diegetic time locks the novels' protagonists in a cycle of stagnation, a defeated Constantine, hemmed in by the gorges of the Rummel, reverberates with the subterranean, circuitous nature of the river's course. Figuring its constrained itinerary and downfall, the torrential waterway devolves into an "exhausted river" (229), a "pseudo-Rummel," conveying a sense of dismal ineffectuality, which also colors Rachid's characterization: "a pseudo-Rachid issuing too late from his father's death, like the [Oued-el-Kebir] prolonging only the [Rummel]'s shadow and its dryness, without restoring its vanquished violence" (trans. 240).[54] A restoration of the prestigious lexeme Guadalquivir to its Arabic etymology, "l'oued el-Kebir" (the great river) is itself construed as a pale reflection of the mythical Andalusian river. This Oued-el-Kebir, depleted of its mythical Andalusian charge, only conjures the aura of another halcyon North African warring past to set current-day abdication in relief: "vanquished, tracked down under the Rock like the Moors driven from Andalusia . . . a futile escape" (238).[55]

Throughout the novel the past is a locus of defeat and loss, whether in the form of hollowed-out mythical signifiers or material architectural ruins. Consummating the impossibility of movement, its resurgence overlays the novel with an irrevocable sense of belatedness. As any forward-moving form of temporality is rendered inert, the inexorable pull toward origins disrupts the line of agency. By "turning defeat into peace," previous generations have entrenched the tribe's abdicated potency: "too many fathers to be born by broad daylight, too many ambitious races disappointed, mingled, confused, constrained to creep upon the ruins" (*Nedjma* trans. 245).[56] Thus Rachid's itinerary evolves from political protest in his school days to seemingly aimless wandering in the streets of Constantine, before his final isolation on the balcony of the *fondouk*, where he will tell stories of entombment and failed ambitions amid the haze of hashish. With its future truncated, the novel's chronology can only attempt to reclaim a mythicized past of grandeur through contemplative reappropriations of the history enshrined in its ruins. Yet the vestiges underlying the novel's poetic production do not quite coincide with the revered "ennobled specters" (233) of the past.[57] These hallowed mementos exude their own approaching demise: Kateb evokes "the remains of the Romans . . . that kind of ruins, where the soul of the multitudes has only time to waste away, engraving their farewell in the rock" (*Nedjma* trans. 232).[58] Upending colonialist readings of Roman ruins as evidence of the land's supposedly Latin heritage, Kateb restores these ruins to their eroded legacy, equating their erection with the impending disappearance of the civilization that produced them. In their stead another sort of ruins filters through Kateb's engagement: "the ruins watermarked from all time" (232), which Kateb evokes contrapuntally, unexpectedly gesturing toward the long-standing debates over the deep nature of Maghrebi identity.[59] Laying the groundwork for a reconsideration of the biological heritage born of multiple historical waves of conquest, these diachronically constituted ruins ("de tous les temps") consecrate the multiple components making up Algerian identity. These ruins "steeped in the blood of our veins" (232) are the vestiges of a complex history of contact and mixing.[60] Taken in its productive ambivalence, this phrase can summon not only the blood shed during battle but also the blood soaking the watermark, the mixed blood of ancestry that makes the watermark legible and that alone can dole out the right interpretation of the complex past—and suggest the appropriate commemoration of its traces. Evoking the most intimate vector of identity, the biological lineage to which one is tributary, this diachronic hybridity gives the present its deep density. "The inestimable ruins of the present" (232), though lacking apter deciphering, are nonetheless perceptible right beneath the translucent surface of time.[61] They are visible only against the light, through the visual excoriation of multiple layers of time in the palimpsest of past accumulations. Relegated to the realm of secrecy, their resurrection requires no more than the right set of circumstances, "the place or the time suitable for seeing them" (232).[62]

Whatever their reach, I read the ruins reclaimed in the text as the metaphorical rendering of Algeria's composite bloodlines away from easy-made narratives of ancestry and identity. Graebner rightly argues that "even Kateb's rejection of the myth of Arab and Islamic unity (problematic in Algeria) does not lead to a less conflicted construction of the past. . . . The ruins are 'Numidian' and therefore Amazigh rather than Arab, but the Amazigh-identified past remains just as difficult to build upon as the glorified Arab conquest" (*History's Place* 273).[63] Through the reclaimed identitarian palimpsest, an undeniable form of hybridity presides over the development of Algerian identity and culture, making any claim to purity incongruous and deceitful. Even Numidian Cirta postdates more ancient, mysterious origins. Kateb evokes "a name older perhaps, perhaps Byzantine; a name perhaps older than Cirta" (*Nedjma* trans. 246).[64] More than an atavistic bloodline, it is a political commitment in favor of independence that defines Algerian belonging. Further along the text characterizes the "nation spread between two continents" as "the Old Numidia where the Roman descendants have succeeded each other" (233).[65] Jocelyne Dakhlia, cited by Tlatli, argues that this Roman component is endowed with a synecdochic quality in Maghrebi languages and collective memory, which proved oblivious to historical stages of conquest and subordinated all invasions of North Africa to the most powerful ancient conquest at the hands of the Romans (*L'Oubli* 52). The novel itself plays up the metonymy: "But it is Corsicans instead of Romans now; all Corsicans, all prison guards, and we play the slaves' roles in the same prison, near the lion pit, and the sons of the Romans do guard duty with rifles on their shoulders" (Kateb, *Nedjma* trans. 56).[66] The phrase *descendants romains*, which recurs several times in the narrative, thus mediates the intrinsic opposition between native and foreign colonial elements in a clear refutation of Bertrand's colonial paradigm of "our ancestors the Romans" (*Les Villes* 8), which also encompassed "Berber" groups. At the other end of the spectrum stand Amazighs and other defenders of North African autonomy from Christian rulers. Kateb underlines that "neither the Numidians nor the Barbary pirates conceived in peace" (*Nedjma* trans.

233), putting the spotlight on the composite ancestry of Numidians united through their mixed offspring in a common position of resistance to the transhistorical "Roman" adversaries.[67] Building on the synecdochic significance of the Roman conquest as a stand-in for all other colonizing invasions, Kateb's text thus posits native resistance to foreign domination as the only form of verified (and desirable) heritage.[68]

Algerian identity is left open-ended, a receptacle for all identifications aligned in the fight against colonialism, an inclusive spectrum reaching as far as African ancestry, through the figure of the black man, and as far as Nedjma's Jewish origins. If a national consciousness is at work within Kateb's text in the form of a desire to mold existence to the law of the ancestors in a land rid of foreign aggression, Soraya Tlatli's analysis points out that this impulse hardly coincides with its historical realization: "[The book's] particular logic proscribes reading it in light of the country's accession (as a fragmented tribal entity) to nationhood" (54). Instead she identifies a "negative sacralization of the native land," which she reads in light of Ibn Khaldun's conception of history. Concerned with the identification and rationalization of historical development, Ibn Khaldun's 1377 *Muqaddima*, the prolegomenon to his *Kitab al-ʿIbar* (The Book of Lessons), which he intended as a history of the Islamic world, located the motor of history in the concept of *ʿasabiyya* (social solidarity). A function of group consciousness in a tribal context, *ʿasabiyya* does not demand blood relations as a prerequisite for the feeling of unity and cohesion that it designates. Its cohesiveness extends beyond the coterminous order of the clan to embrace "any one of social or ideological structures that hold societies together and motivate conquests" (Graebner, *History's Place* 263). The vision of history it relays emphasizes multidirectionality and concomitance among various historical moments following the ebb and flow of dynasties and civilizations. In this respect Ibn Khaldun's conception of history runs against the grain of both colonial understandings of Arab temporality (as a cycle duplicating itself to no end) and teleological visions of time that suppose a linear, deterministic chronology ending in Western modernity.[69] Cognizant of this double negation, Graebner likens the concept to Deleuze's baroque fold: "The Baroque trait twists and turns its folds, pushing them to infinity, fold over fold, one upon the other. The Baroque fold unfurls all the way to infinity" (qtd. in Graebner, *History's Place* 258). This infinitude of ramifications extends the coordinates of Kateb's text to a boundless horizon, capitalizing on this vision of history as a nonsequential narrative rife with circuitous detours and destabilizing returns to question the limits of an Algerian nation yet to be defined.

Construed in its temporal dimension through Ibn Khaldun's conceptions of history, this vision of the national quest resists assimilation into a nation-state structure modeled on Western incarnations. For such is the allure of the protean, transitional period during which the novel was composed. In the post-1945, pre-1954 context of *Nedjma*, with the nascent nationalist war yet to be initiated, political activism has no outcome other than imprisonment, torture, or exile.[70] As Arnaud argues, "Love is impossible, revolt is impossible; it's a dead-end" (*Recherches* 731). Whereas the contours of a future independent Algeria are discernible, the attempt to harness the national sentiment pervading the novel to a teleological nation-building process founders, while the return to an original Nadhor, the tribe's territory serving as the symbolic foundation of identity, yields nothing but death and stasis. A formerly triumphant Nedjma, allegorizing Algeria, eventually falls prey to the inhibiting logic of the tribe, to its atavistic obsession for purity: she is abducted by Si Mabrouk and later sequestered in a closed carriage perpetually traveling the distance between Bône and Constantine. Dispersing her symbolic capital in contradictory episodes, the novel casts Nedjma as "Algeria's 'betweenness' because of her multifaceted, contradictory, and shifting identity encompassing past and future, tribal and national society: she is of culturally mixed and uncertain parentage and has symbolic ties to France" (Woodhull, *Transfigurations* 27). Nedjma becomes a principle of undecidability, figuring both the vivacity and the curtailment of nationalism in the pre-1954 days. In Woodhull's words, "Nedjma is . . . a productive force in, rather than the static ground for, emergent nationalism's affirmation of the cultural heritage" (27). In *Nedjma*, Algeria lies at the meeting point between atavistic impulses to reconstruct the social bonds etiolated by colonialism and a marked evolution toward the future.

It is my argument that if Algeria's emergence is inextricably bound to the historical process of nationalism, it should not be restricted to the contingencies ushered in by the war of independence, and certainly not to the kind of power that came of it. The kind of nationalism the novel fosters both propels and exceeds the nation's historical incarnation in the postcolony. Any reading retroactively infusing *Nedjma* with the validating aura of the liberation struggle would only serve to propagate the myth that FLN rule is the necessary teleological end to the anticolonial process. In turn such a move would problematically restrict *Nedjma* to a mere validation of that myth. In contrast Ibn Khaldun's circuitous theses on history delineate the future adumbrated in *Nedjma* as "the future [of a] heterogeneous nation" (Woodhull, *Transfigurations* 27), which, without refusing inscription into the dynamics of nationalism, reaches beyond the monolithic regime that came to power after 1962. This reframing of *Nedjma* undermines interpretations casting it as an immature harbinger of ulterior, more politically effective forms of national consciousness. It ultimately suggests that *Nedjma* should not be read as the Algerian novel that effected the passage from proteiform national impulses to more politically viable models of nationhood, but rather in terms of its own *pensée mythique*, the "foundation by fiction" of a mythical Algeria mediating "the passage from an allegorical reality to an allegory turned reality" (Farès, *Un passager* 37). Considering the specific period of its elaboration and discounting the alluring magnetism of the impending war as a primary frame of reference is therefore essential for any approach seeking to look beyond the claustrophobic experience of Algerian nationalism presented in the novel. In this respect, restoring Kateb's diegetic world to its transnational reach through the Mediterranean deployment of its revolutionary quest marks a first step in that direction.

OF GHORBA AND ÉTRANGETÉ

"In its 'impersonal and concrete' power, isn't Algiers' Kasbah a labyrinth? It is this usurped power that . . . turns any attempted escape into exile. . . . Ali la Pointe and all the others sentenced to death are children of the polygon. They inhabit a violent death, just as I write from a dead-end" (Kateb, *Le Poète* 176).[71] Such is Kateb's response to Jacques Berque and Jean Duvignaud's investigation into the nature of the polygon—the geometrical figure metonymically presiding over Kateb's entire oeuvre.[72] Keeping in mind the strong metonymic association casting the Algiers casbah (the theater of the infamous Battle of Algiers in 1957, immortalized in Gillo Pontecorvo's 1966 film) as the epitome of Algerian resistance to colonialism, it may be argued that the figure of the polygon evoked in these lines overlays the all-encompassing nation-in-the-making. A principle of defensiveness in the face of aggression ("offensive angles pointing outward" [176]), the polygon ultimately leads to violent death.[73] Its only alternative is permanent desertion, complete expulsion from the all-engulfing dynamics of nationalism through irrevocable exile from a consuming homeland.

In a 1965 text on the Turkish poet Nazim Hikmet Kateb explains, "The Arabic word *gharib* means stranger. *Ghorba* means exile. The Maghreb, a word derived from the same root, was for the Arabs a land of exile. The same word, *ghorba* in Arabic, *gourbet* in Turkish, means both the poet's wandering and the strange presence of the stranger" ("Nazim Hikmet" 236).[74] Capitalizing on the polysemy of the trilateral root, which runs the gamut from strangeness and alienation to nostalgia and wandering with a detour via the conceptual armature of Sufi mystic thought, Kateb's reflections on the concept of *ghorba* illuminate the layering intrinsic to all identities. Through an examination of exile and the predominance of an outsider's positionality saturating Kateb's writing (*l'étranger/ère*, or *gharib*, in his poetic cycle), the novel's critical quest for supposedly pure tribal origins to be used as national foundation gives way to an irrevocable dynamic of "violent dispersion" (Bonn, *Kateb Yacine* 16). It is in confined spaces, such as the prisons where Lakhdar and Rachid are incarcerated, the hospital where Rachid meets Nedjma, and the grotto where Nedjma was conceived, that a narrative of origins is elaborated through revelations, apparitions of the Keblout ancestor, or echoes of previous episodes in the text. In contrast the characters' recurring disappearance introduces the principle of mobility to the core of the novel, which the text itself consistently corroborates through the repetition of the friends' open-ended journey along bifurcate roads that brings the 1956 novel to its temporary ending ("the two shadows fade on the road" [*Nedjma* trans. 46/344]).[75] From this standpoint Nedjma's multiple flights out of imprisonment contribute to preserve her layered complexity from dissolution into this raw, corrosive national force, though at the price of disjunction and loss. Even Rachid's atavistic model of identity and legacy—his anti-Roman stance delineated through the contemplation of the ruins—ultimately succumbs to the dominance of exile as he eventually leaves Algeria with Si Mokhtar, a dynamic recurring both in the novel and in other contemporaneous texts from Kateb's corpus. As one last deviation beyond the bounds of an all-too-restrictive narrative topography, the alternative routes charted by the protagonists' journey undercut the overdetermined space of Constantine and Bône, the two static cities bounding Nedjma's debilitating to and fro itinerary. The choice of ending the novel with the start of a new voyage outside the confines of the tribe's order suggests that the heuristic search for Algeria cannot be fully brought to term without a simultaneous spatial deployment. Linked to the inescapable reality of exile, the reader's encounter with Lakhdar and Mustapha in Bône is marked with the seal of *étrangeté*, or *ghorba*. As for Nedjma, *l'Étrangère*, she is the object of three distinct abductions, which make her the figure most vulnerable to (forced) displacement in the whole novel.

Linking the exile's feeling of estrangement to the deracination from which it ensues, the concept of *ghorba* sheds light on the constitutive presence of heterogeneity within the Algerian nation. As the figure of the Poet inherited from the classical Arabic tradition is endowed with the gift of *étrangeté* (an inherent discrepancy with his environment), the awareness of heterogeneous traditions within national culture becomes the desirable hallmark of a higher order of civilization, which, in Kateb's reading, is not devoid of political undertones. In Kateb's meditations all poets marked with the prestigious seal of *ghorba* are canonized as "martyrs" of the successive oppressive Ottoman regimes, and the text acclaims them as a vector of identification and unity for all opponents to state-sponsored violence ("Nazim Hikmet" 238). This *ghorba* is best synthesized in the tutelary figure of Ibn Khaldun, whose conception of history proved so influential to *Nedjma*. The parallel is also found solidly anchored at the heart of *Le Polygone étoilé* (The Starred Polygon): "Imagine Andalusia in the late Middle Ages. Imagine the golden age of the Arab world in those days. A family from Yemen, established in Sevilla and settled in Tunis gives birth to Abu Zeid Abderrahman Ibn Mohamed. He will be known as Ibn Khaldun" (80).[76] His forced exile and multiple incarcerations in Spain, the Maghreb, and Egypt have made Ibn Khaldun a paradigmatic *gharib*, the exile whose peregrinations are coextensive with the articulation of an ennobling poetic persona. Embodying the halcyon age of al-Andalus, the apex of Arab civilization in Kateb's imaginary, his itinerary constitutes a patent inspiration for the persona of Keblout himself, the ferocious Ancestor reigning over the mystified space of Nadhor. His tribe is depicted in *Nedjma* as "Tolbas, wandering students" (trans. 165), who transited through the twin pillars of Spain and Morocco within which the lingering memory of Arab Andalusia is contained.[77] A pure hypothesis just as uncertain as the peregrinations relayed by the *ghorba* narrative, the genealogy of the tribe emphasizes the indeterminacy of origins and buttresses the supremacy of exile as a foundational category. Alongside it, it brings to the fore the intrinsic syncretism born of the tribe's multiple displacements. The object of several semantic alterations, the very name Keblout is derived from the Turkish word for "broken rope," whose enduring echo can be found in the Arabic "Hbel" (165/116). With the spirit of Ibn Khaldun looming large over the reminiscence, the layered nature of the tribe's history complicates any nativist prejudice in the formation of Algerian identity. Kateb's Algeria emerges from the successive assimilation of foreign elements, exceeding the history of ransacking conquests that have left the country exsanguinated since ancient times. This history is to be read as strata of resistance culminating in the nascent nationalist movement; it is the willingness to join in the fight against colonial aggression that truly brings incorporation into the crucible of Maghrebi history to a close. In fact the Keblout lineage is itself the product of biological syncretism, a process gradually uniting the supposedly pristine Amazigh tribe with the exiled Arabs. Keblout is said to have been ultimately "chosen or adopted by the natives who gradually entered his family and finally made him the elder of the community" (trans. 166).[78]

Suffused with the movement and rhythm of an open-ended poetical mode of writing, the narration recalls the mobility of the ancestor's peregrinations beyond Nadhor, the marching progression of a caravan.[79]As the narrative structure flexibly adjusts to render the multiple, noncongruent temporalities and voices, the ebb and flow of storytelling constantly needs to negotiate the unresolved disparities that make *Nedjma* a novel of circulation—of semes, textual fragments, and recurrent narratives. Propelled by a fluid structure, the never-ending storytelling both molds the story and gives free rein to incursions and additions, to variations and revisions.[80] As words are rearranged into new constellations, new meanings coalesce. They course out of the entropic narrative space of the novel marked with the dark seal of stasis to join disruptive spaces of narration (inserts from notebooks, Keblout's portentous speech, among others), which form "dialogical—not lost—voices" (Raybaud 154). Beyond the confines of the novel, ancillary texts, concurrently partaking of the cyclical structure of Kateb's mythical narrative, divulge new synergies and movements. Kateb's part-journalistic, part-poetic triptych on the Land of the Lotus-Eaters, Djerba, performs such a revelatory function. The texts that compose the Djerbian cycle are "Djerba, l'île de l'étrangère" (1958), introduced as an excerpt from *Le Polygone étoilé* that will nevertheless not be found in the 1966 Seuil edition of the novel; "Le Lotos" (1964), a rewriting of the first text "in the direction of further fictional development" (Kateb, *Oeuvre* 436); and "Les Poissons sautent" (1965).[81] All three texts were published in newspapers and journals: Tunisian *L'Action*, *Dialogues*, and *Révolutions africaines*, respectively. The first two texts, more intimately tied to the narrative blocks developed in *Nedjma* and *Le Polygone étoilé*, provide a coda, a detour of sorts from the seemingly infinite back and forth of Nedjma's forced itinerary. Her exile in Djerba, an island off the coast of southern Tunisia, supplies a continuation to the supposed dead end suspending her fate at the hands of her captors: it is in Djerba where her resistance to the tutelage and coercion forced on her by the male protagonists will be enacted and where she will eventually gain relative agency.

Set in a parallel diegetic dimension, the texts take account of the heroine's continuous mobility out of her Algerian confinement, performing her metaphorical redeployment in the ex-centric yet coterminous Mediterranean space of the island. Thus Kateb mentions a strange woman, "the Stranger fearing neither God nor men, who had sought refuge on the island in the days of the Babylonian captivity. It is said that the Jews . . . had found her in a branch hut near . . . their quarter" ("Djerba").[82] This mythical presence, which Kateb rewrites as another incarnation of the *femme sauvage* (wild woman) permeating his texts, reappears briefly in *Le Polygone étoilé* as "the untraceable amnesiac from the island of the Lotus-Eaters" (148).[83] Herself the daughter of an *étrangère*, Nedjma is consistently touted as hybrid, the product of several consecutive forceful removals and reiterations of her mother's abductions, "the insatiable Frenchwoman . . . three times ravished . . . a Jewess" (*Nedjma* trans. 136).[84] Her variegated descent also harkens back to a constellated African lineage: "the Sudan that unifies us, the sun of the future and the darkness of the land of the dead that comes to us from Upper Egypt and its impersonal, concrete Trinity" (Kateb, "Le Papyrus" 256).[85] This characterization buttresses the porous heritage periodically resurfacing throughout the novel: "For the story of our tribe is not written anywhere, but no thread is ever broken for those who seek their origins" (Kateb, *Nedjma* trans. 192).[86]

Bearing the mark of Kateb's journalistic reportage, the texts recontextualize the quest for Nedjma in a nonnational mythical framework, crossing the search for the Algerian nation with the Homeric episode of the Lotus-Eaters in the *Odyssey*, situated on the island of Djerba. Reported in full form in both "Le Lotos" and "Les Poissons sautent" and constituting by that token the most conspicuous narrative concatenation of the three Djerbian fragments, the intertext of the Homeric story interrogates the attachment to the homeland as a sine qua non for social existence. The "impersonal, concrete Trinity" referenced in relation to Nedjma's heritage overlaps with the ternary rhythm running through the lotus imagery: the jujube trees in Bône, the island of the Lotus-Eaters, and the *fondouk* musicians (Kateb, "Le Papyrus" 256). With all three incarnations of the lotus alluding to the same propensity in three distinct contexts—forgetting, the jujube fruit being one of the possible inspirations behind Homer's lotus—the constellation places at its center the ever elusive, tumultuous relation to memory and origins in an oblique engagement with the cognate process of nation formation and attendant amnesia. It also strings together the three settings of the common quest deployed throughout the narrative cycle in an interlocking geography: the city of Bône, incarnating French colonial rule; the island of Djerba, the meeting point of western and eastern Mediterranean cultures; and the city of Constantine, home to Rachid's *fondouk* and the backdrop to his ruminations on Algeria's past. Encompassing the dialectic of authenticity and modernity in the Algerian stalemate, the triangulation of the quest contains the germs of the eventual transnational evolution portentously announced in *Le Polygone étoilé* ("The untraceable amnesiac from the island of the Lotus-Eaters" [148]).[87]

The narrative braiding of the two storylines—the cross-Mediterranean continuation of the quest for Nedjma and the contrapuntal rewriting of the Lotus-Eaters' episode—takes on full meaning when read in conjunction with the Jewish tradition framing the texts. Accompanied by Si Mabrouk, the preserver of the tribe's legacy, Nedjma fully morphs into *l'Étrangère*. In so doing she arrogates to herself the ahistorical space of the Djerbian legend of a strange woman living on the island prior to the Jews' arrival, whose sepulcher is said to lie beneath the foundation of the Ghriba synagogue—in its literal Arabic meaning, the synagogue of the *Étrangère*—a space incarnating Djerba's complex symbolic position in Kateb's cycle.[88] Paul Sebag dates the arrival of the Jews in Djerba to the first exile, in 586 bc. According to legend, the *kohanim* (priests) who built the Ghriba incorporated fragments from the Temple of Solomon into the foundation of the synagogue, branding the Jewish diaspora to North Africa with the seal of continuity and memory (Sebag 18). The episode is but one of the many tales surrounding the history of the sanctuary, and its transmission adds a syncretic touch to the worship rituals surrounding the synagogue in Jewish tradition. Historically considered the holiest house of worship in all of Djerba, the Ghriba is also the only synagogue to contain Torah scrolls anywhere on the island, and the sanctuary is still the object of a prominent annual pilgrimage attracting worshippers from the entire world. Crossing pagan legend with Jewish ritual, which, in the syncretic space of Djerba, was also deeply imbricated with Muslim worship, the text offsets the plural character of the Djerbian cult: "[The synagogue] originally housed the living quarters of a pagan woman. . . . She died in her hut wrapped in mystery, without ever revealing her religion or her origins; it is said that the Jews fleeing the Babylonian captivity were moved by the fortunes of the Stranger (this is what they would always call her) and honored her with a temple built on the spot where the future synagogue would be erected" ("Djerba").[89] Overlaying the figure of the *Étrangère* with the pagan woman of the legend, Kateb throws into relief the island's symbolic contiguity with his homeland, inscribing it in his narrative cycle as the "genealogical, pluri-confessional, heterodox, progressive, emancipatory space" (qtd. in Aresu, "Arcanes algériens" 182) that colonial Algeria failed to incarnate.

Lying at the heart of a complex web of Mediterranean migrations, Kateb's Djerba is conjured as a geography of movement, long itineraries, extensive territorial crossings, and ritualized returns to specific points that stress its edenic disposition for exiles (it is an "Éden insulaire" [Kateb, "Les Poissons" 156]). Ensconcing the island in the repetitive echo of ritualized journeys, whether across the sea or the desert, Kateb's evocation anchors it in the timelessness of myth, a reading reinforced by the textual allusion to Moses's parting of the Red Sea ahead of the Egyptians' pursuit.[90] The text evokes the Roman road that links the island to the continent, parting the waters of the Gulf of Gabes and symbolically figuring Moses's miraculous passage as he escaped bondage to enter the Promised Land. The biblical story relates to Kateb's cycle in at least two significant ways: in the crossing of the Red Sea, which is reenacted, albeit in the opposite direction, by Rachid and Si Mokhtar's *hajj* in *Nedjma* and also in the projection of the symbolism of the Promised Land onto Djerba. A local legend recounts that when Cyrus the Great authorized all Jews to return to

Jerusalem, the Djerba community refused to bring their exile to an end. Resettled on the Mediterranean island, they made the decision to remain in their new homeland, blending with the local population, and adopting the Arabic language and local surnames. Tasting the sweetness of oblivion in an echo of the ancient Homeric episode, the Jewish community chose to favor the potentiality of the Djerbian present over an obsolescent past with which it could no longer identify.[91] The resting place of many outcasts, the island is characterized by its variegated community, the result of myriad migrations: "Israelites banished after the fall of Nineveh, emancipated Sudanese still in bondage . . . various schismatic, unorthodox Muslims" (Kateb, "Les Poissons" 156).[92] A heterodox community unified by its experience of banishment, Djerba brings together Jewish exiles and Muslims, whose journey from the Arabian Peninsula enacted the same movement from the Middle East into the Maghreb. Reconciled in an oft-forgotten "collective memory of Abraham's children" (154), the two Semitic lines find restored cohesion in a common emblematic patriarch, an olive tree, whose peaceful symbolism encloses the twin *haras*—the Jewish quarter and the Muslim quarter—under the protection of Djerba's tradition of tolerance.[93] "Les Poissons sautent" (The Jumping Fish) thus illuminates a different form of loyalty to the "homeland," one based not so much on points of origin and ancestry as on an elective affinity for a space of peace and hospitality: "The Lotus-Eater never forgets this happy land, this verdant desert in the Middle Sea. . . . [These] hospitable, mysterious [men and women] . . . no temptation ever makes them relinquish their land" (155–56).[94]

Another superimposition adjoins a third exiled figure, the Keblout ancestor, whose itinerary follows the same direction as the Prophet Muhammad's followers: a westward trajectory eventuating in a Maghrebi settlement that consecrates the final crossing of the Red Sea, the definitive passage from Arabia to North Africa. While *Nedjma* generally configures the Mediterranean Sea as a corrosive space of dissolution and bastardized amalgamation establishing the ancestors' ruin ("our fathers; every [*oued*] ransacked, sacrificed to lesser brooks all the way to the point of confluence, the sea where no spring recognizes its sound: agony, aggression, the void—the ocean" [trans. 128]), the crossing of the Red Sea reveals more complex semantics.[95] The prime model of migration evoked by the cycle is the *geste* of the Prophet's paradigmatic caravan marking the start of his exile from Mecca. Cut from the cloth of legend, his westward trajectory is credited with the advent of civilization and progress: "But here they banished him. . . . The ones for whom the Koran was created aren't even at the stage of paganism or in the Stone Age yet" (158).[96] Overlapping with the destiny of the estranged Poet or *gharib*, the Prophet's forced displacement and incorporation of other groups away from the tribal land pollinated the world: "They wouldn't stand for it; it took other peoples, other men to face the immensity" (158).[97] Restoring spirituality to the desert, his progression propelled one of the chief civilizations of the world. Through mobility and crossings, both geographic and biological, its inclusive nature, welcoming of other groups, adumbrates the very blood mixing at the core of Keblout's mixed lineage, the blood mixing that alone can sustain the lofty aspirations of Islam's idiosyncratic spread: "to disseminate [the dream] wherever there was a favorable wind" (158).[98] For caravans in *Nedjma* are endowed with the power of the demiurgic word, capable of fomenting and carrying out revolutions: "The desert was simply the old paradise. . . . Only a revolution could reconquer it" (158).[99] Revealing paradise in the lifeless expanse of the desert, this revolution in the making is intricately bound up with the power of mobility and transculturation ("transplant his dream" [158]), with the arrow-like force of the procession.[100]

In contrast the Keblout tribe's passage to the Maghreb is steeped in bitter disenchantment: "Here, between Egypt and Arabia, the Keblout fathers passed, tossed about on the sea like ourselves, on the morrow of a defeat. They lost an empire. We are losing only a tribe" (*Nedjma* trans. 171).[101] Originally imbued with a similarly epic aura, it is the eventual settlement in North Africa (Kateb refers to Eastern Algeria as "the site of the disaster [les lieux du désastre]") that brought ill fortune to the prosperous tribe. The empire to which they can no longer lay claim, the Golden Age of Islamic civilization, is but a faint halo surrounding the tribe's oral history. Settlement, or to put it differently, sedentariness as the refusal to set out on a civilizing march ("ils n'ont pas voulu marcher" [112]), brings about the internal dispersion that exile eschews: the sedentary branches of the Keblouti tribes that remained in the ancestors' land form "the decimated tribe" (166).[102] If the colonial exploitation of Algeria is unequivocally invoked as the poison having caused the tribe's decimation, it seems that the nature of the remedy is shrouded in more mystery. For the postlapsarian reality of Algeria, Kateb substitutes the allure of broader horizons. The mention of the tribe's loss immediately conjures the specter of the lost daughter born to a French mother loved in Marseille. Si Mokhtar's proposed solution to the tribe's disappearance—the incestuous pairing of the two siblings in an illegitimate and unsanctioned union—fails miserably, leading to his own demise and Nedjma's captivity: "And the Keblout blood will recover its warmth, regain its old thickness. . . . But hear what I say: You will never marry her" (trans. 172).[103]

Djerba's variegated and complex legendary substrate provided Kateb with an alluring context for the resetting of the nationalist quest. Combining rejection of the debilitating past with a strong legacy of hybridity, Djerba seems in fact to inhabit the symbolic space left vacant by an early nationalist Algeria decidedly averse to its mythical calling. A series of echoes in some of the main descriptions of the locales buttresses the analogy. Occurring through the visual exploration afforded by the train ride along the coastline, the reader's initial encounter with Bône in *Nedjma* is redolent of the opening description of Djerba. Bône materializes as a "sightlessness streaked with rippling ochre and ultramarine" (*Nedjma* trans. 92), Djerba as an "ochre, green, blue, and white immensity, a deep plain surging out of the water that submerges it on all sides" ("Djerba").[104] In addition, the emphasis on the insularity of both spaces prolongs the correlation between Djerba and Algeria as *al-jaza'ir* (islands), the Arabic name of Algeria, a characteristic appropriated in Kateb's rendering of Bône: "the city decomposing in architectural islands" (*Nedjma* trans. 92).[105] The narration conjures up the space of the island in terms of intermediacy, as a repository of influences born of multifarious transmaritime mobility. Situated at the confluence of land and sea, Djerba appears as a terraqueous space. Capaciously holding heterogeneous elements in tension, it functions as an extension of the Mediterranean as *pontos*—Massimo Cacciari's conceptual representation of the sea in its etymological complexity as both body of water and bridge. Its depiction as a "deep plain surging out of the water that submerges it on all sides" marks the contiguity of land and gushing water, a characteristic reaffirmed in the remark that "the land breeze succeeds the sea wind" ("Djerba").[106] The island itself, capitalizing on its natural confinement, bears the imprint of elusiveness: "It fades away and resists scrutiny," as does its immediate semantics; the island is evoked as "Meninx," the obscure moniker of an ancient Carthaginian trading post on its southeastern shore.[107] While the evocation of the land is marked with the supple, undulating cadence of the sea tide, Djerba is conceived in its abstract materiality as color, contrasts, and movement, a site where blurred shapes are imbued with oneiric distance.

Taking the depiction further, "Les Poissons sautent," Kateb's 1965 rewriting of the previous texts, pictures Djerba as an indefinable space of mixing between Orient and Occident, between Greece and Egypt. Lying at the threshold of all major civilizations of the ancient Mediterranean, Djerba is shown to have thrived from its multiple legacies, most visible in the island's distinctively syncretic ceramic tradition: "The hand follows the curves inherited from Egypt and ancient Greece" (153).[108] The syntagmatic accumulation of these two types of savoir faire speaks to a nonhierarchical learning process, where the shapes favored by the craft come from an undifferentiated, integrated common pool. This contiguity, inviting a possible commingling of historically discrete elements, constitutes the island's chief characteristic. A crucible of sorts, the mirage-like space of Djerba performs a continuum between elements typically perceived as opposites. Thus its matrix merges Egypt and Greece, two spaces that dominant classical scholarship has rendered as incommensurable civilizational models, a perspective positioning Kateb as an early precursor of later works that put to the fore the African and Semitic lineage of Ancient Greek civilization (Bernal). Taken as a principle of continuity and convergence, Djerba therefore breaks down barriers that were thought impermeable. In another echo of the terraqueous quality of Djerba, water and earth, universally conceived as forming two of the four discrete elements, are undone in their discreteness, as Kateb reports that fish and caravans collide in the third space of the Roman road linking the island to the mainland. A porous line of demarcation—between land and water, but also mainland and island—it undermines Djerba's insularity.

Unsurprisingly the Djerbian texts stay clear of offering any determinant resolution of the multiple tensions hindering the unfolding of nationalism in the novel. Yet the substitution of Djerba for a deadlocked Algeria permits a revisitation of the issue of hybridity in its relation to nation-building. Freed from the negative rendering of oblivion lurking under the surface of the Homeric text, Djerba emerges as the resilient Meninx transforming potentially cataclysmic infiltrations into a bountiful ferment for tolerance and peaceful community formation: "The island never kept the same name, like those polyandrous lovers lavishing on each spouse and each lover the same diabolical virgin's unquenchable love, while shifting or abolishing . . .

all bearings" ("Le Lotos" 152–53).[109] As immune from debilitating atavism as it is sensitive to the pressing needs of Algerian nationalism, Djerba maintains its allegorical juxtaposition with Algeria, symbolically supplementing it with a transitory, myth-infused space wherein to hone the very workings of its allegorical aspirations—and wherein to lay claim to their possible actualization through the Revolution: "It is where Si Mabrouk came to negotiate the weapons. They arrived in Constantine in fish boxes" (Kateb, "Les Poissons" 153).[110] Harkening back to the fish colliding against caravans along the Djerbian Roman way, these weapons are charged with the revolutionary potential of the many itineraries that came to an end on that very road. Reactivating the *geste* of the Prophet's westbound journey—and of Keblout's original migration—Djerba's revolutionary potential dispels the ineffectuality of the early Algerian nationalist ferment saturating *Nedjma.* For Nedjma's claustration in the itinerant carriage consecrates first and foremost the depletion of her allegorical poetic potential. The repository of the tribe's honor, she becomes the object of mystification—the obsessive quest for pure tribal origins as the source of collective identity—rather than fully deployed myth. In the novel's last encounter her allegorical density is reduced to a sterile, univocal symbol at cross-purposes with the historical agency that the nationalist élan of the novel portended. In contrast the Djerbian epilogue stages long-awaited deliverance from confinement as Nedjma flees the island with the assistance of foreign sailors: "It is said that she beseeched the sailors and planned everything herself" ("Le Lotos" 150).[111] Through her scheme she implements of her own accord the premeditated escape that Mourad failed to carry out in Bône: "She offered to marry him if he would take her to Algiers where she hoped to realize her dreams as an 'enlightened' woman; they planned an elopement" (*Nedjma* trans. 111).[112] As Nedjma finally leaves the shores of the island for an unknown future, orchestrating her final journey with finesse and resourcefulness, the contours of a possibly independent Algeria glisten in the distance.

Far from the perpetuation of a "single, unified Algeria" (Bensmaïa, *Experimental Nations* 23), Kateb's *Nedjma* performs a preemptive suspension of monological myth, favoring instead the etymological *fabula* at the root of the "fabuleux passé," its legendary reconstruction: "his ghost consigned to this pathetic blind man's bluff stumbling over the fabulous past" (trans. 223).[113] As the space of Djerba dispels the pernicious aftermath of tribal atavism, supplying instead a model of felicitous mixing between strata of historical migrations, it affords a revaluation of the value of hybridity as the imperishable part of *étrangeté* at the core of Algerian identity. Farès overlays this caesura with the power to reveal the true nature of the Algerian nation ("la vraie patrie de l'Algérie" [*Un passager* 74])—what he calls "paganism" from an aesthetic point of view. Farès's own reading evokes a possible excoriating of identity, a stripping away of all waves of conquests concealing the true bedrock of "pagan" Algerian identity. In contrast Kateb's transnational deployment of the figure of the "pagan woman" in the space of Djerba, in the political sense invoked by Farès (he speaks of "crossing the expression of the Revolution with the expression of paganism" [*Nedjma* trans. 158]), eschews the danger of a pointless, debilitating quest for origins.[114] In a corrective echo of the model advocated by Farès, Kateb's opus reincorporates historical hybridity and estrangement as the two pillars of an Algerian identity in the making. His Djerbian cycle realigns the Revolution with the allegorization of the nascent, fluctuating national myth away from any duplicitous, mystifying monological impulse. Debunking all origins through jumbled chronology and hazardous geographical coordinates, Kateb expresses an unconditional refusal of absolutes, a fundamental mistrust of totalizing perspectives. To quote Glissant's insightful analysis, "He knew very well, in an instinctive manner . . . that everything is imbricated, intertwined. . . . Kateb had an intuitive understanding of the world's abundant diversity, which made him . . . the writer who best expressed Algerian identity, but who also relativized it best" (qtd. in Boudraa 201). In this respect Kateb's Mediterranean mythical *poétique* might well have been the most influential rendering of Algeria's vital diversity for the corpus of writing that was to reclaim his work as a foundational national narrative—its representation henceforth always underlying any attempt at thinking the national community.

CHAPTER 2

Andalusia as Trauma

The Legacies of Convivencia

Africa begins at the Pyrenees. This is why Roblès is Algerian twice over, adjoining Spanish blood to Berber vitality like many of us.

—Camus, "Notre ami Roblès"

An admixture of Spanish blood, imbued with hidalgo pride and a keen sense of honor, and the sempiternal vigor of the "Berber," the noble savage ubiquitous in racialized constructions of Algerian identity starting in the 1890s—such is the distribution evoked by Camus in his delineation of Algerian identity.[1] Situating literary creativity in the opacity of blood ("dans l'obscurité du sang" ["Notre ami" 3]), Camus's judgment reactivates the hybrid heritage of Algerian colonial fiction.[2] This amalgam could be read as a literal rendition of the racial and cultural legacy of al-Andalus—the nearly eight centuries of Muslim rule over parts of southern Europe.[3] The long-standing shorthand for felicitous mixing and cultural florescence, al-Andalus—as both historical moment consisting of dates and events and mythopoetic trope of interfaith dialogue and intellectual creativity among Jews, Muslims, and Christians—has suffused the cultural memory of the Arab world as its Golden Age. The concept figures both the deployment of the history of Islam within the Iberian Peninsula—the "Moorish" substratum of Spain's long-repressed identity (Majid, *We Are All Moors*), a construct to which Camus's conclusion obliquely alludes—and the possibly peaceful coexistence of the three monotheistic religions. Through the influential concept of *convivencia* the unified construct of al-Andalus stands in sharp contrast to prevalent, if disquieting, contemporary notions of a clash of civilizations threatening the future of Western civilization.

In the Maghreb the trope has been mobilized as an alternative to failed nationalist experiments. In the context of what Bensmaïa dubbed the "interruption of the myth," "demystification" proves crucial to expose the distorted reality offered by a totalitarian state.[4] Once the moment of Kateb's national allegorization has definitely passed, other "mything" processes must be activated to displace ossified structures of allegorization (Bensmaïa *Experimental Nations* 28). The trope of Andalusian *convivencia* that I examine has been used as one such alternative to state-sponsored identitarian constructs. In a Maghrebi context the persistent fascination with al-Andalus's spirit of tolerance has been mobilized as the object of a melancholy reading of the national past by resilient subjects refusing to acknowledge contemporaneous regimes of power as the incarnation of the national ideal. In addition the stubborn search for alternatives to the totalizing model provided by the nation-state insufflates new life into al-Andalus's concern with the status of minorities and their incorporation into social life. Resonant with the inflection of the post-Reconquista "traumatic viewpoint" following the seizure of Granada in 1492 ("point de vue traumatique" [Khatibi, *Par dessus* 124]) and the de facto end of Muslim rule over Spain, the memory of al-Andalus is deployed as a traumatic chiasmus (124). As the ghostly presence of trauma colors the Arab world's relationship to Spain and the West, its resurgence partakes of unconscious mechanisms producing longing for this unforgettable past.

The object of centuries of appropriations, the memory of al-Andalus vibrates with increased potential today. Reverberating on Braudel's delineation of the maritime border between Spain and North Africa as a "frontière insuffisante" (qtd. in Liang et al. 2), the Andalusian trope examined in these pages aims to deploy the full scope of Mediterranean connectivity that brings together the shores of the Strait of Gibraltar in an inseparable unit.[5] Born of the historical sedimentation of the Andalusian hiatus—the Umayyad dynasty, the *muluk al-tawa'if* (Taifa States) in the eleventh century, the Almoravids (1086–1147), the Almohads (1147–1212), and the entrenched Kingdom of Granada, the last remnant of Muslim rule, which fell to the forces of Ferdinand and Isabelle in 1492—this transmaritime legacy of contact was extended through the colonial conquest of the Maghreb, the phantasmatic ultimate stage in the completion of the Reconquista. From the fifteenth century on, both Portugal and Spain founded fortified cities along the Atlantic coast of Morocco, while Spain claimed possession of Mediterranean enclaves, some of them still existing today (e.g., Ceuta and Melilla, infamous today for their barbed-wire border fences). A

Spanish protectorate regime was established over northern Morocco in 1912, which lasted until the 1956 Independence. Entwined in this long-standing history of interactions, which can be seen today in the clandestine migrations once more connecting the Maghreb to the Spanish peninsula (Flesler), the imaginative potential of al-Andalus remains unobstructed on both sides of the Strait.

Stretching beyond verified historical events, the trope of al-Andalus stands out for its aesthetic malleability and elusive intangibility. The Andalusian signifier is an echo chamber for the multiple forms of transaction and passage between contiguous bodies of texts that it historically facilitated through translations, appropriations, or other forms of cultural transmission. It carries with it the vibration of metaphoricity in its most etymological sense: the "transfer [of] the meaning of home and belonging, across the 'middle passage,' or the central European steppes, across those distances, and cultural differences, that span the imagined community of the nation-people" (Bhabha 291). In her insightful reading of Bhabha, Claudia Esposito hints at another "middle passage," the Mediterranean, as "a space across which new iterations of belonging are formed and in which writers make the invisible visible" (xxii). Unfettered by any form of stable affiliation or fixed coincidence with recorded history, the revelatory power of this unhinged mediation endows al-Andalus with the effusive richness of mythical topoi. Leaving behind the burden of historiographic verifiability, the reconstructed site of al-Andalus cuts across history and space and makes itself permeable to nostalgic, imaginative narratives sympathetic to equivocality and embellishments. Reconfigured as a pure principle of *convivencia*, it unites antagonistic spaces with its intersectional deployment. The Andalusian trope thus becomes a multifaceted signifier containing the germs of an imagined, transnational, transconfessional, and multilingual community. Revered as the epitome of civilization, it is held in inconclusive tension against embodied forms of community throughout history. Al-Andalus forms a framework within which to potentially expose the failings of successive regimes of power. To quote Justin Stearns, it constitutes a "promise of common humanity that regardless of historic accuracy offers a productive answer to contemporary challenges . . . not as a past to be lamented, the memory of which should be elegized, but as a call for political and social action in the present" (370), a judgment destined for variable fortunes in different contexts.

THEORIZING CONVIVENCIA

In his consideration of the development of Arabic literature in relation to the dynamics of nation formation, William Granara has defined a heuristic "Andalusian chronotope" as an "interfaith utopia," a topos "of mythological dimension which can only be reached by way of both time and space travel" (58). Tributary to its Bakhtinian intertext (the chronotope as a "literary artistic [figure where] spatial and temporal indicators are fused into one carefully thought-out concrete whole" [Bakhtin 84]), Granara's concept allows for the bridging of the gap between the text in which al-Andalus is mobilized and the context that saw its emergence: it effects an "allegorization of contemporary political problems that, mapped onto the literary, enables fantasies of a better life" (Granara 60). Restoring the ties between the aesthetic reconstruction mediated by the text and the political energies underlying it, Granara's concept goes beyond a mere reiteration of the topos of nostalgia for the glorious past (or, in the Arabic context of Granara's analysis, *al-hanin ila al-madi al-majid*). Taking its cue from St Augustine's "extensio animae" in book 11 of the *Confessions*, this tripartite approach spans past, present, and future, uniting in a dynamic sense of time the evolution from the memorialization of a Golden Age of Arab civilization to the "sight of the present state of affairs" and the meditation on a more promising future. The site of multiple projections, Granara's Andalusian chronotope is remarkable for its enduring relevance to the discussion of various epochs in the development of the Arab novel. Through his reading of historical novels by Jurji Zaydan, 'Ali al-Jarim, and Radwa 'Ashur, Granara explores the various moments of historical consciousness at work within the texts in their sustained, if reluctant, engagement with the movement of Arab nationalism. These forms of historical consciousness deny a strict correspondence with the moments in which they are formed. These correctives populate the differential space between a revered ideal and a present failing to live up to the comparison. They pave the way for noncoincident visions to emerge, for hauntings to be performed, revealing the specific weft of present political circumstances.

Extending the relevance of this historical consciousness to the context of minorities, Yael Halevi-Wise recalibrates the Andalusian trope of *convivencia* to the Jewish Sephardic context (the experience of Jews in medieval Spain), reading it as a "prism through which we examine different ways in which creative authors use the history and heritage of Spain's Jews to describe their own national preoccupations at a time of heightened political consciousness . . . [and which is] remarkably well-suited to reimagining the image and status of political minorities in competing national agendas" (1).[6] Unbinding the trope from its incarnation as a marker of Sephardic ethnic identity and self-representation, her argument embraces all manifestations of the use of Sepharad (Jewish Spain) by writers of different times, places, and backgrounds as a mythicized platform from which to examine cross-cultural patterns of interaction. Halevi-Wise reads it as a postulate of interactive identity cutting across confessional, national, and linguistic lines. In this use Sephardism becomes a metaphor, a "form of literary expression that functions politically during heightened moments of historical consciousness in diverse national contexts" (5). The Andalusian trope that I excavate shares significant semantic space with Granara's Andalusian chronotope and Halevi-Wise's Sephardism. The model of Andalusian *convivencia* mobilized by the writers featured in this chapter is the product of historical truncation and selective memorialization. Indeed drawing on Anouar Majid's *Freedom and Orthodoxy*, Nouri Gana has argued that a certain degree of romanticization is inseparable from appropriations of al-Andalus in our "post-Andalusian," dystopian moment of inflexible cultural determinations ("In Search" 231). As such, any nostalgic mobilization of al-Andalus offers a mystified engagement with the past.

Recent scholarship on the concept of nostalgia—literally, the longing for home, or the affliction resulting from the loss of something necessary to one's self-identity—has brought forward its distorting power. Construing al-Andalus as a site of nostalgia imbues it with suspicious connotations, questioning the political legitimacy of the voice speaking in a nostalgic tone. For nostalgia is but "a universal but aberrant yearning for an irrecoverable past; a reality-distorting emotionalism triggered by thoughts of home . . . an understandable but destabilizing force infecting our politics with irrationality, unreality, and impracticality" (Kimberley Smith 507). Taking the argument further, Welch and McGonagle affirm that "to be nostalgic is to be trapped between memory and fantasy in a way which is unhelpful and unhealthy, and which almost inevitably implies a conservative and reactionary politics" (22). Producing a critical reflection on al-Andalus requires attending to the nostalgic origins of the very project the term came to designate. Early Umayyad Andalusia itself bore the distinctive mark of nostalgia for the lost Umayyad caliphate of Damascus, the homeland of the Andalusian ruler Abd-al-Rahman I. Jerrylynn Dodds reports that a memorial cult for the original Umayyad capital developed in the Andalusian emirate, which provided the newly conquered city with a model to emulate politically and culturally. Cordoba was to become a powerful reincarnation of Damascus that would eclipse the artistic and architectural dominance of Abbasid Baghdad in the Arab world. Given the irremediable clout of nostalgia in considerations of al-Andalus, articulating a critical model that can successfully untangle the concept from elegiac memorials of loss and their conservative aftermath seems to be the first task for any exploration of its political usefulness.

Svetlana Boym's reflection on nostalgia has done precisely that. The cultural critic distinguishes between two interrelated forms of the concept: restorative nostalgia and reflective nostalgia. Restorative nostalgia highlights *nostos* and a return to roots (41). Oblivious to its entanglements with myths of origins, this kind of nostalgia overlaps with revivalist nationalism and purports to establish a purer form of "national past and future" (49). Reflective nostalgia dwells on the myriad possibilities encapsulated in the pain of loss to address the ambivalence of modes of belonging. The product of subjective experience, it offers a meditation on the texture of time, on the palimpsestic layering of temporalities and levels of consciousness. Teetering between political activism and a sterile reiteration of nostalgic bereavement, Andalusian *convivencia* as reflective nostalgia functions as a processing agent in a photographic sense, revealing the ghostly presence of the past under the dense texture of the present. Renouncing the teleology of homecoming, it betrays fascination for ruins and ghosts and reveals the afterglow of loss. It blossoms as a cultural template, the benchmark against which societies throughout history are reevaluated and defined anew. It filters through the faults of contemporaneous political systems and unhinges social representation from the flawed structures of a rebarbative state. Ultimately it becomes a model for redistributing difference in our contemporary postcolonial societies. Periodically reappropriated across genres and disciplines (from history to literature, philosophy, and the arts), al-Andalus thus emerges as a vector of investigation into the nature of culture and heritage in the historically diverse spaces dotting the soft contours of the Mediterranean. It is a heuristic gesture directly engaging the many forms of disconnection and violence saturating late postcolonial incarnations of statehood—and, in the context of the war on terror, a vessel to mediate the West's anxious relationship to the Muslim world (Shannon).

In this chapter I examine reflective nostalgic mobilizations of al-Andalus by Maghrebi writers in the throes of our postcolonial, "post-*convivencia*" world. Abdelkébir Khatibi's Andalusian trope seeks to untangle Mediterranean "communal relationships of solidarity" from their more exclusive pendant, "communitarian nostalgia," a concept "that makes it difficult to conceive the plurality of the Mediterranean, its ability to overcome borders, multiplying meetings, exchanges, and friendships" (Cassano, *Southern Thought* 148). Khatibi's triangulation of existence beyond France and Morocco restores the space of contemporary Spain to a dialogic encounter with modern Morocco with the aim of moving beyond the deeply ingrained structures of trauma overdetermining the Arab world's relation to its contiguous neighbor since 1492. In contrast, and in direct relation to his earlier musings on the power of literary allegorization in the works of Kateb, Nabile Farès's dystopian reflection on the truncated subject's ontological stillbirth ("re-tour-né") silently acquiesces to the irreparable rift forever separating the self from its constitutive other. Giving in to the pervasive influence of politically unconvincing "tristesse," Farès's "dark star of Andalusia," poised halfway between Nerval's melancholic black sun and Nedjma's black star of blood, remains mired in the stasis of undifferentiated time and perpetual estrangement. A similar sense of nostalgic hopelessness permeates Colette Fellous's oblique appropriation of al-Andalus as an unspecific principle of coexistence. Bringing the symbolic potential of the trope to bear on the issue of minority existence within the postcolonial nation, Fellous's urban allegory (Avenue de France as allegory of the Tunisian nation) bears the mark of the narrator's unresolved post-traumatic estrangement from the fabric of postcolonial Tunisia. In this respect Farès's and Fellous's writing closely coincides with the deployment of Deleuze's concept of the virtual, defined as that which is "not opposed to the real but to the actual" and whose symbolic potential eschews the uneven battle of actualized politics (208–9). Through the willful desertion of the arena of political praxis to the benefit of lyrical estrangement, Farès and Fellous can therefore be construed as performing the negative counterpart to the positive moment of allegorization coeval with the development of nationalism in Kateb. At the end of the arc of national realization their writing embodies a fundamental sense of unmitigatable belatedness casting the Mediterranean as a mythicized refuge averse to political inflections.

SITUATING AL-ANDALUS

Maria Rosa Menocal's influential 2002 *Ornament of the World* lays bare the fabric of harmonious coexistence between communities in the Andalusian microcosm. The "culture of tolerance" that Menocal's subtitle announces rests on connectedness: "This was the chapter of Europe's culture when Jews, Christians, and Muslims lived side by side and, despite their intractable differences and enduring hostilities, nourished a complex culture of tolerance . . . [which] found its expression in the often unconscious acceptance that contradictions—within oneself, as well as within one's culture—could be positive and productive" (11). A cultural and literary survey of the 750 years of Muslim rule over Spain from the ninth-century caliphate of Abd-al-Rahman III to the last rulers of Granada in 1492, Menocal's opus incorporates the voices of contemporaneous commenters from all segments of Andalusia: the Christian Paul Alvarus's account of the spread of Arabo-Islamic culture in Cordoba, Ibn Hazm's "quixotic" defense of the Umayyads (114), and the Arabized Jewish poet turned soldier Samuel the Nagid, among others. But beyond the reading of a wide-ranging corpus of medieval Iberian literature, Menocal's objective aligns with a rehabilitation of Arabic scholarship in a transcultural context, emphasizing the centrality of translations and collaborations between faiths and languages for the transmission of knowledge on a continental scale. And indeed examples of such dialogue and transmission abound. Jean-Claude Xuereb describes a school of translation in Toledo in which Jewish scholars would translate Arabic versions of Aristotle into Latin or vernacular languages (he mentions Castilian). Similarly Menocal focuses on the figure of Petrus Alfonsi, a twelfth-century Jewish convert who made accessible Hebrew and Arabic scholarship to Latin readers beyond the confines of Iberia (he worked in exile in England), emphasizing the permeability and contact existing between languages and literary traditions. The interpenetration of Latin, Arabic, and vernacular languages for the twin purposes of scholarship and imperialism was not restricted to Andalusia and endured far beyond the Fall of Granada. A striking example of this dynamic can be found in a Latin translation of the Qur'an in 1698 under the care of a Vatican cleric at a time when Arabic was widely taught and spoken in Counter-Reformation Rome (Bevilacqua).

This idyllic vision of Andalusian history has been vehemently contested by medievalists who have been eager to restore the many intricacies of Spanish medieval history. Recent work has brought to the fore the relative "intolerance" of the Almohad period, a reality that in fact Menocal's book had acknowledged too (Balta et al. 8). Thus Pascal Buresi engages in a direct critique of *The Ornament of the World* on account of its inaccurate reading of the *dhimma*, or minority status, of non-Muslims in al-Andalus. Beyond the mythical recoding of the Andalusian topos as a locus of harmonious collaboration, subsequent recuperations of al-Andalus have emphasized its inextricable entwinement with the politically charged competition between incompatible memories. If the 1492 recapture of Granada was memorialized as a glorious *lieu de mémoire* in Spanish historiography (through the self-celebratory formula *la toma de Granada*), it was concurrently enshrined in the memory of the populations expelled from the Iberian peninsula as an event of catastrophic magnitude (the Fall of Granada, or *suqut Gharnata*, shortly followed by the expulsion of the Moors and the Jews), illuminating conflicting appropriations of the same trope of medieval Andalusia across contexts (Shannon). The end of the ancient world of Mediterranean interconnectedness thus gave way to a more fractured form of colonial modernity centered on the (North) Atlantic world. In this post-Andalusian context tension grew between a newly galvanized, increasingly hegemonic colonial West and a vanishing Mediterranean world of connectivity.

Inaugurating the recentering of the Spanish nation on Catholicism with religious homogenization and racial expunging through the *limpieza de sangre* statutes, the Catholic monarchs' 1492 victory forcibly ruptured the intertwined development of the three cultures bound together during the eight-century Andalusian hiatus.[7] Fallen back into the fold of European modernity's divisive rhetoric, post-Reconquista Spain developed its racialized legal apparatus to successfully shift the grounds for Christian identity from professed religion to genealogical lineage. In this respect Spain distanced itself from its amalgamated Andalusian legacy to emerge as a leading world power in the race for imperial ascendency. As Tabea Linhard has shown, "with the reconquest of al-Andalus and the ensuing conquest of the Americas, Spain became an empire firmly grounded in enslavement, exclusion, and the resulting homogenization of language and religion within the empire's boundaries" (5), a dynamic that predated the 1492 expulsion but nevertheless culminated in it.[8] The concurrent onset of a new era of transatlantic development—the point of origin of Europe's colonial modernity, which would connect the former Mediterranean center to the Atlantic circuits of commerce—ensured its definitive integration into Europe after centuries of Mediterranean existence: "Spain was the beginning of modernity in Europe and the beginning of coloniality outside Europe" (Mignolo, *Local Histories* 51).[9] From the early days of the conquest of the Americas, resistance to the Andalusian heritage catalyzed Spain's aspirations. It also mediated its process of national formation and the development of its historiographic efforts. In the enduring post-Andalusian, divisive world order of Western modernity born of the rubble of Mediterranean shared history, Spain's identity emerged from the eradication of cross-confessional contact. It materialized in the form of anti-Jewish and anti-Muslim violence, mass conversions, and the establishment of the Inquisition, until very recent revaluations of its Muslim past fractured the monolithic narrative of the Catholic monarchs' history.

Yet, regardless of its historical exactitude, this troping of al-Andalus as *conviviencia* has displayed astonishing longevity and resilience across history, embracing its romanticized, phantasmagorical roots with a passion characteristic of those doomed quests of origins shrouded in the haze of an already lost, irrecoverable past—a past from which nostalgic subjects can nevertheless never quite recover (Gana, "In Search"). Laying exclusive claim to the Andalusian semantic space, this strategic mobilization of medieval Spain produces a cross-cultural, cross-confessional imaginary among the three cultures of cohabitation. Across the increasingly coercive "post-Andalusian" East-West divide, it revivifies the obscured afterlives of the Andalusian moment—whether transnational, plurilingual, or literary. Medieval Iberian literature bore the imprint of this interpenetration, its languages "translat[ing] each other, gloss[ing] each other, calqu[ing] each other, transliterat[ing] each other . . . appear[ing] side by side in texts and inscriptions," as Karla Mallette argues with regard to medieval Sicily, another space of marked interaction (261). Spanish scholars' recrudescent assessment of their nation's Arab heritage gained momentum with the publication of fictional texts mobilizing the heritage of al-Andalus. Recent debates surrounding expelled Andalusian Jewish communities' right to Spanish citizenship have foregrounded more intricate narratives of cultural transaction than earlier scholarship augured. Spanish nationalist approaches to al-Andalus have emphasized the uniqueness of Muslim Spain, construing Andalusian Islam as "hispanified" (Ramón Menéndez Pidal, *La España del Cid*, qtd. in Liang et al. 12). As Liang et al. argue, Menéndez Pidal ultimately sought to assert Spain's uniqueness and al-Andalus as a space incommensurable with the rest of the Arab world. His distinction between medieval Spain and the rest of the Arab world, which was perceived as backward, reinforced the narratives of European colonialism in North Africa with which his perspective was entwined. In his and other modern historiographic narratives the Maghreb was considered a stagnant, static space, whose accession to modernity was to be mediated by colonial efforts.[10] Américo Castro, a contemporary of Menéndez Pidal, took the opposite route and recast the history of Spain in light of its Andalusian legacy in a patent jab at Franco's authoritarian rule. With the neologism *convivencia*, coined in 1948 as a political tool, his analysis cast light on the reciprocal interactions of the three cultures of medieval Iberia, even if each of them was to maintain its idiosyncratic characteristics.[11]

Taking these insights further, Juan Goytisolo explores the legacy of Spain's variegated past in an eponymous 1992 essay, "El legado andalusí," written on the occasion of the quincentennial commemoration of the 1492 expulsion. Castigating the event for its hollowness (he calls the past commemorated "trunco," or truncated), Goytisolo argues that the grandiloquent celebration is no more than "an exorcism for a guilty conscience" that consecrates the death of al-Andalus as a lived ideal.[12] From this "purifying ethnocide," which he compares in *Cuaderno de Sarajevo* to the contemporaneous siege of Sarajevo, comes the determination to illuminate Spain's "nuanced Occidentalism," the Semitic influence ("el factor semita," inclusive of both Jews and Muslims) ingrained into the nation's weft, as the mark of a felicitous uniqueness rather than a liability for Spain's accession to modernity within Europe.[13] Goytisolo even suggests that it is only by embracing this distinctiveness that Spain can ever lay claim to that modernity: "We are distinctively European, we are *exceedingly* European."[14] Against the dominant Hellenic genealogy of Europe, Spain's ancestry must necessarily incorporate the Arab roots of European culture.

Although Goytisolo confines the argument to the realm of the arts, its resounding political aftermath cannot be ignored. Throughout this modular history of interaction and overlaps, the aura of Andalusian *convivencia* has persisted unmarred in collective memory. In Andalusia itself the enduring heritage of al-Andalus spurred dissenting modes of social formation. Thus the sharp increase in conversions to Islam among Andalusians speaks to a desire to embrace the region's distinctive legacy. The inspiration behind Andalusian nationalism, al-Andalus was appropriated by intellectuals and political movements alike. Emphasizing the uniqueness of the region, poets such as Federico García Lorca located in Andalusia's multicultural legacy the root of its incommensurability to Spain. Blas Infantes, the "father of the Andalusian Fatherland" (Padre de la Patria Andaluza), drew political claims to self-governance from this idiosyncrasy. They eventually resulted in the ratification of the Estatuto autónomo de Andalucía (Statute of Autonomy of Andalusia), a statute that Andalusia shares with the bilingual regions home to Spain's three historical nationalities (Catalonia, the Basque Country, and Galicia). And it is today in the name of al-Andalus that the independence party Liberación andaluza (Andalusian Liberation) campaigns for a sovereign state where the descendants of *moriscos* can live in total independence from the Spanish nation (Martin-Márquez 302). Although independence is nowhere on the horizon, these identitarian claims have been met with relative consideration by the Spanish state. In 1992 accords were signed that granted Islam official status as an established religion in Spain, thereby recognizing its crucial importance in the makeup of Spain's identity. The fact that these kinds of symbolic gestures coexist with much less hospitable realities such as the SIVE anti-immigration border protection system or the endemic marginalization of Muslim populations throughout the country certainly mitigates their thrust. Whether these initiatives, as well as institutional forums for cross-cultural dialogue such as the state-sponsored Fundación Tres Culturas in Sevilla, are really gestures toward possible reconciliation or additional strategies for managing ethnic and religious difference is up for debate.[15] Yet they are undeniable signs of Spain's increasing willingness to come to terms with its hybrid past, even if the 2005 train bombings in Madrid inflected its relation to the Muslim world toward more defiance and enmity and delineated a "nueva convivencia" (Shannon) defined along the lines of containment.

Andalusia's past never quite galvanized comparable institutional energies in the Maghreb as it did in Spain, but the fading memory of the Muslim empires over southern Europe nonetheless animated a distinct form of cultural memorialization immune from the nostalgia permeating Sephardic memories of al-Andalus. In the wake of the expulsion of the Moriscos in 1609, Ahmed Ibn Muhammad al-Maqqari, a Moroccan historian, penned two magisterial volumes evoking the legendary history of al-Andalus. *Nafh al-Tib min Ghusn al-Andalus al-Ratib*, partially translated into English in the nineteenth century as *History of the Mohammedan Dynasties in Spain*, is a compilation of Andalusian geography, history, and literature, as well as a biography of the Granadan writer Ibn al-Khatib, underlining the relevance of the Andalusian past to conceptions of the Maghreb's historical existence. Yet al-Maqqari indulges in no narrative of loss. In the seventeenth century, in which he writes, al-Andalus has not yet become an object of longing (Stearns 366–68). The rise of the concept of *firdaus al-mafqud*, or lost paradise, is concomitant with the arrival of the first Arab and Muslim travelers to Europe and Andalusia one century later, at a time of increased European dominance over the remnants of a weakened Ottoman Empire.[16]

In Maghrebi literature evocations of al-Andalus, whether nostalgic or satirical, are persistently entwined with considerations of national identity. Allusions to *convivencia* as a political project enforceable in our polarized moment (Fabre, *L'Héritage andalou*) often facilitate the preaching of a tolerant, moderate Islam of coexistence with Western ideals and, no less significant, Judaism (Meddeb, *The Malady of Islam* and *Phantasia*; Khemir). In his two volumes dedicated to the *geste* of the Amazigh conquest of Andalusia, *Birth at Dawn* and *Mother Spring*, the Moroccan writer Driss Chraïbi disentangles the purity of the Islamic world and an idealized *umma* from the reality of social discord in the Arab world (Rey-Mimoso-Ruiz). Rewriting Andalusian Islam as the product of Amazigh probity, the novels are an indirect indictment of Arabness and its model of community. In Andalus a new *umma* can be founded free from the taint of Arab decadence. In a similar vein *La Prise de Gibraltar* (The Taking of Gibraltar) by the Algerian Rachid Boudjedra severs al-Andalus from the evocation of a halcyon Arab past. Debunking the myth of the Andalusian conquest, the novel unhinges identity from the great Arab narratives, whose ethnocentrism it demystifies. The Moroccan authors associated with the journal *Souffles/Anfas* similarly refuse the weighty Andalusian heritage. As Arnold Rothe argues, they have conjured the memory of al-Andalus as an oneiric, intangible, ghostly presence, rife with bloody rivers and severed heads in Mohammed

Khaïr-Eddine's *Une Odeur de mantèque* (A Smell of Fat) and decadence and dystopian hallucination in Abdellatif Laâbi's *L'Oeil et la nuit* (The Eye and the Night), or, in Laâbi's "Méditations à Grenade," as a site of solidarity for the victims of fascism on either side of the Straits: "Los Moros! Los Rojos!" (114).[17] If the returns performed by Khaïr-Eddine and Laâbi yield nothing more than disillusion, Khatibi's visions of Granada thrive on their inconclusive nature. His return home oscillates between familiarity ("Étrange impression de *revenir* en Espagne" [Khatibi and Hassoun, *Le Même livre* 95]), a quest for origins (tracing the steps of the ancestors in *La Mémoire tatouée*), and a conquest through the overlaying of his itinerary onto that of American soldiers in the same book (Rothe 82–83). What transpires from this variegated corpus is that, in the fractured post-Andalusian context, both locales on either side of the Strait have fallen prey to an "illusion" (*La Mémoire tatouée* qtd. in Rothe 82).

FROM TRAUMATIC CHIASMUS TO VIRTUAL ESTRANGEMENT (KHATIBI, FARÈS)

Khatibi wrote "Au-delà du trauma," for the first symposium of Spanish and Arab writers in Ronda (Andalusia) in 1985, and it was published in Spanish translation in the catalogue for the 2003 exhibit *Triangle of al-Andalus* in Rabat. Here Khatibi questions the inheritance of the Andalusian moment in Moroccan identitarian constructions and identifies a ruptured "symbolic genealogy" of writers and artists, superbly condensed in the formula "To live, to die, to survive between Spain and the Arabs, in a writing . . . and thinking experience" (*Par dessus* 124).[18] Addressing the entanglements of language and nation in the wake of the Andalusian experience, Khatibi casts his gaze on the modes of writing that could probe the aftermath of the traumatic disunion. Yet this inquiry is not simply a matter of reincarnating a vanished past, "the lost paradise" of al-Andalus. "The power of the unforgotten between the Arabs and the Spaniards" (125) resides most acutely in the nearly imperceptible traces of trauma, in their pervasion of Arabic poetical discourse.[19] There the traumatic separation has induced an ontological form of nostalgia discernible in the corpus's original, rough prosody. Speaking to the melancholy aura of Arabic lyricism, Khatibi alludes to the remembrance of loss as the "song of the unforgotten and the unforgettable. In this respect, Spain is but another name for the passion for this rememoration" (125–26).[20] Anachronistically recast as the source of Arabic elegiac expression, the amorous evocation of the Spanish alter ego demands acceptance of Arab culture's traumatic 1492 truncation, the awareness of a throbbing phantom limb once amputated that is as integral to one's sense of self as it is impervious to possession. It delineates a post-traumatic liturgy that makes room for the marvelous possibilities of the new: today's Spain in all its unassimilability, the prime vehicle for the poet's participation in the order of the world. Retrospectively the signifier *Spain*, which Khatibi uses metonymically for *Andalusia*, spans two interrelated, partially overlapping notions. The first is physical, a space lying at the confluence of land and water that still remains entangled in the web of its historical relationship to the Maghreb through the pervasive phenomenon of African migrations (Flesler); the second is poetic, come to life in the poet's imagination by virtue of its embedded history ("Au-delà du trauma" 126). Khatibi engages the second, the trope of Spain meant to serve as an underlying map of desire in a projected cinematic script that never quite comes to fruition, like an ardent lover: "This duplicity, or rather, this multiplicity of histories, cultures, and languages . . . [its] secret is only revealed to he who deciphers it through love" (126).[21] The realm of an aesthetic experience ("une expérience esthétique," 127), this amorous heuristics reveals the irrepressible alterity at the heart of Arab culture, setting up comparison as the foundation for one's relation to the world: "This historical Spain has taught the Arabs to pit themselves against the Other, to know him and misjudge him in the same gesture of appropriation and expropriation," a moment of awareness coeval with the peak of Islamic civilization in the western Mediterranean (127).[22] For those who arrive too late to drink from the fountain of Andalusian coexistence, the power of writing is paramount to enact the melancholia sparking remembrance. The rehearsal of facts, real or reconstructed through writing, presents the sole remedy to the loss of complex forms of being in the wake of the "traumatic chiasmus" (124) induced by the collapse of Moorish Europe: "We return to a past that is still alive, to an exiled part of our beings, to the strangeness of our past" (127).[23] Yet it is also a remembrance that extends beyond the stifling entanglements of sterile recollection. It is a taking stock of the past with an eye to the future, to the post-Andalusian world order, which in the context of Spain implies gesturing toward its former colonial Latin American empire (Mignolo, "The Many Faces").

Circling back to the *ghorba* reclaimed by Kateb as the hallmark of hybrid Maghrebi subjectivities, the French *étrangeté*, which Khatibi mobilizes, connotes the disquieting uncanny that sharply emerges in contrast to the familiar. It is the alienation of affect lying at the core of estrangement from one's self-perceived identity, the literal banishment of exile. Deploying the unresolved dialectic of sameness and alterity at the core of identity formation, identity surges as a "reconciliation . . . with our foreign [*étranger*] heart in this country" ("Au-delà du trauma" 128).[24] The space of Spain emerges as a question of thought and art beyond nostalgic exoticism. It restores the missing segments of the self by mirroring the constitutive absence against which it is calibrated. Denying the other and its constitutive role amounts to indulging in a mortiferous, self-destructive dynamic. In its endorsement of the never-ending process of mourning as a mode of apprehension (he mentions "l'être endeuillé," the mourning self), Khatibi delineates a militant process of memory that confronts the historical plurality of Arab identity head-on. This vision builds on the rhetoric of *Maghreb pluriel* and its indictment of a postulation of identity resting on blind self-denial and resentment in the name of an illusory purity of culture. In contrast Khatibi proposes a triangulation of desire and existence. He adds the third space of Spain to the Morocco-France dyad, the two poles of postcolonial history and identity, creating an "indestructible link of symbolic filiation" hinging on the contiguous, overlapping forms of identity born of this rapprochement ("Au-delà du trauma" 132).[25] Only a poetic move beyond trauma can ever aspire to reactivate this ethos of encounter. It implies the articulation of a "geopolitical form of writing that would break with folkloric visions and melancholy complaints, a form of writing that would reveal its mythological depth, which lies deep within our common identity, as if this encounter were to be written anew on the pages of a palimpsest—like an overdue letter" (133).[26] Through it an "intercontinental and interscriptural narrative" will take shape, along which the Maghrebi text enters in communion with the world (135).[27] Reconfigured as a disincarnate, purely symbolic principle, Spain materializes as a blank surface, a projection screen upon which the writer imagines a life beyond trauma in contact with the world: "Spain is a matter of writing. . . . It isn't self-possessed, it isn't possessed by anybody, it is this other space where the experience of living, of dying, of surviving beyond trauma compels us to embrace the becoming-world of modern narrative" (135).[28]

It is such a form of post-traumatic, contiguous writing in the layered, palimpsestic space of a mythicized Maghrebi-Spanish continuum that Farès's 1994 *Le Miroir de Cordoue* crafts. Farès wrote the deconstructed narrative following his 1975 visit to Cordoba, where he was invited to attend a Muslim prayer in the *mezquita* turned cathedral. Under the spell of the tolerance imbuing the event, Farès developed the idea of a film memorializing the historical milestone and approached the Algerian government, requesting that a team be assembled and mandated to record the event. The film was never produced, but a narrative of the experience materialized in the form of a disjointed meditation on the nature of identity, interspersed with recollections from his sojourn in Spain and the encounters and reunions it facilitated. Rife with echoes of the *convivencia* of yore, the text also gathers draft scenarios for the film project, which Farès composed, together with a few final poems, during a visit to the city fifteen years later. The narrative can be characterized as a peregrination through time, aiming to reconstruct the conflicted identity of what Farès calls the "pays d'Al." A mythicized rendition of Algeria since precolonial times, the book evokes the land mostly through references to the narrator's childhood in various urban and rural spaces: Tlemcen in Western Algeria, a settlement of Andalusian Jews and Moriscos arrived from Spain over the course of history, but also Cordoba, through contrastive allusions to the mythical Golden Age that preceded the 1492 expulsion. The ahistorical, mythicized site of al-Andalus is readily substituted for any form of spatiotemporal fixity. Reverberating on Farès's literary preoccupations from the early days of *Un passager de l'Occident*, the text posits exile from one's immediate circumstances as the only mode of apprehension of "reality," a concept always safely neutralized by scare quotes. As if the subject could never fully inhabit the space of enunciation, personal and possessive pronouns are always followed by a question mark, endlessly interrogating the possibility of univocal identity. Reconfiguring the self as a vacillation, a principle of nonconformity and nonidentity, Farès's ontology marks out a dynamic of transition and translation that revisits, deflects, and destabilizes signification and existence. Emphasizing the porosity of time through recurrent tropes and motifs, this perennial back and forth dynamically interrogates past and present history in an attempt to delineate the differential nature of all identification in postlapsarian, postexpulsion Algeria—*expulsion* understood as Iberia's rejection of its others in 1492, but also as the expunging of all European colonial populations from the postcolonial nation soon to be formed.

The first section, "The End of the Abbasids," deploys a rhetoric of excruciating transfiguration, which Farès presents as a transmigration of the soul between various potential selves: "It is indeed easier to pass into other bodies than we think; we refuse to see that the actual metempsychosis that we actually undergo during life prevents us from believing in the identity . . . of our vital organs . . . without which life is no more than pure . . . interrogation" (*Le Miroir* 19).[29] The self materializes from the traumatic severing of physical birth when the subject enters a melancholic space of unicity experienced through the loss of the "other part of myself: dead, suppressed . . . 'Us.' (?) him and me (?) perceptible at the same time, in the same movement of life, of sensations" (13).[30] Birth itself is likened to expulsion and death (Farès's original "expulsion beyond being" [12]).[31] Through this physiological frustration, duplicating the historical Andalusian frustration, the subject's mournful birth emerges as an ontological refusal to adopt any fixed identity located within tyrannical genealogies and socioreligious rituals. The self is born "carried forth from the Vacuum, in the absence of a name" (15).[32] The unequivocal boundaries that Farès's narrator evokes—primogeniture as a principle of social hierarchy that determines one's place in what is depicted as a traditional hierarchy of abuse—bear the mark of rigidity. This order of segregation crystallizes a bifurcate vision of reality, reminiscent of Khatibi's "traumatic chiasmus": "Two world then two: perfectly seen, identified, one of which (the second one) is not the opposite or the mirror image of the other, but, the exact measure of its separation . . . its frustration" (39).[33] Congruent with this precarious ontology, the relationship to the coterminous Other always already lost dons the shape of a dialogue. It is Farès's prime "inter-diction" (18) as both exchange and prohibition that mediates the narrative voice's fundamental denegation of the dominant order of things, his ubiquitous "refus" (17). Echoing Khatibi's multiple "denial" ("dénégation"), the willful destruction of otherness in the self, Farès's "imaginary destruction of [his] own genealogy" evinces the self-damaging violence characteristic of subjects in the throes of multiple crises of filiation and self-estrangement (Khatibi, *Par dessus* 132).

Khatibi's "indestructible link of symbolic filiation" between Morocco and Spain ("Au-delà du trauma" 132) is reactivated in truncated form in Farès's "chain of beings, and, divisions" (*Le Miroir* 55), a collocation that breeds *affabulation* as a tactical distantiation from "reality" (53).[34] Farès's phantasmagoria partakes of a kaleidoscopic aesthetic of subjectivity, which capitalizes on the specular nature of Cordoba. Rife with the visual shimmers of its diffracting surface, "Cordoba resembles a lake that, like a shattered mirror, blinds the traveler. And this is how he, too, sees Cordoba, or, rather, how he loses himself, in her, in multiple sentences, which name him differently, each time: in a fragmentation" (11).[35] Analogously prolonging the diffracting surface of the lake, the white canvass of the screen on which the diegetic film is meant to be projected mediates fragmentation and loss. In turn the boundary between social groups and the flat surface where the performance of the self can be played out, the ubiquitous white screen of self-performance always marks isolation. At the apex of the first section, the rhythm of the book accelerates to its precipitated climax: the end of the performance of the self and the temptation of murder, the killing of this brother who has usurped power, the alter ego who must be eradicated for the self to emerge. The screen is finally torn apart: "The screen is split open; [it] opens the other half of the Heart" (67–68).[36] Prefiguring the impending "confrontation between communities" (56), the episode assimilated to the foundation of "pays d'Al" is steeped in the blood of fratricides (66). "The death of the other" (70) unites in its semantics the blood brother and the coterminous other brought about by colonialism, who is not necessarily French and could quite possibly be Spanish: "this other—whom I believed to be: other—and who may have been me: who was me, at the very moment when the judgments . . . came to be" (69).[37] Breaching the insularity in which subjectivity is ensconced, the tearing of the screen brings both confinement and self-performance to an opportune end. Through the tear a new form of intersubjective interaction materializes, which the next two sections of the text will carry forth. The logic of separation is no longer a measure of difference obliquely interfering with social configurations. It is recast as a historical aberration and marginalized by the recuperation of a common position of otherness underlying subjectivity. Although self and brother, self and other are annihilated in the inescapable fratricide mandated by the time's ethos of segregation, their previous existence of common marginality and contact endures: "(We then were close, rid of fear, or, irreversibility) (for we had taken the chance of living, in the world, the border, marginality). . . . Here, the rupture, change happened" (68–69).[38] The fractured postcolonial subject infected with the dualism of colonial logic is redefined precisely from this new mode of reaching out to the other, finally inhabiting the space standing between identity and difference—the space of reclaimed marginal coexistence.

Contrasting with the dominance of separation, the concept of willful and categorical estrangement ("éloignement" [*Le Miroir* 91]) comes to mediate existence within the postcolony. The fractures underpinning national construction are to be construed in light of a great "error," whose lingering presence overdetermines any reading of the past: "There is only one error that I have wanted . . . to rectify" (73).[39] It is "a crack in the present, born of the error of the past" (96).[40] This error lies at the intersection of Algerian history and Andalusia, in their respective amnesias and exclusions. The "ChezNous" (OurCountry) encapsulating the narrator's national life is a site of doxas and multiple boundaries: "'OurCountry,' the Mirage of all desires, pasts, histories 'We 'We" (92).[41] In the revised imaginary of the Spanish-Maghrebi contact zone, the stubborn, redundant repetition of "ChezNous" is undercut by the destabilizing power of its lowercase variant, "nous," substituting the structure of hospitality for the exclusive momentum of patriotism: "I heard from Pedro, and, Juana, who live, now (1975: maybe you could go and see them, and, invite them to come here, to 'our' country—simply to mark out the difference 'o' between individuals 'o' and nationals 'O—') on the Spanish coast, in Alicante" (93).[42] This "nous" is inflected with the ethos of inclusivity that pervades the farm of the narrator's youth, a secluded space where all communities coexisted before a fire burned it to the ground moments before the violence of the War of Independence flared up. Rid of capitalization, it recalls Algeria's multiple destinies and incarnations through less codified, more subjective experiences of collective existence: "'we' who lived on the borders between worlds, and, differences—accepted within the narrow boundaries, defined, by social hierarchies, and, their shortcomings" (93).[43] It is a "nous" tolerant of alternative valences of national existence, of fluctuating definitions of a collective: "There are several meanings to the word 'citizenship' and to this 'we' contrary to what we might have believed some time ago: internal, visible rifts: exiles; hopelessness; estrangement" (93).[44]

Exile as ontological necessity can be construed as one such incarnation of this estrangement. Replacing Hegel's Egypt as a transactional space between Orient and Occident in a renewed historical dialectic, Algeria incarnates the "one country . . . in charge of organizing passages between [both worlds]: Jazirat El Maghrib [the island of the Maghreb/of the West, in an echo of Algeria's Arabic name], the land where the unfamiliar makes its sweet passage!" (*Le Miroir* 101).[45] Aligned with the reaffirmation of Algeria's long historical destiny at the crossroads of multiple passages, the necessity of mobility looms larger. It undoes the solipsistic, misanthropic "pleasure of interdiction" (100) that has come to exclusively claim all social interactions.[46] This interdiction relies on monolingual, monological models of identity and religious belonging. One such model reigns supreme over the Kairouan mosque, the oldest mosque in the Maghreb and one of its most revered spiritual sites, dating back to the early days of the Muslim conquest. In Kairouan identity is encapsulated in the question "Are you Muslim?," a question only the faithful recitation of the *shahada* ("There is no God but Allah, and Muhammad is the messenger of Allah") can presume to answer (100). Farès suggests that the declaration of faith, a prerequisite to entering the prayer room, relegates spirituality to the desiccated rigidity of formulaic words, emptying them out of the luminescence of shared communion in prayer and silence: "the tender light of reminiscence. Not the ecstasy of the law, but, the original simplicity of hospitality . . . There is no light in the self that does not take root in the light of the Other" (101).[47] This model of openness, in contrast, seems to pervade Farès's experience of Cordoban culture, where the possibility of dialogue supplants the endless reiteration of belief as a mode of engagement with the world. Restoring the predominance of the temporal over the ritualized, Farès's Cordoban spirituality is a function of social interaction. It is epitomized by the alternative formula significantly couched in Spanish: "You don't agree with me, but it is of no consequence . . . of no consequence" (104).[48] A subversion of the imperative of *shahada* as a self-duplicating, normative form of identity, the echoing Spanish words "no importa . . . no importa" decline self-definition on pluralistic, heterogeneous registers. Between the two polarized spaces al-Jaza'ir (the Islands, Algeria's name in Arabic) serves as mediator, setting Algeria at the heart of the spiritual spectrum. Farès's configuration infuses the Orient with a mournful sensibility in remembrance of the ideals that have taken root in the West (gender equality, freedom, meaningful romantic relationships [104]). Vindicating the desire for another land, this mediation performs the kind of amorous heuristics delineated by Khatibi. Redolent of Ibn Hazm's ideal of seduction and pleasure in his eponymous treatise on love, the "Doves of exile"

(101) enact the logic of encounter metonymically evoked through the cross-confessional prayer at the Cordoba mosque-cathedral.[49] From the anamorphic superimposition of the two sites of Cordoba and Kairouan arises the newly minted, mythical site "Cordouan" (102), which allies the prestige of the Tunisian holy city with the inclusive tolerance and spatial versatility of Andalusian history (a Mosque turned cathedral turned mosque for a day).

Significantly this configuration is not followed by any political effect: the film that was to memorialize this unique moment of coexistence is never actually made, for fear of cultural rehabilitation, or "mystification," under the influence of an unscrupulous government (*Le Miroir* 135). If the narrative's imaginary space strives to move beyond the Arabia-Maghreb-Cordoba-Tlemcen trajectory of deployment and dystopian return, the book nevertheless ends with military barracks and the reiteration of a scene of conscription. In Tlemcen, language, which had been held in check in the sections on al-Andalus, finally gets out of joint to the point of unintelligibility. It is what Farès calls "the delirium of the Founder" (129), as the attempt to fold the singular self into the collective of the community devolves into psychological and historical dispersal.[50] As the narrator later confesses in a letter to his exiled friend Nourredine, "Being in contact with the inside of ideology has cost me my mental balance" (134).[51] Tlemcen is associated with a later moment in Maghrebi and Andalusian history: the Almoravide conquest, resemanticized as the "al-Mors-Avides" (literally, those avidly chomping at the bit [125]), a dynasty indicted for its austerity and rigid interpretation of religious law. It is also evocative of the return of expelled Andalusian communities after 1492, who chose the city for their resettlement and made it into one of the high cultural centers of the Maghreb, especially with regard to music. Apprehended in its layered complexity, Tlemcen collapses several layers of history: the national Algerian narrative finding its root in Islam and Mecca (presented as the ghostly voice of the novel's last section) and, beneath it, that of Almoravide rule indicted for making Algeria a land of barracks and spiritual austerity.

To preserve its integrity, Farès's Andalusia needs to remain imagined, immaterial, capitalizing on the etymological sense of *u-topia*, that which does not have a place and cannot be situated or actualized: "Andalusia remains this incomplete site" (*Le Miroir* 140).[52] Endowed with symbolic potential, this virtual space nevertheless falls short of political implementation. Unsurprisingly what remains of the narrative morphs into a series of poems—as approximate remembrance, language irreducible to the confines of a collective voice, expression resistant to the obliterating order of epistemic violence and subjective dispersal. The curse of the dark star of Andalusia, "l'étoile obscure de l'Andalousie," curtails the historical potential of the Andalusian myth. Farès's transnational ideal predicated on an Andalusia of *convivencia* is never to be actualized as a replacement for a deficient nation-state. The return it performs is mired in the passages of time, fusing past, present, and future into an atemporal site of memory incommensurate with historical unfolding: "A strange blend of dreaming, and, 'remembrance': my visit here looks exactly like a previously experienced already completed voyage" (115).[53] "Cordouan's site of return" (102) eventually falls prey to the same logic of debilitating stasis.[54] If it eschews the ulterior "détournement" (corruption [102]) of Islam's original spirit in monological Kairouan, this revised Andalusian space of exile in turn succumbs to the fate of being "re-tour-né," delineated as an incapacitating "return Future behind me always—as if live turned-back-and-reborn: you can *regression* you I cultural easily understand past present future: all the same" (130).[55] Both "returned" and "reborn," or reborn through its return, the "re-tour-né" paradigm emphasizes the ontological stillbirth phonetically encapsulated in the word—an echo of the mournful birth into the world under the sign of fracture and frustration, the original "expulsion beyond being" (12). In this restricted model of temporal existence, the fertile cultural narrative of Cordouan teeters on its intrinsic limits. Estrangement is to remain virtual, mired in the stasis of undifferentiated time, at cross-purposes with historical inscription.

Although Farès's concept also marks an inability to move beyond the past, it stays clear of any transformative potential. Impotence prevails, and nostalgia is sublimated into a lyrical aesthetic invalidating its social density: "It's because we proceed—both of us—from the same sadness [*tristesse*], and, from the same civilization" (*Le Miroir* 134).[56] The silent acquiescence to the irreparable original rift asserts the pervasive influence of politically unconvincing *tristesse*. In its place Farès's reconstruction of al-Andalus proposes a sort of decentered, trans-Mediterranean "experimental nation" aligned with Bensmaïa's concept, which reverberates with Deleuze's definition of the virtual as "a nation above all nations that writers have had to imagine or explore as if they were territories to rediscover and stake out, step by step, countries to invent and to draw while creating one's language" (qtd. in Bensmaïa, *Experimental Nations* 8). In his poem to his lost friend Farès's narrator announces, "I'll leave early tomorrow (again) for a new exile" (140), opening up narrative space to an ever-deferred arrival and performing the process of his own endless transmigration.[57] Recuperating the fundamental dispersion mediated by the reflecting surface of the eponymous broken Cordoban mirror (*psyche* as both mirror and self, in all the density of the Greek polysemy), the specular relation to the Other is placed under the double sign of fracture and mendacity—*speculum*, or mirror, as speculation (Zemmouri 243), the tactical "simulation" (*Le Miroir* 53) at the heart of estrangement. Trapped in the circularity of the ultimate return ("They return to the world" [141] is the first line of the final poem bringing the volume to a close), displacement is curtailed as "retour[-né]."[58] As future and past are fused in an enduring sense of belatedness, the curse of al-Andalus's original traumatic chiasmus and the permeating sense of its impossible repair endure. In the face of ontological truncation shrouded in the recesses of mythical time, the subject remains eternally displaced. The hope of a humanistic Mediterranean leads to truncation, the eternal frustration of history.

FELLOUS'S IMPERATIVE OF RECIPROCITY, OR THE AMBIVALENCE OF ESTRANGEMENT

> I like bringing this birthplace to life, not like an image of nostalgia or of a lost land, but truly like a site of resistance, a force that would help sew strongly together fragments of reality, whether they be projected very far, in exile, scattered across the world or on the contrary motionless, nestled within the self, wonderfully sedentary.
>
> —Colette Fellous, in Samia Kassab-Charfi, "Entretien avec Colette Fellous"

The social promise inherent in Andalusian *convivencia* requires consideration of the idiosyncratic position and claims of historical minorities.[59] Engaging Maghrebi multiculturalism requires attending to the historic relationship between the Muslim majority and the historically significant Jewish communities of the Andalusian diaspora (the "Andalusians," or "andalous" fleeing the Christian Reconquista of the fourteenth century, followed by the Moriscos in 1609) and other, mostly Sephardic movements.[60] The myth of a common, syncretic Andalusian origin came to nourish an imaginary of interaction and peaceful cohabitation in the Maghrebi crucible among

Jews, Muslims, and Christians that remains particularly vivacious to this day, especially in Tunisia.[61] Conflated with the mythical diversity born of Tunisia's central position at the heart of the Mediterranean (Audisio, *Sel de la mer*), this foundational cosmopolitanism has crystallized around critical historical figures who embody Tunisia's irreducible plurality—among them, Elissa, the founder of Carthage, whose recurring evocation mediates Tunisia's own sense of nativism, and Sidi-Mahrez, the medieval saint whom tradition credits for first assigning space for a Jewish quarter (*hara*) to be established within the city's walls, thereby offering protection to the Jewish community, previously forced to leave the city every night (Haddad de Paz).[62] The desire for increased consideration of heterogeneity within the confines of the nation speaks to the forms of internal exclusion within postcolonial states, whose coming of age often coincided with the undermining of postcolonial dreams of equality and social justice. Springing from the distinctive standpoint of minority narratives, the Andalusian trope engages the legacy of the medieval *dhimma*. The literal designation of the status granted by the Qur'an to those who are to be "protected" (i.e., all monotheistic minorities in *dar al-islam*, the lands of Islam), the *dhimma* question has often been converted into a semantic marker of Islamic societies' level of tolerance. Reading it alternatively as an incontrovertible sign of Islam's being open to alterity or as an implicit denigration of these communities relegated to a marginalized, second-tier legal position, critics and historians have subordinated the historical application of the concept to the broader narrative that it came to buttress. The *dhimma* question thus became shorthand for measuring the degree of *convivencia* in al-Andalus, erecting the juridical rights granted by the Islamic rulers as the prime determining factor even though it never constituted more than a legal apparatus that could be respected or ignored to various degrees. Buresi denounces such instrumentalizations of the concept as a quest for essentialist readings of Islam, a practice depriving the actual minorities of historical agency (30–31). It is indeed on this issue of agency in its relation to diversity that contemporary revivifications of the issue of *convivencia* touch. How indeed to empower marginal subject positions? How does the mirror of Andalusian coexistence hold up to our theoretical frameworks for multiculturalism?

Granara construes 'Ali al-Jarim's social-realist use of the trope of interfaith coexistence as a call for unity among society's segments. (The plot of al-Jarim's novel takes place during a waning eleventh-century

Umayyad caliphate embattled by the rise of petty kingdoms.) Emphasizing the importance of solidarity and commonality of purpose in a time of disunity, Granara argues that the author ushers in the constitutive heteroglossia of medieval Cordoba as evidence of its nuanced, nontotalizing take on social existence. In Granara's words, "the urban landscape for discordant voices and identities, of conflicting ideas and point of view," is a model for the clandestine resistance to monological order that it obliquely encourages (67). Such is the tremendous modularity of the "shifting metaphor" of al-Andalus (Ellis-House, "Al-Andalus"), which may concurrently signify deep-seated unity behind the banner of Arabness and Islam and resistance to the same ideals.[63] As a site of disharmony and unaligned identities, the Maghrebi-Andalusian continuum presents the most compelling metaphorical counterpoint to the nation-state born of independence, most notably through its assumption of the positionality and advocacy of minorities.

In his preface to Albert Memmi's autobiographical novel, *La Statue de Sel*, Camus offers an unusually direct engagement with the complexities of Jewish identity in the Maghreb, declaring that the book centers on "the impossibility to be anything specific for a French-educated Tunisian Jew" (in Memmi 9).[64] Camus locates this outsider's ethos at the intersection of the world's refusal to accept what being a Jewish subject entails and of the latter's own rejection of the world. This negative reciprocity creates an ambivalent, fractured sense of self that can flourish only in undetermined spaces, in a movement of estrangement from dichotomous identity rhetoric—and thus largely in disaffiliation from the politics of Tunisian nation-building. Read in that perspective, Camus' identification resounds powerfully with the trope of the "imaginary Jew," the assimilated Jewish intellectual whose identity "becomes a quest, a questioning, a perpetual invention" (Le Rider 244).[65] The "desubstantialization of the assimilated Jew's identity" (244) is confined to postmodern models of subjectivity, which swirl in the constant interrogations and displacements of this specific form of existence.[66]

Close to fifty years after the publication of Memmi's text, Fellous's autobiographical narrative, *Avenue de France*, redeploys this principle of instability in the context of her émigré Francophone Jewish Franco-Tunisian identity. Reinscribing seemingly haphazard mobility into her identitarian equation, Fellous avails herself of a fragmented aesthetic that frees her writing from the yoke of critical accounts based on narrow considerations, such as an author's place of origin. Distancing her narrative from possible Jamesonian allegorical readings, Fellous touts her outsider's position on the margins of the nation as the prerequisite to writing. By favoring impressionistic perambulations of the mind throughout history and space, her prose unsettles ready-made conceptions that circumscribe postcolonial authorship to the lines of group affiliation. In their place Fellous reasserts the need for individuation and differentiation from any and all totalizing logic. For, to echo other haunting words from Camus's preface to Memmi's book, "a writer is most significantly defined by the—nostalgic—inability to blend anonymously in a class or a race" (10).[67] Thus Fellous's narrator isn't merely Jewish nor fully Tunisian. She inhabits the ever mobile, unstable space at the heart of things ("au coeur des choses" is one of the book's leitmotivs), crafting her identity-in-movement through her amblings across multiple, nearly interchangeable spaces. Redrawing the contours of community membership along the lines of alternative historical migrations (from the southern shore of Europe for the most part), Fellous places new value on patterns of relentless individuation. She limns a singular take on identity that thrives on the subversive power of peripherality—and on the potentiality of reclaimed estrangement.

Reactivating the trope of Andalusian *convivencia* beyond a thematization of Sepharad (the novel barely even mentions Spain), her haphazard narrative highlights the inclusive diversity that, in her eyes, defines her choice of microcosm: l'Avenue de France, the main colonial thoroughfare connecting the Tunisian capital's *ville nouvelle* to the World Heritage Site of the Arab medina. Carefully weaving personal memories and national temporal landmarks, Fellous delineates a history of affect in which the protagonist's immersion in her family archives dredges up scores of historical events. Once pieced together they reconstruct the arc of recent Tunisian history and stake a claim to the syncretic multiplicity underlying its course. A space of interaction and exchange, the avenue functions in the manner of a palimpsest, melding two distinct yet embedded narratives: the protagonist's life, rife with echoes of past generations, and the history of Tunisia since the days of colonization: "Everything is right here, visible through the surface. My life and yours. Between us lie the measure of a hundred years and the history of France" (91).[68] Banking on the Arabic lexical overlap between *Tunis* the city and *Tunis* the country, the narrative thus seamlessly unites the space of the narrator's urban life to the out-of-field expanse of the Tunisian nation, whose diegetic existence is circumscribed to punctual episodes entangled in the cosmopolitan geography of the text. Along the multiple incarnations of the novel's avenue of choice, it is therefore the history of Tunisia as a whole that the narrative figures, starting with the advent of the French protectorate in 1881: "Avenue de France, forever. An entire country has just been drawn within a few meters [Avenue de France, toujours. Un pays entier vient d'être dessiné sur quelques mètres]" (31).

The celebrated, idealized space of mixture and encounters characteristic of the eponymous thoroughfare finds its materialization in the abundance of lists that dot the narrative. One egregious example of this agglomerating logic can be found in the depiction of the heteroclite inventory of the Piperno store bordering the avenue. In the disorderly accumulation of sundry objects, the Mediterranean flavor of the early protectorate years stands out, softening the blow that the impending discussion of colonialism is bound to bring. The "Tunisian Curiosities," as Piperno himself dubs them, are in fact a mix of Roman lamps, iridescent chandeliers, Oriental rugs, and damask upholstery. This happy East-meets-West capharnaum, "an entire population of objects" (31), paves the way for myriad profuse lists bringing together other "populations" of diverse geographic and religious origins in a felicitous *mélange* where the narrative voice finds its natural place: "Come on in, there is still room. Angelvin, Meyer, Montelateci, Valentin, Cohen, Bortoli, Disegni, Massuque, Fellous, Fourcade, Rondot, Conti, Verzani, Moulin, Licari, Nuée, Achir, Fescheville, Bugui, Ville, Piperno, Borg, Gagliardo, Sangès, Cattan, Teynier, Viola, Licari, Kloth, d'Amico, Ladislas, Saliba, Galano, Saba, Baccouche, Mariani, Zerafa, Cardoso. There is a role for each of you. It is a performance in progress in the year 1893" (32–33).[69] At the end of the avenue the Porte de France gateway separates this make-believe cosmopolitan city ("ville d'opérette") from the Arab medina. Despite the clear Gallicization of many of the patronymics, Iberian origins stand side by side with Italian and Sephardic lineages, which often collide in shared histories of Mediterranean crossings. The name Piperno itself, which is promoted to the role of organizing principle behind the apparently chaotic list of family names, is a case in point since the name is found mostly in Livorno, Italy, where it is one of the most prominent Jewish names, as is incidentally the Disegni family name, also mentioned in the list (Luzzati). The Fellous family name too is inconspicuously inserted into the list, comfortably ensconced at the heart of this new population, where the Jewish community looms large. Within this community the narrator is at home: "They form one single body, the tissue of my tongue" (31), the physical, almost ontological contiguity between them enabling the writing process and the life it composes.[70]

This display of foundational, capacious hospitality reshapes subjective identity around the incorporation of the ancestors, as the polysemy of the word *langue* as tongue and language suggests. Captured in the depth of her gaze ("My memory is intact; it runs underneath my eyelids" [29], and "They all move very slowly underneath my eyelids" [31]), the ghosts of her family's past blur the lines between corporeality and recollection, making the body the site of remembrance, the material source of collective expression.[71] The narrative unfolds in the echoes of the recurring phrase "There is still room," rewriting the national community in that early moment of the protectorate to reveal additional space, inclusiveness—the possibility of belonging. True to the extended geographic scale of the project, this hospitality is concurrently redirected toward a more open form of community affiliation since the colonial ideal of pan-Mediterranean, transconfessional inclusion can be seen at work in the text: "[We need to] pull the curtain, to subdue this whole pandemonium. My prayer is open to all, whether Arab, French, Maltese, Greek, Italian, Corsican, Berber, Jewish, Sicilian, Egyptian, Palestinian, Portuguese, Uzbek, Armenian, Lebanese, Chinese, Albanese, Turk, Afghan, English, Mexican, or Argentine" (27–28).[72] Rife with colonial echoes perceptible in the denomination of the main ethnic groups making up colonial North Africa, the list extends the hospitality at the core of the book beyond the limits of the colonial Mediterranean, in a dialogue with the world's diversity. This hybrid body within which the narrator finds her moorings touts the mark of felicitous coexistence, in the spirit of a Mediterranean history of integration, which supposedly saturates the semantic space of its representation. Coextensive with the cosmopolitan *grana* Jewish community, with which the narrator mostly identifies despite her mixed origins, this Mediterranean model takes precedence over any fervent alignment with the identitarian rhetoric of Tunisian nationalism.[73]

Yet an increasingly polarized international context imposed its pervasive fault lines onto the delicate balance of community relations in Tunisia, calling into question the peaceful coexistence of communities the text invokes.[74] Closing the curtain on the commotion of the avenue's historical evolution thus sets up the narrative as a replacement for historical events, legitimizing the fictional world it propounds as the only effective remedy against momentous historical mishaps. Taking to extremes Hayden White's vision of history as literary narrative, the narration instills fiction at the core of events, in lieu of events, reinventing time and history through the rendition of her experience: "This stroll suits me. It is like a prayer that I invent at the center of each second and that helps me along . . . 1860, 1865,1909, 1913, 1924, 1938, 1943, 1948, 1950" (26).[75] The insistence on the theatricality and performativity of the new colonial regime (Tunisia is independent in 1956) takes to task its legitimacy. It suggests that, in a make-believe world where everything exists only on account of a willing suspension of disbelief, the order of things may simply be a matter of representation. Through the eminently subjective focus of the narrative, time is reduced to an enumeration of dates animated only by the reeling litany accompanying the perambulation through space and time. No history exists but the one re-created, eluded, and eventually rewritten as the affective story of a place.

This pervasive distrust of the ineluctable course of a history of events betrays a fascination with the poetic potential of mythicized visions of a circulatory past of tolerance and mixing—a gesture redolent of the troping of Andalusian history, here centered on the era of the French protectorate. Partaking of a restorative effort to correct the inequity of the present, a romanticized vision of the colonial past is conjured, in which the Jewish community occupies a central role more aligned with its historical significance in the Tunisian capital.[76] With the establishment of the French protectorate in 1881, the Jewish community found itself split among several languages (French was soon to be become the de facto language of instruction with the emergence and flourishing of the Alliance Israélite Universelle schools) and multiple, concurrent loyalties.[77] While the vast majority of the Tunisian Jewish community (the *twansa*) had been subject to the *dhimmi* protection status granted by Muslim authorities to the People of the Book for centuries, the arrival of the French portended a more felicitous political status. With the advent of colonialism dawned the promise of French citizenship, which took decades to come to fruition.[78] The new colonial power was eventually welcomed as a purveyor of universal human rights, pandering to the desire for international recognition that inclusion in the French nation permitted. Incorporation into the French regime of citizenship was thus on the ascendant, as was acculturation to colonial mores. Just as the Fellous family name found its place at the core of the heteroclite list for Piperno's store, so the Jewish community found in the protectorate a sympathetic form of governance. While the incongruity and illegitimacy of the colonial regime is consistently emphasized ("as if it were normal. Normal to set up a country within another, normal to sign treaties" [32]), it nonetheless appears that the protectorate is also the only structure to offer the narrator a path to political legitimacy.[79] An alienated "we" gives way to an empowered "I," which defines itself only in relation to the colonial power: "France became my country right then and there. I didn't have to think about it or ask permission, I just followed instructions" (32).[80] Through this identification the narrator joins the community of settlers, those she follows off the boat and greets on the wharf, those whose voyage becomes her own: "[France] invited me along. It's as simple as that" (32).[81]

This assimilation generates a deep fracture within the self, a definitive truncation of the precolonial Arab heritage. To disappear to better exist: such is the fundamental, strategic ploy by which the narrator writes herself out of the historically actualized Tunisian nation inhospitable to the Jewish community to better write herself back in, in relation to a fully decentered nation in the virtual mode. The embedded narrative structure, abounding in prolepses, analepses, and other types of chronological shuffling, defamiliarizes the reader and precludes a sequential, teleological reading. Instead it foregrounds an expressive mode of rupture and discrepancy born of the violence of colonialism. Identity surges from this to and fro. It is reconceptualized as identity in movement, a legacy inherited from the immigrant Jews who arrived in Tunisia at the turn of the century by the boatload. Recasting the narrative voice's inability to function within the delimited space of rooted identity, the desire to belong, to be anchored and defined is sublimated into a moving map of sites, a series of visual representations attempting to capture the purely imaginary abstracted through visual encoding: "Your place of birth, please? I always need to think about it for a few seconds before I repeat in one go: Tunis comma Tunisia. All places of origin irritate me, it is something else that I seek, I will say it again, it is a geometric figure, a drawing, an arabesque, a line of fire, a history inscribed into the very architecture of the city. Maybe a color" (140).[82] This willful, consistent estrangement echoes Farès's tactical self-exclusion from the strictures of the "actual." Evocative of Nadia Khouri-Dagher's paradigm of "la

Nouvelle Andalousie," a relational model of identity characterized by concurrent double allegiance to one's native culture and Western culture and ideals, this strategic positioning intersects with multiple synchronous affiliations. Affording the possibility of rebirth, it figures a dynamic imbued with a modernity more attuned to the fluctuating modes of existence of our global world. It is enigmatically evocative of the echoes of the multiple languages reverberating through the writer's most intimate memories: "I really need multiple affiliations, I almost said multiple births, and I always feel more alive when I hear multiple languages around me. I also believe that this is precisely where modernity comes to life" (in Kassab-Charfi, "Entretien" 149).[83]

Playing up the importance of detachment from contemporaneous considerations ("I don't believe in the truth of immanent things [Fellous 91]), the narrator casts the influx of Mediterranean immigrants as an utterly fictitious dynamic far removed from the colonialist underpinnings of the protectorate regime ("They were moved to make the journey toward this make-believe country by these sentences" [84]), even though the vessels that bring them to Tunisia partake of the forces of colonialism, since the introduction of the steamship in Mediterranean waters in 1833 accelerated the colonial exploitation of the Maghreb (Crowley).[84] Attempting to distance her chronicle from political readings, the narrator turns the spotlight on the importance of detachment and amnesia: "One does not need to have a country to exist. One just needs to exist, one needs to move on, to not hang on to everything" (Fellous 92).[85] The novel calls into question the omnipresence of a national frame of reference responding to the mutilations perpetrated by colonialism, a violence the narrative voice nevertheless denounces. Instead it doles out a humanist perspective laying claim to the world, "the world [that] was given to us [and that] we need to . . . give back" (92).[86] The narrator construes the world as a space marked by global relationality and hospitality, even if it implies the loss of one's specificities to the detriment of self-actualization: "To make [the world] exist is already to give it back. But to give it back is also to disappear. And through disappearance, we make [the world] appear more clearly, don't we?" (92).[87] This reclaiming of universality, remarkable for its depoliticized deployment, is presented as a deliberate choice, a selective engagement with the patrimony of the past. It is a choice that can be duplicated in the present to encourage new models of coexistence between communities, keeping in tension the two conflicting imperatives of self-estrangement and responsibility to one's community (or family, if nothing else): "You tried to forget the humiliations, the beatings, the fires, the murders. You chose to remember the unobtrusive friendship, the tolerance, the intimacy, the taste for a common culture, a common land, music" (92).[88]

This stubborn reactivation of the ideal of *convivencia* gives the narrative its momentum. The narrator's task consists in giving the world back to the ones who have lost it and whom the course of history has marginalized and dispossessed: "saving them all . . . speaking for them . . . gathering their story, illuminating it" (Fellous 59).[89] The book opens with the profession of a moral obligation to mutual cooperation and reciprocation as an ideal for generations to take forward: "The world was given to me; I must give it back" (9).[90] And indeed the moral law reemerges periodically throughout the narrative. Through the law the desire to participate in the world's great rule of exchange is linked to a central, deeply anchored position at the heart of things: "To be here, then, at the heart of things" (11).[91] This twofold participation is mediated by the process of writing as the book born of its meandering course becomes an allegory of life itself: "I say book, but I mean life. . . . These words hear each other, beckon to each other, they both accomplish the same work, one takes, the other gives back, always this inescapable law. To be here, then, at the heart of things" (11).[92] If the give and take to which these lines allude brings up the possibility of an unequal movement between things, the threat is soon defused by a reaffirmation of the narrator's sense of responsibility when crafting her life ("to make my life by hand . . . It is now time . . . to give back" [62]) and by her familial duty inherent in her ambivalent position at the end of a long lineage (she speaks of the "impossible challenge of the last born" [59]).[93]

The epiphany comes in the shape of a cry, a strident voice striating the Parisian afternoon, introducing in its wake a sense of loss, a crack at the heart of things. Upsetting the narrator's certainties and reactivating long-existing anxieties, the unknown source of this cry emphasizes its oppressive effect. An intimate echo of the self, the cry is an interruption of life, of the quotidian that has lulled the narrator away from the burden of her contradictions. An irrupting interpellation, the cry functions as a forceful reminder of the irrepressible magnetism of the past, of its presence as the foundation of any future. For the cry is birth, original cry, passage from limbo into life: "There a heart starts beating without warning, the world has just been born, please tell me what time is it at la Nation?" (Fellous 23).[94] "La Nation" operates as shorthand for the Place de la Nation in Paris, where the cry was heard, but it is also a reminder of the narrator's inescapable homeland. It seamlessly weaves together her current life in exile in France and her disparate geography of wandering: "Every day at the same time, whether I am in Seville, in Paris, in Rouen, in Tangier, in Palermo, in Florence, in New York, in Samarkand or in Lisboa, I instinctively rush back to all those years that I have never spent over there in Tunisia" (23).[95] Commandeering voice and obscured influence at once, Tunisia stands as the authoritative ordering principle in absentia, whose recollection oscillates between delight and tyranny: "At the same time, I know that it is my prison" (23).[96]

The cry is construed (possibly misconstrued) as a call from the past in the voice of the narrator's ancestors, whose interpellation forces a reactivation of far-reaching affiliations. The true nature of this immersion into the past is revealed in a later dialogue, in response to the forefathers' prompting. It comes in the guise of a confession, the acknowledgment of a life-altering episode: the suspension of her brother's right to the benefits of Tunisian citizenship. After being arrested in 1967 for approaching girls on the street, her brother was essentially convicted for not speaking Arabic and for having chosen to leave Tunisia for France. Ultimately the conviction is ascribed to his identity ("They don't know who they are talking to anymore, my brother or an entire community" [Fellous 242]).[97] The incident results from an incomprehensible concatenation of events all mediated through administrative Arabic, a language that excludes her brother in the same way French had excluded their Arabic-speaking grandfather in 1879. Two years prior to the establishment of the French protectorate, the fourteen-year-old forefather stopped to pick up an apple that an elegant French gentleman ambling down the street had dropped. Without a word he returned the fruit, only to be greeted by words he did not understand, possibly "Thank you" or "You thief!" (109).[98] Forever changing the life with which they intersected, these French words stand at the core of the family's history under the protectorate. They have spurred the desire to assimilate and the family's eventual failure to merge into the nationalist order of Bourguibisme after independence. Containing the germs of the second episode of linguistic incommensurability, the apple scene on the Avenue de France sanctions the Jewish community's inescapable estrangement, visiting the ancestors' distress upon their descendants. Holding the whole book in tension, it signals the ordering power of this constitutive aphasia in the face of the chiasmic linguistic traumas that frame the narrative in an echo of the violence binding colonization and decolonization. From 1879 to 1967 the Avenue de France is indeed the story of an "itinerary," what Laâbi has defined as "the crossing, inscribed in the language of the writing, of a sociocultural field subjected to violence" (qtd. in Scharfman 137).

Consummating the Jewish community's exacerbated minoritarian position, the core incident of the brother's arrest becomes the primal scene intertextually overdetermining other instances where the family's sense of helplessness bursts forth. The same voicelessness colors the ghostly enunciation and occasional aphasia that materialize every time the self risks disintegration, a dynamic extending beyond the purview of the narrative voice. When evoking her mother's near death from the bombing during the German occupation of Tunis, the narrator notes the same aphasia, leaving the stage to André Gide's depiction of the ordeals of war: "all that [my mother] could never tell me, what she preferred not to say" (Fellous 55).[99] Marked with the same expressive limitations, the scene renders the mother's ontological anxiety of disappearance. The volatile nature of wartime brutality, compounded by the perceptible if veiled Nazi presence in the city, suggests another mapping of violence evocative of more pernicious forms of obliteration. In the face of the growing fascist threat, the unease of an increasingly vulnerable Jewish population finds its way to the surface of the text. The mother's powerlessness to protect her children from the violence of the blast, the trauma endured by the child she carried as a result of the detonation (he will develop an aggressive medical condition), the brother's inability to extricate himself from the administrative trap ultimately depriving him of his rights as a Tunisian, and the narrator's commitment to save all of them bespeak the family's sense of beleaguerment. It can be argued that the entire novel and the act of writing itself follow from this feeling of hopeless marginalization. Conceived as a testimony in the name of those who cannot speak, the story is the material instantiation of the imperative of compensation and equity that opens the volume: "I am not in my mother's womb this time, I need to make my life by hand, the world was given to me, it is now time to give it back. . . . I embrace this world in the making" (Fellous 62).[100] The retelling of the story proceeds from the pledge formed from a mother's womb, before lived existence, during the first crossing to France, undertaken to consult a prominent professor regarding her brother's medical condition. Replicating the original journey, a second crossing tears asunder the fragile balance of communities, definitively tolling the knell on any possible long-term inscription into the fabric of Tunisian society—the narrator's departure to study in France in 1967, a handful of days after the end of the Six-Day War, which marked a turning point in Arab-Jewish relations in Tunisia and across the Arab world.[101]

The spectrality of the narrator's voice, a function of her haunting by the voices of the past, is coextensive with a sense of dispossession. It is a sort of ventriloquism in absentia that marks with its cadence her very inscription at the heart of her family. The text insists on the unreliable nature of the narrator; her memory fails her and her perspective on events is partial, obstructed. The aphasia that this truncated vision begets likens the narrator to a phantasmatic presence: "I watch, I cannot find any word yet, I am an unborn child. I can see, but I cannot speak. I am like the dead" (Fellous 49).[102] As the lines of demarcation separating the living from the dead, the vocal from the voiceless, get scrambled, the incorporation of the dead ancestors into the narrative voice proceeds. Yet the syntactic structure of the simile "Je suis *comme* les morts," inserting comparison at the heart of what should have been similitude, splits the narrator's position from those ghosts, and marks spectrality with irrevocable estrangement rather than complete incorporation. In fact she soon recovers her memory: "There, I now recognize Bette Davis's face. The film is called *Dangerous*" (50).[103] Between the two avowals, in the oscillation between nascent remembrance and the pull toward dissolution, stands a maternal confession uttered in anger, begrudging the lives born of her unhappy union: "On that day [the day she met her husband] I should have worn slippers and none of this mess would have happened" (50).[104] Encapsulating the whole paradox of being alive while being supposed to have never been born, the formula "Je suis comme les morts" emphasizes the discrepant subject position from which the narrative emanates. Significantly the narrative voice recedes in the background at the time of the mother's confession, which is reported in free direct speech. In its wake, the attempted incorporation of the ancestors' voices operates as an attempt to find one's place. It marks an effort to legitimize one's existence, to appropriate a family structure that could circumscribe an existence made of constant suppression from one's immediate environment: "I stay with them, I am a part of their history, even if I am a stranger" (148).[105] A reverted echo of the "hypermnesia" that critics have often associated with Jewish Tunisian literature (Kassab-Charfi, "Architecture"; Latiri Carpenter), the hypomnesia displayed throughout the novel betrays a dissonant position, an exclusion from lineage spurring the quest for an appeased form of belonging.

This appeasement will not come, and it is ultimately the desire for disappearance that will prevail: "I can do it all, even die" (Fellous 232).[106] The text is mired in the undertow of dissolution reclaimed as an ideal. Clustered around a beach scene in which a little girl contemplates dispersal into the vast sea at her feet, the maritime reminiscences punctuating the novel betray a deep-seated sense of profound bleakness. This endless *tristesse* surges from the contemplation of one's death as a perpetual, disintegrative swim into the blue line of the horizon. From the initial description of the cry and its immediate evocation of the lost Tunisian years that the narrator has the moral obligation to restitute, the threat of erasure looms in the distance as an ineluctable finality: "I want to toy with [the world]. I also want to distance myself from it and to practice disappearing" (24).[107] The insertion of this seemingly casual admission belies the ostensible felicitous intellectual *cabotage* of the narrative voice to reveal a gloomy undercurrent beneath the display of hospitality concluding the fragment: "Come on in, there is still room" (25).[108] Against the grain of this fantasized capaciousness for inclusion, the narrator's own estrangement resounds. Through her willful dissipation—letting herself disappear to better let others speak through her in this desired haunting by the voice of the ancestors—the narrator's openness onto the world is declined in the mode of the virtual, of a fantasy never to be actualized. Existence follows perpetual flux and displacement—from inscription into the fabric of family life and community but also from the weave of national histories inimical to minority representation. The ghostly voice ordering the disposition of memories, Tunisia nevertheless stops short of incarnation, an inaccessible ideal. Its potential *convivencia* materializes only through an erratic text as invested in its delineation as it is in its undoing. The narrator's multiple forms of traumatic truncation underpin the spatial projection of her identity. Through the scattered, disparate geographies of existence that she reclaims, across religious and civilizational boundaries and afoul of historical processes of identity formation, another collocation of identity is forged where Tunisianness is redefined as a diffraction open onto the world. Reminiscent of Glissant's archipelago for Kassab-Charfi, this identity-in-relation is conspicuous for its depoliticized universalism, its reluctance to lay claim to any rooted form of affiliation. Hélé Béji associates movement to national consciousness and fixity to a nationalism tending toward totalitarianism, what she calls "nationalitarianism" (19). In her wake Fellous locates Tunisia in the nonactualized space of relation, in the quintessential spirit of *convivencia* that animates her mythicized vision of the Tunisian national construct—the transhistorical (and indeed ahistorical) nostalgia-imbued Avenue de France. Unable to replace the dismissed subject of official history by an effective, self-enacting community, Fellous's Tunisianness remains unclaimed in its collective instantiation. It is affixed to her fragmentary mode of consciousness, at the receiving end of a concatenation of traumas inducing dispersion and nomadism. Fellous's cosmopolitan subject considers herself to be "part of a world, a circle of belonging that transcends the limited ties of kinship and country to embrace the whole of humanity. However, because one cannot *see* the universe, the world, or humanity, the cosmopolitan optic is not one of perceptual experience but of the imagination" (Cheah 26).

Fellous's use of the ahistorical, mythical matrix of Andalusian convivencia in *Avenue de France* engages the steadfast residue of Tunisian multiculturalism. The multiple traumatic fractures that have marked the deployment of her identitarian paradigm enforce an insider/outsider viewpoint throughout the narrative that brings to the fore other forms of historical consciousness than the ones rooted in conventional models of identity. Hovering between persecution and historical *conviviencia*, her Tunisian "national consciousness" (Béji) mediates a nostalgic form of doubling that summons the lingering past haunting the dystopian present. The transposability of Fellous's configuration is a function of its unrealizable character. It subverts any clear sense of self. Identity surges in the seams between the subject's multiple incarnations and blossoms in the ethical imperative of remembrance and voicing.

Fellous's construct (as well as Farès's) does not take as its melancholic object a perfected form of nationalism that would fully circumscribe the national community and include all of its segments in utopian congruence. The destiny of diversity that it highlights is to inhabit the space of the virtual. Yet its nostalgic prism reveals the incommensurability of minority experiences to national narratives. Undoing the multiple forms of silencing performed by rigidified forms of power, this writing reveals the willfully perpetuated opacities and blind spots marring national narratives. By circulating a different representation of the past, it opens a breech within the monolith of official memory. If these two alignments stay short of realization, other configurations pursue the reactivation of repressed alternative affiliation further in the direction of political claims. Malika Mokeddem's *N'zid* is one such text.

CHAPTER 3

Traumatic Allegories

Mediterranean Nomadism and Melancholia in Malika Mokeddem's N'zid

[Being] singular plural in such a way that the singularity of each is indissociable from its being-with-many and *because*, in general, a singularity is indissociable from a plurality.

—Jean-Luc Nancy, *Being Singular Plural*

In a recent article on serial torture, Ross Chambers defines the traumatic event as "an event that is both violent and unprecedented in the experience of the victim. . . . Something is happening that has no referent to which it might be compared. Consequently it cannot be known because it cannot be recognized; it is the raw sensation of unfiltered violence" (39). Such a definition lays emphasis on the key importance of the quest for a figural form of representation for something which is, by definition, unlike anything else. How can an event partake of the referentiality constitutive of literature if it is by nature unique, unprecedented, and incomparable—if, in other words, it defies representation? Just as the subaltern stands to lose its intrinsic subalternity upon becoming represented, the traumatic event crosses into the realm of the untraumatic as soon as it is harnessed to figural rendering. To qualify as trauma, Chambers concludes, an event must be narrated through the figural mode of allegory, or suggestion. Such is the avenue through which the traumatic event can be extricated from the realm of the unspeakable without falling back into an evidentiary mode of reading. With the doubling afforded by allegorical coding, trauma can be released from voicelessness and gain legibility within the economy of the written word. This is not to say, however, that allegorical inscription endows trauma with the clarity of unambiguous meaning. The object of allegory is by nature elusive. In its ever-deferred form, losing all transparency and inscription, it collides with the uncanny object of Benjaminian nostalgia, the leftover trace of a past now unreachable and therefore incomprehensible. Like the pile of rubble or the majestic ruins evoking a vanished past, allegory recaptures only the lingering afterglow of events, stopping short of restituting their concrete presence and determination. Allegory is by definition suggestive, an approximate mode of interpretation. For, as Chambers argues, "[allegory's] object is not necessarily identified, the recognition of its object being left to the reader, who may well discover it to be infinitely elusive" (40). This dynamic is suffused with the manifold afterlives of violence associated with trauma. The source of this violence and its cause remain shrouded in mystery as the reader is left with the uneasiness of a failed deciphering, "the kind of recognition that is an acknowledgement of one's not-knowing" (41). For allegory is "*nothing but* clues, indicators, symbols and referents," as its object remains forever inscrutable (40).

In this chapter I seek to illuminate how Malika Mokeddem's novel *N'zid* (2001) espouses allegory to stage the complex aftermath of multiple forms of traumatic exclusion from the comforting bounds of national belonging. The fractal narrative of a woman's literal quest for identity across the Mediterranean in the wake of an amnesia-causing attack, Mokeddem's novel follows Nora Carson's nautical peregrinations from the Aegean Sea to the Catalan village of Cadaqués. Waking up alone and nameless after an attack by the Armed Islamic Group, the novel's half-Irish, half-Algerian, French-born protagonist sets as her prime objective to reconstruct the line of events that have led to the novel's incipit. Adrift on a boat she doesn't recognize, Nora first tries to secure a sense of self and history through anamnesis. As the attempt to fashion new identities for herself falls short, Nora resorts to allegorical sketches to retrieve fragments of her history. As memories begin to resurface, loosening the grip of trauma over her destiny, Nora rekindles her relationships with key characters from her past, who dispel the lingering traces of her amnesia. Having fully recovered her memory, she is free to engage in an analytical reading of her past in relation to the history of Algeria, confronting historical traumas and working toward the resolution of past sins in a future-oriented perspective.

Despite the ostensible nomadic sensibility of Mokeddem's style, the novel ruminates on the reality of being at odds with a national construct inimical to difference—gender difference within the oppressive patriarchal order common to all Mediterranean societies, a form of inequality enshrined in the 1984 Algerian Family Code that relegates women to the position of lifelong legal minors, or other forms of minoritarian positionalities. Entangled with considerations of class and models of plurilingualism (or lack thereof), marginalized identities often overlap with literal voicelessness in the postcolonial nation's Arab(ophone) construct. What Béji has dubbed "nationalitarisme" in the case of postcolonial Tunisia (the co-opting of the transformative potential of a newly expressed national consciousness in the service of increasingly authoritarian regimes) could just as well be applied to FLN rule in post-1965 Algeria. Corrupting the promise of decolonization, the systematic anchoring of identity in the twin concepts of nationalism and Islam made for the emergence of a disquieting state structure exclusive of the many nuances of the national community and perpetuating the marginalization and silencing of vast segments of Algerian society (Sansal). In response to scripted and prescriptive forms of identity, Mokeddem's novel resorts to allegory to write over the dominant rhetoric of nation-building, attempting to inflect it toward more inclusive forms of self-definition that do not suppress diversity. Capitalizing on the current reflection on critical melancholia discussed in the introduction, I suggest that the narrative ultimately performs a working through of trauma, which concurrently doles out an appeased reading of national identity in a more inclusive mode.

In Mokeddem's paradigm the Mediterranean figures prominently as a geographical space of oblivion, an ethos of intersubjective encounter, and a fundamental principle of instability and opacity within self and nation. Being at one with the sea means revisiting exhausted, overly coded tropes of the self, the community, the nation. It implies insufflating a new life force into them. As the plot progresses, Nora recovers a history peppered with personal and family trauma, ranging from her mother's return to Algeria, which left her in the care of a surrogate Algerian maternal figure, to the disappearance of her friend Jean Rollan and the murder of her lover, Jamil, at the hands of Islamists. Reconfiguring the Mediterranean Sea as a space of plural identities, the narrative of her anamnestic quest opens the text to consideration of various performative practices and facilitates the emergence of female subjectivity in complex relation to the framework of the nation. Beyond the diegetic quest, the protagonist's seafaring ethos generates a renewed trope of nomadism mediated by the novel's allegorical aesthetic. This nomadism of the sea, in contrast to Mokeddem's famed desert nomadism, is a purveyor of multifarious hybridity in an intersubjective framework. It rewrites the Mediterranean not so much as a no-man's-land of pure detachment but rather as a rich, sedimented space where a philosophy of singularity can develop in fertile dialogue with a sense of intersubjective existence. In Mokeddem's early fiction desert nomadism functions at the service of a revised national pact in post–civil war Algeria. A form of motion inspired by the author's own nomadic ancestry in the "smooth" space of the desert, the concept conveys nostalgia for an authentic Maghreb unsullied by the tactics of political dominance and personal gain.[1] Following Mokeddem's personal maxim and her deliberate reclaiming of a nomadic aesthetic, critics read her early fiction through the lens of Deleuze and Guattari's nomadological model (Orlando, "Écriture"; Agar-Mendousse, *Violence et créativité*; Mertz-Baumgartner).

In contrast *N'zid*'s performance of a nomadism of the sea, which I call Mediterranean nomadism, functions as a new form of displacement that extends beyond the confines of the national community and the three cultures brought together by the colonial encounter. This new configuration highlights the necessity of actualized forms of identity coextensive with a reinvigorated, pluralized conception of the nation. Many critical accounts of the novel have emphasized its postidentitarian postulates, reading the sea exclusively in terms of a "smooth space," or "nonspace" (Brahimi; Aubry), where identity is reconfigured as free-flowing and undetermined—the plane of deterritorialization's deployment (Carlson; El-Nossery; Helm). In contrast, I suggest that Mokeddem alternately endows the sea with characteristics of both "smooth" and "striated" spaces: smooth space whenever Nora is seeking refuge in the temporary amnesia offered by a romanticized, aestheticized Mediterranean, and striated space, incontrovertibly subjugated to the tight constellation of ports dotting the shoreline. The sea is inescapably crisscrossed, teeming with irrepressible others: "There is too much traffic, too many propellers, triumphantly chopping up the sea, breaking it and churning it up in between the strait's ports" (Mokeddem, *N'zid* 67).[2] Against deterritorialized readings I argue that the connectivity mediated by the sea performs the subject's reincorporation into the national community through the melancholic working through of trauma. Under the double aegis of singularity and reciprocity, which echoes Nancy's concept of "singulier-pluriel," this vision redraws the contours of *algérianité* to include an appeased remembrance of its traumatic past. Progressively confronting and working through the subject's past on the individual and collective levels, Mokeddem's writing is confined to an "écriture d'apaisement" (Agar-Mendousse, *Violence et créativité* 110). This Mediterranean form of identity is more attuned to the outside world, and the transitive forms of contact that it affords mediate the novel's persistent attempts to reflect on the fraught issue of national identity.

UNDOING ALLEGORY, DEBUNKING POSTIDENTITY

In *Assia Djebar: Out of Algeria,* Jane Hiddleston has convincingly argued that Algerian texts from the 1990s can be characterized as mournful texts expressing the progressive acceptance of the loss of an identifiable Algerian identity. And indeed the unbridled violence sweeping across the country during the infamous Black Decade had much to do with the residual sense of chaos that left its imprint on the national unconscious.[3] In the wake of resurgent violence the emergent political and cultural crisis triggered deep-rooted disenchantment toward the possible grasping and embracing of what being Algerian meant. As any nuanced identity configuration evaporated under the pressure of political polarization, the possibility of delineating productive forms of engagement with one's history or genealogy was significantly jeopardized. Algeria as a historical site and complex cultural entity dissipated in the haze of chaos, while myriad narratives testified to the immateriality of its presence. Displaying the aesthetic marking of trauma, these texts reconfigured *algérianité* as the object of loss, the melancholy core of writing. *N'zid* is no exception to this trend. Linguistically and otherwise Algeria is lived as a lack, a coreless focal point, what Anne Donadey has dubbed in the context of another amnesia "the nodal point of suffering," which the subject's traumatic narrative must "approach . . . as slowly as possible" ("L'Expression littéraire" 71). Nora's attack by Islamists constitutes the core episode of "unfiltered violence" evoked in Chambers's definition of the traumatic event. In its wake, after amnesia has set in, Nora finds herself unable to reconcile her shattered psyche with the memory of the attack. The narrative presents the devastating event as trauma precisely by emphasizing its elusiveness and lack of direct and obvious characterization. The fracturing of the self is embodied in an internal voice that gives substance to what Inge Boer describes as "the voice of trauma . . . a voice that assaults the subject, a voice that is separated from her but not leaving her alone" (62). The interpretive odyssey of reading that takes place throughout the novel is a function of this fractured aesthetic. It ensures that the traumatic event is approached cautiously, its meaning parsed out progressively through the indirect vehicle of allegory, which alone can create adequate conditions for its expression (Ross Chambers). By bringing the focus back to the segregating nature of the subject's trauma, allegory thus bears the mark of a distant perspective born of the authority of the traumatic event over its immediate aftermath.

Nora's initial withdrawal after the attack is echoed in the physical distance from Algeria afforded by the voyage at sea, which places Nora at a safe distance from the events unfurling in the country. Her wandering across the sea is the objective manifestation of the unhoming of the subject in the wake of trauma. It enables the process of anamnesis or, more broadly, the return to origins. In the amniotic space of the sea the vacillation of identity revisited on the performative mode lends itself to Nora's temporary estrangement from her immediate position. It is through the absolute solipsism of sailing and the total disintegration of the self in the infinite expanse of the sea that she first succeeds in reining in her ontological anxiety. Denying any claim to social mediation, this model of singularization functions as a curative process remedying the deleterious effects of trauma. Ensconcing herself in the comfort of healing solitude, she is able to give in to the relief provided by amnesia: "No more past. No more land. Not even their nostalgia . . . before the wave of oblivion washes over" (*N'zid* 22).[4]

Dismantling prescriptive identity protocols, her Mediterranean form of deterritorialization is a first step toward escaping the narrow strictures of rigid identity patterns to recover the complexities of her history. The wandering underlying *N'zid*'s narrative structure reverberates as a journey into language and alternative modes of signification. Suffusing the surface of the "corps-texte," a text-body continuum echoing the damaged cortex at the root of the amnesia, this contiguity between body and text extends into the blending of second- and third-person narrative fragments. The second-person voice of anamnesis in italics, addressing the estranged self as "you," and the third-person omniscient narrative voice provide analysis and insight into otherwise scattered episodes. From the interlacing of these two voices the narrative unfurls, encapsulating the rootlessness ("errance") of orality and the autobiographical recollections at the heart of anamnesis. It is in the unstable, fluid space in which both voices are intertwined that the protagonist can perform her fractal identities and negotiate a space of resistance to any form of overdetermination. The reading of the signs inscribed onto the surface of the body generates the narrative on the page, as do Nora's ad hoc drawings, through which anamnesis is performed. In a reciprocal move the body engenders the text just as the text engenders the increasing awareness of Nora's bodily experiences. The reconstruction of the self takes place on the screen of the blank page being written as the blank space of the sea is being charted. It confines the protagonist's existence to a poetic composition seemingly divorced from any form of inscription into history. Following the arc of Nora's recollections, performativity takes precedence as the subject's dominant mode of relation to the world. It encourages an exacerbated form of singularity oblivious to community allegiance. The point of contact and means of communication between members of the community, language appears as a bankrupt tool, meretriciously disguised and distorted. Appropriating Mallarmé's rejection of "the language of the tribe," in this case the tribe indicted for causing the death of Nora's mother, the novel breaks down the structuring elements of a common linguistic imaginary into unrecognizable elliptical fragments that are subjected to singular use and subversion in the wake of trauma.

Throughout the novel Nora's performances interweave intellectual and affective experiences to exceed frameworks of localization bound to narrowly defined cultures and temporalities. Mokeddem's rewriting of the self in the mode of unstable, fractal "performative encounters" (Rosello, *France and the Maghreb*) thus effectively exposes the intrinsic fictitiousness of all identity narratives. Refusing what Mireille Rosello has called "over-determined protocols of encounters," the text delineates new modes of engagement with alterity that burst open binary logics of identification and contact, the "dual metaphors of coupling" that restrict and predetermine the outcome of any future encounter between opposed polarities. In this respect Nora's imaginative rewritings of the self can be likened to Rosello's concept of a literary "mosaic that take[s] into account a multiplicity of religious, ethnic, and gendered specificities" (*France and the Maghreb* 165). In these early episodes Nora revisits a constellation of defined identities centered on national or religious models of belonging. Her performative peregrination across the Mediterranean makes them susceptible to resemanticization. Questioning claims to absolute definitions, *N'zid* foregrounds the mutual imbrications of all Mediterranean cultures in the formation of subjective and collective identities in the region.

The playfulness characterizing Nora's engagement with onomastic coding is a case in point. Rejecting national affiliation, she takes to task the all-pervasive power of the state, whose authoritarian logic forces clear-cut identification and predetermined self-definition on the two-pronged basis of lineage and geography. Nora compensates for her loss of identity and memory by creating transnational aliases and forging identities that all share a form of Mediterranean inclusiveness. These performances construct a utopian transnationalism reminiscent of the Mediterranean myths of the twentieth century (Audisio's or even Camus's), where identities were conceived as syncretic and relational rather than clearly circumscribed in spite of the incontrovertible reality of colonial segregation. This vision reconfigures the sea as a multifarious site of contact and collaboration rather than tension and friction among different religions and cultural models. It casts the Mediterranean as a space of contiguity where Western and Islamic civilizations can peacefully coexist in a renewed mythical Andalusian Golden Age. Nora's three reconstructed identities testify to the syncretic quality of the Mediterranean: Myriam Dors, an identity supplied by papers found by chance in the boat, whose origins are shrouded in the same sense of mystery as the other circumstances at the origin of her journey; Ghoula, a Lebanese artist fleeing the Civil War in Lebanon, named after the devouring ogress of Maghrebi folk tales in a gesture that substitutes the logic of myth for that of national history; and Eva Poulos, the epitome of Mediterranean hybridity: "My parents were Greek . . . What were they? My father, a Copt, my mother, Jewish. I was born in Paris. A pure Franco-Greco-Judeo-Christiano-Arabo-atheist" (*N'zid* 64).[5] This aesthetic of accumulation undermines the stable reference to the Greco-Judeo-Christian genealogy of Mediterranean descent. It calls in question the root of French colonial modernity, as well as the relevance of its sweeping progression across Greece and Rome on its way to western Europe, which posited the French colonial conquest of the Maghreb as the last stage of the alleged Greco-Roman destiny of the Mediterranean. Each of these identities is in itself a performance, that of a simulacrum that does not rest on any stable basis. Instead the playful recourse to an endless string of signifiers destabilizes the very notion of identity resting on the principle of strict correspondence. The basis of the patronymic system of identification, the name as a decipherable identifying mark reflecting lineage and social identity, gives way to a never-ending flow of signs devoid of any stable meaning. As onomastics becomes a fluctuating process, the novel thus hampers cognition and intelligibility. Meaning can be grasped only through its inscription in contentious, simultaneous linguistic and cultural logics. Thus the name *Nora* may be read as Irish or Arabic; the name *Myriam* as Hebrew, Muslim, or Christian. In the novel identity becomes a choice, a performance, not an essence that one has no choice but to embrace and express. The pendant of the loss of memory, the loss of fixed identities, and their attendant restrictions emancipates Nora from any constricting bind. Although memory is what guarantees the bond between the community and the self, the securing of one's place within the group, it is also "a ghetto, a purgatory" (52).[6] Once the rupture with the community and the collective order of meaning that is language has been consummated, the self appears to be released from social definition, free to roam the seas and consider identity from a critical perspective.

A first reading of *N'zid* might thus lead one to conclude that the structural ploy of the journey at sea in the throes of amnesia offers a postnational take on the issue of identity. The protagonist pursues her ostensibly aimless drifting in apparent bliss, marking any relation to a possible motherland (itself an ambivalent concept given Nora's fractured lineage) as antiquated at best and very likely nefarious. The first part of the novel enacts a total disintegration of the subject in the aquatic materiality of the Mediterranean. (Nora's first sensation upon waking up is suggestively the feeling of being "engulfed by nothingness" [11]).[7] It stages an evolution from a rational subject tied to a clear-cut sense of social existence to the unreflecting *hic et nunc* of physical sensations, which is experienced with a certain degree of *jouissance*. Female subjectivity emanates from sensuous immersion in the scents and colors of the Mediterranean, in a move harkening back to the felicitous primitivism bordering on animality that French colonial writers celebrated. Not least among them stands Gabriel Audisio, whose "liquid continent" metaphor reappears in *N'zid*: "This liquid continent belongs to her" (68).[8] "Your skin has eaten your brain. Soon you'll grow fur or scales on your skin," claims Nora's inner voice with delight, rejoicing in the blank slate that this cutaneous form of memory ("mémoire cutanée") affords her (*N'zid* 22; Elbaz 265).[9] Ostensibly giving way to a characterization of movement as pure difference, the novel appears to rewrite the protagonist's nomadic itinerary as absolute deferral and nonidentity, that is, as absolute allegory in the etymological sense of the Latin *absolutus*, that which is fully detached. Drifting freely on the surface of the Mediterranean, Nora may be construed to join other nomadic subjects, "free-floating signifiers without psychic and material investment in one or more given particular geopolitical spaces" (Lionnet and Shih 8). In its unmooring from any clear process of reference, the overarching allegorical structure of the text thus seems to associate mobility with a deterritorialized subject position generative of a postidentitarian mode of being.

In contrast with this Deleuze-inspired nomadological reading, I suggest in the wake of Mireille Rosello that Mokeddem's use of allegory stretches language to its representational limits and reveals zones of opacity and contradiction within itself. Taking the point further, I argue that this aesthetic significantly complicates the text's ostensible analogy between Nora's diegetic nomadism and its extolling of pure difference; it also reveals that her inalienable singularity is ultimately contingent on recognition by others. A careful examination of the layered nature of allegorical representation in the sketching episodes punctuating the diegesis sheds light on the disconnect between narrative and image—and on the semantic instability that this fracture generates. Two intertwined forms of allegorical imagery, pictorial and verbal, undergird Mokeddem's novel and the process of identity reconstruction it enacts. The novel's double allegorical aesthetic borrows from the realm of the visual through the recourse to various episodes of sketching carried out by the protagonist in an effort to jog her deficient memory. These sketches provide a forum amenable to surges of memory with the aim of reconstructing the original traumatic event that Nora has repressed, hoping to gain access to her personal history and an inherent sense of historicity. The corrupt words of the tribe prove unsuccessful in providing a suitable mode of expression for the subject's anamnesis. In turn these images act as sites where memory erupts, as blank spaces where singular readings of identity and national belonging can crystallize. Due to their visual nature, vignettes function first and foremost on the synchronic level: each drawing proposes to encapsulate and illuminate the many layers of one circumscribed episode in a single image meant to be taken in and deciphered at one take. Creating a bubble of time removed from the imperatives of sequential temporality, the process of sketching facilitates the artist's appropriation of the blank page. It also lends itself to the unfolding of an anamnestic process generative of identity and subjectivity. However, because the novel does not include actual drawings, the reader's access to the allegorical reality they depict is necessarily mediated by the narrative, whose unfolding obeys the rules of sequentiality. The novel thus puts two conflicting modes of temporality in tension: the synchrony of sketches with the diachrony of the narrative unfolding in the real time of reading, itself a mode of representation that, in the context of the novel, comes entangled with the strictures of national time and teleological history. Mokeddem's segmentation of Nora's experience in these vignettes extracts it from collective history and allows singular time to surface. In the process it produces a distinct form of sequentiality—a repetition proceeding from the progressive work of anamnesis as vignettes morph into comic strips marked by the use of recurrent symbols. For synchronic and diachronic readings need to be produced in combination to successfully read allegory (and subjectivity) through diegetic time.

The now canonical allegorical episode of the encounter between a nomadic, translucent jellyfish and a community-oriented sea urchin deep in his rocky sea bed reveals the complex dynamics of representation at the heart of *N'zid*. Rosello interprets Mokeddem's allegorical use of sea creatures as conflicting modes of being in the world—sedentary and nomadic—in light of what she calls "performative encounters," where "the protagonists of the encounter . . . construct a unique relationship with the idea of duality, hybridity, and inbetweenness" (*France and the Maghreb* 165). Her first impulse, Rosello tells us, was to see in this allegorical episode the antithesis of her performative encounter model. A diaphanous, subtle jellyfish attempts a close relationship with a rooted sea urchin blind to her transparency, only to find that its spines are a direct threat to its physical integrity. Discomfited the jellyfish has no choice but to move away, bemoaning the shortsightedness of her companion. At first blush the irreconcilability of the models is patent; most critics agree that the jellyfish stands for the open-minded, mobile drifter, whereas the urchin incarnates defensive subjectivity barricaded in a logic of intolerance. In short, neither one can successfully coexist with the other. The urchin's defensiveness, which is very clearly indicted for the failure of the encounter, translates as indifference toward alternative modes of being. There seems to be little space left for possible interaction.

However, as Rosello argues, a closer look at the narrative reveals minute imperfections in the oppositional logic. Subtle shifts appear within the text that expose binaries and essentialized protocols of difference as being no more than vacillating constructs. They reveal zones of ambiguity and tension and undercut the idealized nomadism and open-mindedness to which the jellyfish aspires. Belying the nomadic fluidity advocated throughout the text, both types of allegory ultimately come undone. The supposed clarity and authority of Mokeddem's dichotomous model of social relations, centered on the irreconcilable poles of the sedentary and the nomadic, are eventually cut across by currents of indeterminacy. As Rosello notes, a careful reading cannot fail to see that the subtle nomadic figure is in fact rather lacking in subtlety and seems to be rather bogged down by the weight of its heavy-handed dichotomous symbolism. The narrative voice's setting up of the jellyfish as a detached drifter is compromised by the very rigidity of the visual symbolism marking it as such. Mokeddem's text thus fails to carry into prose the ethereal quality of the jellyfish sketch, which is ultimately as tributary to a dualistic, prescriptive interpretive grid as the sea urchin's exclusionary worldview.

Within the context of her argument Rosello reads this opacity undercutting seemingly Manichaean representations as a breeding ground for subjective practices of hybridity freed from the strictures of ready-made identitarian narratives—the perfect illustration of her productive "performative encounter" model. She identifies a "fracture . . . between the drawing and the text" of allegory, an analysis to which I am indebted (*France and the Maghreb* 168). Bringing these insights to bear on my own reading, I take this fundamental ambivalence as a harbinger of the novel's narrative unreliability, of a fracturing of allegorical meaning that reinforces allegory's traumatic resonance. In the first half of *N'zid* the attempt to restore identity bears the mark of violence and incompletion. The narrative undermines the ostensible allegorical meaning of the drawing it is meant to faithfully reproduce and locks the jellyfish symbol in a cycle of undoing. In this context allegory marks a conflicted form of being following trauma. It deploys Nora's fragmented consciousness and her inability to fully inhabit any subject position, even that of a rootless nomad in the oblique mode of allegory that her drawing postulates. In this respect the sentence "Here is someone who uses fiction as a screen between him and the world" (43), a phrase Nora uses to ponder Loïc's resistance to her questions, could also be applied to her.[10]

The jellyfish symbolism will recur several times in the course of the novel, in the guise of a sketch or as an embodiment of the Gorgon Medusa. These uncanny echoes share conceptual space with Deleuze's notion of repetition as a conduit of "non-exchangeable and non-substitutable singularities. . . . To repeat is to behave in a certain manner, but in relation to something unique or singular which has no equal or equivalent. And perhaps this repetition . . . echoes . . . a more secret vibration which animates it, a more profound, internal repetition within the singular" (1). In an uncanny reiteration of Deleuze's words, Nora's inner voice exclaims, "You are like your drawings. Lines. Shapes. Vibrations without caption," only to add, "She thought 'fate' while saying 'drawing'" (*N'zid* 43).[11] The paronomastic overlap between *destin* (fate) and *dessin* (drawing) underlines the promise of a proteiform destiny more akin to a constellation of plural potentialities than to a set sense of *fatum.* In this slippage between the two, agency appears, undermining externally imposed structures. These deep vibrations color the subject's identity with the hue of ambivalence. Reminiscent of Deleuze's "profound, internal repetition within the [nonexchangeable and nonsubstitutable] singular," they link the diffracted course of Nora's anamnesis to the expression of her inalienable right to uniqueness. Her singularity vibration is said to be "sans légende," that is, devoid of any fixed reading, whether caption or legend in keeping with the polysemy of the French. Beyond the obvious reference to the complex relationship between the written word of the text (*legend* in its acceptation as explicative *caption*) and the visual drawing it evokes, the mention of legend also gestures to the text as myth, *legenda,* that which must be read—by others—for meaning to emerge.

It is precisely in such moments of allegorical opacity that Nora's singularity unfolds, developing at cross-purposes with clear-cut oppositions between nomadic and sedentary subject positions. Against any form of predetermination Nora's sense of self erupts in all its complexity and ambiguity, inhabiting the differential space between the drawing and the text. Subjectivization takes shape in the interstices between pure detachment and staunch forms of rootedness. It irrupts in the ghostly voice haunting the clear symbolism of the narrative, which it simultaneously undercuts. To return to Rosello's argument, the allegorical world of anamnesis is itself tributary to unpredictable modulations of identity reaching far beyond dichotomous visions of subjectivity. Located on the intuitive level of vibrations, it transcends words and definitive legends, the only legend being that there is none.

This disjunction between allegorical meaning and text thus adds another layer of reality to the text's univocal and supposedly truthful message. It exposes its hollowness and contradictions and forces a reassessment of its signification. This resistance to ready-made forms of determination suggests that the narrative voice possesses at its core a kernel of inscrutability that makes univocal representation impossible within the economy of the novel, whether in art form or through language. In this context drawing appears as an alternative mode of writing that would not be tributary to the intrinsic shortcomings of language in an overdetermined postcolonial situation, possibly because pictorial expression lies precisely beyond the bounds of diegesis.[12] The failure of allegorical transmission undermines the credibility of the novel's championing of a purely nomadic form of being. Whether narratorial intent or an instance of the failed deciphering induced by the very nature of traumatic allegorical expression, as Ross Chambers argues, it calls into question the desirability of absolute unaccountability and detachment that could be thought to underpin the narrative's heuristic model. In this respect the equivocal relation between word and image permits us to reassess the overarching valence of Mokeddem's supposed allegory of postidentity throughout the novel. With the labile use of allegory, signification is breached. Singularity emerges in the tension between exterior forms of determination associated with the rigidity of all collectives and the irrepressible desire to forgo any form of predetermined identity—in other words, *between* the urchin's and the jellyfish's positions.

The deconstruction of this dual allegorical reading unearths the social entanglements inherent in Mokeddem's post-traumatic mode of narration. It debunks the narrative's model for a deterritorialized form of being and points to the irrepressible haunting by the phantoms of the past. It thus invites us to rethink the nature of Nora's alternative forms of resistance to the repressive social covenant embodied by the nation-state. It spells out the need to move beyond Deleuze's abstract, otherless form of nomadism embodied in the jellyfish-urchin episode and other vignettes throughout the book, instead reincorporating the other into the economy of the novel as a necessary interlocutor—if only to restore the wholeness of the self after trauma, to read and parse the *legenda*.

BEYOND THE SINGULAR: A MEDITERRANEAN NOMADISM OF TRANSITIVITY

> An empty subjectivity, the estrangement of a subject who becomes ontologically stateless, intransitive (he is nobody's other), with no correlate, no genitive construction, with no country of arrival. A new person.
>
> —Catherine Malabou, *Ontologie de l'accident*

The novel gestures toward Mokeddem's well-recognized trope of desert nomadism in a series of striking parallels that contrast the blue expanse of the Mediterranean Sea to the endless desert of her previous novels.[13] Brinda Mehta's authoritative "Geographies of Space" excavates the political potential of Mokeddem's trope of the desert—a paean to circular trajectories cutting across more rigidified forms of territorialized social affiliation. Replete with Deleuzian echoes, her analysis invests the "desert steppe" of the writer's nomadic writing with both geographical liminality and racial hybridity. In Mehta's words, "[Mokeddem's] novels represent the problematics of racial, geographical, and cultural interstitiality whereby in-betweenness becomes a space of resistance, ambiguity, and exile as reflected by the author's personal situation as an Algerian immigrant writer in France who nevertheless suffers from the existential angst of uprootedness" (1). Her ties to her original culture have been severed, but these "truncated affiliations" enable her searing critique of patriarchy and the other forms of oppression afflicting Algeria, the incontestable home (1). Similarly Valerie Orlando posits this complex re-creation of the self from the distance of exile as the sine qua non for feminist praxis as no freedom is to be found within the coercive order of the patriarchal nation. In the context of Mokeddem's most renowned novel, *L'Interdite*, Orlando defines deterritorialization as a "break with traditional peripheries, which induces [women] to explore a new identity." She continues, "This concept . . . defined by Gilles Deleuze and Félix Guattari . . . [as] an 'asignifying rupture' ['rupture asignifiante'] . . . performs a fracture with former landmarks and a certain freedom with regards to origins. This rupture spawns a re-creation of subjectivity through new principles. . . . [It] perpetuates itself as 'abstract lines in movement freed from the task of representing the world' with the aim of constructing 'a new type of reality'" ("Écriture" 105). Such a characterization of female writing in exile has been prevalent in the field of Maghrebi studies. Indeed one of the primary missions of Maghrebi literary criticism has been identifying patterns and dynamics through which traditionally silent women were gaining representation and agency in the process of writing, mostly in the form of autobiographical expression (among others, see Segarra, *Leur pesant de poudre*; Chaulet Achour, "Autobiographies d'algériennes"). Alison Rice argues that "women [in Algeria] do not have the possibility of taking the floor, much less the pen," and emphasizes the "present challenges women in Algeria inevitably face" (*Polygraphies* 89). In a deterritorialized perspective the successful disavowal of tradition can take place only through physical displacement and the elaboration of a redefined, more fluid form of identity born of motion. Reflecting this intellectual allegiance to mobile and fluid modes of affiliation, Orlando concludes that "these women writers have become nomads who find their subjectivities in new areas" (*Nomadic Voices* 105). Beyond the text this quest also eventuates in the construction of a political standpoint from which the female militant self can gain a voice and contribute to changing the perception of women and their role in society. Each woman writer is therefore entrusted with the task of collective representation, each of their texts shouldering the onus of changing the material conditions of speaking and writing for generations of women to come. In the context of the Algerian Civil War of the 1990s, the imperative certainly reverberates with significant moral undertones.

From Mehta's perspective this imperative is intricately bound to the elaboration of a narrative of origins, supported by oral cultures, that maps the desert as a site for memory and knowledge of the past in the face of obliterating dynamics. Taking her cue from Khatibi's text "The Colonial Labyrinth," she aligns the space of the desert with its urban corollary, the medina. Under the sign of spatial fluidity, the embodied subject delineates a "movement of 'deambulation,' or a culturally determined psychology of evasion" as a strategy of resistance against restraining social networks ("Geographies of Space" 25). In Mehta's words, "[The subject's] mind . . . ultimately frees itself when she embraces the multiplicity of the rhizome . . . the *juste milieu* of a liberating nomadic consciousness" (31). In a nutshell the "nomadic consciousness of the ancestors represents an effective negotiation of the multiple alienations of alterity by respecting the primacy of 'natural law' over institutionalized dominance" (31). In this interpretation Mokeddem's mobility beyond her Algerian homeland effects a transgressive crossing of the fault lines between home and exilic destinations in a pattern generative of female subjectivity and literary nonconformity. Her "horizontality of vision" emerges as "the motivator of a holistic prismatic sensibility in which physical nomadism complements spiritual or cosmic nomadism as the sign of an elevated sense of consciousness" (Mehta, "Geographies of Space" 7). Mehta means Deleuzian nomadology, which stands in sharp contrast to "established hierarchies" and other such malicious forms of stasis (7). The transversality it affords panders to a form of "primordial thought, a preinstitutionalized way of thinking that eludes systematization and favors intellectual wanderings wherein knowledge is perceived in terms of a universal cosmovision" (7). Reminiscent of Amrouche's introduction to his *Chants Berbères de Kabylie* and its characterization of the innocence of pristine Kabylian culture, this melancholic perception bears the mark of pure abstraction and, in the otherless perspective that it proposes, resonates with the empty cosmopolitanism of wandering that Christopher L. Miller has deftly characterized (*Nationalists*). Trudy Agar-Mendousse's articulation of an "ethics of nomadism" encompassing "hybridity . . . tolerance, imagination and independence" ("Counterviolence" 192) in Mokeddem's novel *Les Hommes qui Marchent* ascribes this dynamic to the inherent solipsism of a subject at cross-purposes with any sense of community, a subject limited to the contact afforded by "verbal nomadism" toward her captive audience. Only through scriptural nomadism does the subject gain access to her "line of flight" from masculine oppression (Agar-Mendousse, "Counterviolence" 193). In the context of female subjectivity, such configurations of mobility restrict agency to the nonspace of the written page, which Agar-Mendousse collapses into the third space of madness, a creative site par excellence and the female subject's only space for emancipation. What she depicts as Mokeddem's ethical nomadism of pure deterritorialization is thus recast as absolute resistance, violence without actual physical aggression. In this context subjectivity can be accomplished only through an escapist dynamic mediated by the act of writing, in contradiction to any sort of collective. It is evocative of Catherine Malabou's model of "empty subjectivity" cited as epigraph to this section.

Mokeddem's later Mediterranean nomadism reactivates this distinctive desert trope, revising it in the context of maritime mobility. Through this Mediterranean propulsion reaching beyond the confines of Algeria, the subject exceeds the nation and rewrites it. Yet in contradiction to the escapism identified by readings of Mokeddem's desert nomadism, I suggest that this transnational rewriting of identity materializes as a working through of trauma. As Dominick LaCapra writes, "[Working through] is intimately bound up with the possibility of ethically responsible action and critical judgment on the part of someone who strives for the position of an agent and may thereby counteract his or her own experience of victimhood" (186). Emphasizing the political substrate of any process seeking to resolve past traumas, Rosello argues that "working through the past is both a practice and something between a politics and an ethics, something that could be called an agenda" (*The Reparative* 17). For Nora, amnesia appears as what Mokeddem has termed in the suggestively titled *Je dois tout à ton oubli* "a vital accident of memory" (38), enabling a deeper view of identity. At the core of working through, the ethical necessity of haunting—preserving alterity within the self through the melancholic incorporation of other repressed voices—looms large, shifting the weight of trauma from the purely individual to the collective.[14]

In the manner of the politics of mourning proposed by David Eng and David Kazanjian—an ethical project whereby the past "remains steadfastly alive for the political work of the present" (5)—the question resonating through haunting is less concerned with what is lost than what has survived, what has been used, appropriated, reconstructed, and denominated anew: "*how* loss is apprehended and history is named—how that apprehension and naming produce the phenomenon of 'what remains'" (6). This emphasis on "what remains" eventuates in a "politics of mourning that might be active rather than reactive, prescient rather than nostalgic, abundant rather than lacking, social rather than solipsistic, militant rather than reactionary" (1).[15] In the context of *N'zid*, engaging with the past's many ghosts induces a reflection on the power and nature of collective existence and on the kind of community that a post-traumatic consideration of remains can postulate. Against an ossified, partial, state-sponsored politics of memory, Nora's performative melancholia preserves these resilient phantom voices of Algeria, giving them prominence within a political countermemory. Engaging in a "back and forth movement between incorporation—which results in being 'habitée' [haunted]—and introjection—which results in being 'apaisée' [appeased]" (Donadey, "Introjection and Incorporation" 87–88), this gesture implies performing critical resistance to the obliterating politics of national commemoration identified by Khanna and to the instances of national forgetting that they purvey. The coming to terms encapsulated in the act of working through necessarily implies contact and confrontation with actual others—whether protagonists or victims of the 1990s cycle of violence that engulfed all subjects in its endless aftermath. It means enacting a nonpathological performance of remembering and a restitution of the country's plural past in the direction of a brighter future.

Redeployed on a transnational plane of contact between North and South (and East and West), Nora's nomadism should not be mistaken for a sort of virtual nomadology in which the attraction to pure, abstract difference unmoors the subject from any sense of (or desire for) identity markers. In this respect it belies the impulse to construe her dealings with difference as a "purely internal or self-differing difference, a difference that excludes any constitutive mediation between the differed" (Hallward 162). Difference is here the basis of a new inclusive collective salvaged from erasure and restored to vocality. In Mokeddem's text, as in the case of Djebar, the displaced perspective purveyed by exile constitutes a "gradual shift away from a positioned Algerian identity or genealogy" (Hiddleston, *Assia Djebar* 4). Yet it also extends to "a discovery of Algeria's singular-plurality, and ultimately to an ongoing preoccupation with its loss" (5). A borrowing from Nancy's philosophy, the reference to "Algeria's singular-plurality" (its "singulier pluriel" character in the original French) emphasizes the incontrovertible fact that there can be no existence without coexistence, no being without a pull toward others. As Nancy's epigraph to this chapter suggests, singularities always exist in relation. They are born of encounters: "Plural singularity . . . *because*, in general, a singularity is indissociable from a plurality" (*Being Singular Plural* 32). The intrinsic plurality of the Algerian national community is evoked by this codependency, recasting the singular in connection with a constitutive other. As *N'zid* evolves toward recognition of this indelible law of collective existence, the imprint of trauma becomes erased.

Loosening Nora's solipsistic frame of reference, the novel opens subjectivity to fruitful influences and interactions. Its usefulness notwithstanding, the temporary passage through a detached, absolute form of singularity is to be understood precisely in those terms: as a transitory step toward a more involved form of engagement with the world. As Nora's inner voice presciently admonishes, "It won't be that easy for you. The sea is only a reprieve" (30).[16] Nancy's singular-plural addresses the need to suffuse any singular engagement with the loss of Algeria with the memory of the collective. In this sense trauma does not obliterate the elusive centrality of Algeria in Mokeddem's narrative of remembrance, nor the significance of community, and it should certainly not be read as being generative of a form of identity exclusive of intersubjective contact. What it denotes is rather a wounded form of subjectivity (*trauma* as wound in its Greek etymological sense) at cross-purposes with selective framings of national history. Through the evocation of those "who carry several torn lands within . . . who live between demands and ruptures" (22), a category in which Nora is in good standing, the text sheds light on a fracture perceptible throughout her musings on identity.[17] This rift flags the persistent presence of the nation as the ghostly voice underlying the narrative despite Nora's professed desired for nonidentity. It is a disjunction proceeding from the tension between the un-homing of a free-floating subject drifting on the surface of the sea and her very real longing for the safety and comfort provided by the possible reclaiming of a nation.

Present in absentia, Algeria remains the framework of reference even if the coercive identity narratives it puts forth are purposefully dismissed as restrictive and overdetermining. A few pages before the jellyfish-urchin encounter, a first diegetic sketch offers a clear illustration of the process—and of its limitations. The drawing is of a small fried jellyfish being devoured by a sun turned eye turned octopus. The sequential reading of the cartoon strips highlights the transformation of the celestial body from a luminescent presence watching over the depiction of an idyllic Mediterranean seascape to a harbinger of tragedy. The drawing stages the progressive fading away of sunlight into a pool of blood, irreversibly blurring the line between sea and sky: "The entire sea is reduced to a small roasted jellyfish which he [the sun-octopus] gulps down with delight" (31).[18] With the insight granted by the recognition of repetitive patterns, the reader is immediately able to decipher the obvious allegorical implications of the jellyfish's dreadful fate. However, the scene gains new purchase in light of the new symbolism of the eye turned octopus. The eye is suffused with the dual meaning of the Arabic lexeme *ʿayn* (meaning both "eye" and "spring," the latter reverberating with the same polysemy as the French *source* [173]). In a later sketch the eye-*ʿayn* becomes the embodiment of the lost Algerian mother, who preferred an uncertain return to an idealized motherland to the reality of family life in France, though an unconventional one. Evoking the powerful aura of the motherland, the voracious sun curtails the power of the would-be nomadic jellyfish and its desirable mobility free of restrictive boundaries. A few pages after the original drawing Nora's italicized deep voice shifts from her original dichotomous discourse to a tacit acknowledgment of the omnipotence of memory and one's inescapable history: "You simply cannot inhabit another body. Or rewrite your story. . . . Enough with remembrance! You didn't lose your memory, you escaped its straitjacket, didn't you?" (52).[19]

With any escape from the prison house of history out of reach, the only remedy comes from confronting the past in its entirety to dole out an appeased, comprehensive reading of it. Christiane Chaulet Achour's analysis of the novel along the lines of a process enacting a "maîtrise de la mémoire" restores identity to the core of the quest ("Renaître et poursuivre" 190). After all, Nora suffers from "memory problems, not amnesia" (Mokeddem, *N'zid* 59).[20] This distinction suggests that it is only by coming to terms with one's past that renewal or rebirth is possible, lending credence to the polysemy undergirding the novel (the Algerian Arabic verb form *n'zid* meaning both "I continue" and " I am reborn"). Through the intersubjective model of singularity developed in the second half of the novel, the national pact is redrawn along new lines of inclusion derived from a reconsideration of national history beyond any obliterating or repressive intent. The plurality consubstantial to this renewed national construct is first predicated on the smallest possible unit of community relation: Nora's one-to-one encounters with a number of characters, each incarnating a different facet of Algeria's legacy and potential future.

Interestingly, most of the novel's epiphanies about her past are either mediated by the sketches Nora makes of her loved ones or volunteered by her two companions on her journey: Zana, her surrogate mother awaiting her return in Montpellier, and Loïc Lemoine, her seafaring male alter ego. The diegetic *passage obligé* of her encounter with Loïc undoes the effects of long-term denial and trauma-induced amnesia. It is only through intersubjective dialogue, especially with subjects of the opposite sex in the absence of any discernible form of female solidarity, that a clear sense of self can be captured. Indeed, as Chaulet-Achour has noted, "there are other women in whom [Nora] can confide . . . but the real dialogue happens on the feminine singular/masculine plural mode. It is in relation to (and in the eyes of) the

Other that the female protagonist . . . rebels, or surrenders" ("Renaître et poursuivre" 190).

In turn fellow sailor, resented threat to her solitude, friend, guardian, and romantic interest, the pivotal figure of Loïc comes to inhabit the ambiguous position of otherness in Mokeddem's dichotomous allegory, the would-be urchin to Nora's jellyfish. It is through Loïc's diegetic mediation that the narrative fruitfully bridges the gap between male and female, singular and plural. The tension between a diaphanous, unidentifiable nomadic subjectivity and a rooted communitarian subject is the familiar reading grid overdetermining Nora's preliminary brush with Loïc, curtailing the endless possibilities encapsulated in their actual encounter. Their first meeting in the multifarious space of the sea initially sparks the same defiant, apprehensive reaction in Nora as every other boat sighting. In each occurrence the presence of others is generative of unease and fear (which the narrative voice renders as "terre/ur," or "fear of the land," as Nora's sense of panic surges from the apprehension of having to be confronted to the gaze of "terrien[s]," rooted subjects [Mokeddem, *N'zid* 39]). As Loïc's boat starts following a parallel course, a contrapuntal subjectivity insinuates itself into Nora's well-oiled monadic machine. Unsurprisingly this first contact is a failure, reinforcing her isolation; passing her boat, Loïc neglects to return her gaze. Her jellyfish-like diaphaneity earns her the same fate as her marine avatar; her nautical companion fails to notice her, "as if she and her boat did not exist" (36).[21] This denial calls her existence into question as transparency soon morphs into the threat of delusion: "She thought that he himself might have been an optical illusion" (36).[22] Bypassing interconnectedness, reciprocity functions on the level of the simulacrum: only their potential virtuality unites the pair. Their absolute abstraction from the material circumstances of a localizable, identifiable positionality determines the development of their allegorical representation. It also obliterates any alternative form of identity. Without the other's gaze validating her existence, the subject is threatened with disappearance, with complete abstraction (and thus obliteration) from the material world.

Through her interaction with Loïc, the traumatic allegorical mode of representation thus far favored in the novel recedes, leaving the front stage to a more dialogic form of investigation. Nora's inner voice says, "[My] 'I' has swelled under his [Loïc's] sea gaze" (*N'zid* 51).[23] The shift occurs during yet another key allegorical episode, this time featuring a hermit crab. A crustacean proverbially known for hiding in empty shells, the creature epitomizes the desire to inhabit a different identity. Exposing once more the heavy-handed symbolism encumbering the narrative voice, Loïc is recoded through the hermit crab allegory as an impostor. Belying the implied wisdom and asceticism of his legal surname (Lemoine, "the monk"), Loïc is said to be "décalé" (out of synch [50]), running against the grain of the expectations of his lineage and the power of onomastics. Shedding first and last names to the benefit of dissident monikers (*l'inutile*, "the superfluous," after the name of his boat), he becomes another embodiment of the failure to live up to others' expectations. Originally attributed to Loïc, these characteristics are soon synthesized in Nora. The narrative voice concludes, "A hermit crab? It swims the same waters as a jellyfish, doesn't it?" (52), cutting across the neat dichotomy between nomadic and sedentary groups and offering a third, in-between, mutually inhabitable position where the two friends can meet.[24] This logic of contact is endowed with deep-reaching implications as it is through this face-to-face encounter with Loïc that Nora decides to reenter the world and regain political and social agency, renouncing once and for all her evasive alter egos: "No more Ghoula. She's gone with Hermit Crab" (51).[25] With this shared inability to conform, the two drifters engage in a new kinship that mediates Nora's sense of self. Significantly it is during a charged dialogue with Loïc that she is first able to articulate a coherent subject position using the first-person pronoun *je*, albeit in the midst of a performance of identity: "Being able to say 'je' is making her feel weak in the knee. She starts melting under his gaze" (47).[26] Although the *je* is phonetically echoed in the *jeu* (game) of identity games in a diffracting gesture ("startled, she passionately throws herself into the game" [47]), the shift is consummated and inaugurates a new era of interaction and understanding, the start of a new collective.[27]

From this perspective the substitution of a regional plane of deployment restores legible coordinates to an inscrutable, exsanguinated Algeria all but succumbing to its spectral condition. Nora's diegetic self-invention remains tributary to intent readings of her legend by others, to encounters and relational dynamics proceeding from her peripatetic lifestyle. And indeed it is in many ways through her use of mobility that Mokeddem engages with the fractured form of subjectivity inherited from the many violences and discontinuities littering Algerian history. Perturbing the tyranny of all-encompassing national narratives touting Arabness and Islam, *N'zid* delineates an alternative mode of *algérianité* marked by connectivity within the expansive framework of the Mediterranean. Mokeddem's transnational vision of identity swells from her actual physical peregrinations and dialogic intercultural interaction. It forestalls the possible aporia lurking in the background of any invocation of an imponderable Algeria. Beyond externally imposed frames of identity and narrow models of subjectivity, Nora's transnational trajectory gives momentum to her dismantling of monolithic identitarian constructs. If it marks the text with its fluid cadence, this nomadism of the sea is depicted as a form of being in the world generative of alternative models of social interaction that, if they do not sacrifice the individual in the name of the collective, do not for all that sacrifice the collective in the name of the individual. Mokeddem's Mediterranean trope thus functions outside the narrow strictures of a purely aestheticizing approach to identity and displacement. It emerges instead as a strategic channel of opposition to exacerbated nationalism and narrow definitions of subjectivity anchored in violence-ridden Algeria, but nevertheless in constant tension with the nation. Mokeddem's nomadism of the sea enacts reciprocity, redrawing the core principles at the base of Algeria's concept of community.

N'ZID AS WORKING THROUGH: GHOSTLY VOICES OF ALGERIA

Jamil, Nora's Algerian lover, acts as a catalyzer for the elaboration of an intersubjective model of singularity leading to the appeased working through of her heritage. This process can be apprehended only through a willful confrontation with the violence besmirching Algeria's history, from the symbolic foundational act of terrorism that inaugurated the birth of the FLN on November 1, 1954 (the first attack on French forces), to the more recent episode of the civil war—a continuum echoed in her personal history in her mother's disappearance and Jamil's eventual death at the hands of terrorists. If Mokeddem's text teeters on the recognition of Algeria's fundamental elusiveness, the shift from allegory to an *écriture d'apaisement* speaks to the reluctance to accept the poetics of loss and renunciation evoked by Hiddleston in the context of Djebar's fiction. Instead the text's aesthetic evolution bespeaks a stubborn determination to acknowledge trauma and confront it, not to encourage its aftermath in a debilitating cycle of victimhood and powerlessness. Anamnesis is the primum mobile of this process. Since amnesia only foments oblivion and the perpetuation of an ill-construed, uncircumscribable use of violence, only a working through of trauma can function politically as the foundation of an appeased collective. *N'zid* suggests a poetics of melancholia eager to uncover and makes strategic use of the longing for a fuller past that needs to be confronted, voiced, and reappropriated if any political change is to be enacted (Khanna 27).

Permanently warding off the curse of nonidentity, and therefore ontological disappearance, Jamil reminds Nora, "You aren't from nowhere. You are a liminal being. This nowhere, this nonplace, dooms you to nonexistence" (Mokeddem, *N'zid* 161).[28] Their first encounter in the Catalan maritime village of Cadaqués, halfway between their two worlds, inaugurates a logic of reciprocity and completion. Just as Nora epitomizes the fluidity of the sea, Jamil represents the immensity of the desert. From their passionate embrace surges the hope for a collective open onto the world: it is said that Jamil "rediscovers [the desert] in her" (163), that is, in relation to the sea that Nora metonymically embodies.[29] This renewed trope of the desert doesn't bear the stigma of years of stasis and atrophy with which its most recent instantiations in Mokeddem's corpus have been tainted. It is a desert that the encounter with the sea has fertilized, a renewed space of origins that the detour through the Mediterranean has once more imbued with the authentic fluidity that had once been its inalienable privilege: "Now he travels the world as his music requires. Now foreign lands return him to himself, to the live body of his lute, to its strings where the sea gets entangled. . . . Now the sea is his other desert" (162–63).[30] The exacerbation of the musical discourse born of the cross-maritime encounter with other cultures gestures back to Jamil's own identity quest. His musical production, consisting of performance and composition, partakes of what the narrative dubs "the flamboyant language of the desert" (164).[31] It is an entranced mode of expression born of the lute's voluptuousness, a dissolution of all exclusive categories that predicate subjectivity on opposition to others. This irreverent, fulgurant language extends beyond the strictures of musical idioms, spanning the gap between the two lovers and their ambient environment. Nora's drawings, Jamil's music, and the Mediterranean sea "all proceed from the same essence: the attempt to tame all the senses of surrender" (164).[32] Rife with polysemic echoes ("sens" as sensuousness and meaning; "abandon" as dereliction and indulgence for one's desires), the text reverberates with the combined effects of sensualism as a mode of cognition and resistance to dissatisfactory modes of identity. Jamil's alternative language retains symbolic purchase against the many forms of "the dislocations and the dispossessions" ascribed to fixed forms of being (162).[33] The term *déshérence* is particularly striking at this juncture as it intimates a searing critique of historical forms of affiliation based on the prevalence of family ties in both private and public life.[34]

Jamil's surrogate genealogy of elective affinities ("this lineage which skipped his parents' fossilized generation and restored his ancestors' identity to him" [205]) reveals a space of critical engagement with history.[35] This alternative configuration exposes the crisis of values stemming from the tainted foundational myths at the origin of the modern Algerian nation. In the process it sheds revelatory light on the truncated nature of the Algerian national genealogies born of the blood of patricide that has been only partially memorialized (and more readily repressed) in official discourses of monumentalization.[36] From their first contact Jamil illuminates Nora's Algerianness: his first diegetic appearance lends no other clue than a voice speaking Algerian Arabic, "the voice that recognizes her as belonging to this language," a recognition that makes her melt with gratitude.[37] A "return" to Algeria, the mother's land, is presented as being ultimately inescapable. It is the logical end-product of Nora's love story with Jamil and the propeller of the diegesis in the second part of the novel—the part bearing the mark of anamnesis performed mostly through recourse to a realist aesthetic of appeasement at odds with the allegorical rendition of trauma. Jamil "helped her restore the missing part of her being, Algeria, even if she has not yet set foot in the country. . . . One day, she may have the chance to dock there" (163-64).[38]

Shortly after the episode with Loïc, Nora finds herself drawing yet another jellyfish. However, this one stands out for its anthropomorphism and its unsettling likeness to her: "Under the tip of her pencil, a jellyfish reveals a human face for the first time—her face. She dances to a lute's lament" (98).[39] Immediately following the mention of the lute, a struggle between desert and sea is evoked, which ultimately freezes the free-floating rhythm of the waves. "Zid! Continue!" implores the narrative voice, in a striking reversal of the polarities instituted by the text's original amnesia. Enjoined to prove himself in the eyes of the narrator, the musician performs an aesthetic of melancholia that wells with each note of the lute, materializes with each line of Nora's pencil sketching the scene, and unfurls with each wave on the hull of Nora's boat. Substituting the vehicle of artistic creation for the duplicitous power of logos, "the music haunts the sketch . . . short-circuits the threat of words" (98).[40] This masculine voice wafting up from the dunes of the desert is Jamil's, whose direct experience of the violence of Algeria works as a foil to Nora's abstract knowledge of her mother's land. Affording her a deeper identification with the country, he paves the way for a reconstruction of her identity in relation to the collective of the Algerian nation. The conflation of drawing, music, and maritime errantry identifies the multiple vehicles through which "dissonance" arises (160), at the interstices between exclusive absolutes from which stems a complex sense of self. Doing away with debilitating nostalgia, Jamil's lute "transforms . . . this bereavement and the ones to follow in virtuouso pieces, turning melancholia into voluptuousness" (204).[41] It restores the repressed memory of more tolerant forms of Islam (in his case Sufism through his lute playing) as correctives in the face of the radicalization of discourses of piety. Jamil soon morphs into a symbolic embodiment of another Algeria more respectful of diversity and plural memories. His is an embodied Algeria in the colors of the Mediterranean, stripped of its cavernous, devouring inscrutability, where wanderers could come to rest and where Nora could finally find her place. Nora's incessant commemoration of Jamil's message through her art, a doubling of the music through sketching, completes the circle of his mediation and relays it after his death. The combination of both artistic models (music and sketches) lies at the core of Mokeddem's singular liturgy of commemoration in the wake of traumatic violence. Nora's frenetic urge to commit Jamil's history of dissent to memory takes the shape of a comic-strip album, suggestively named "N'zid" in a familiar echo of the title of Jamil's musical project. There the novel affirms anew the lovers' unshakable resolve to crosscut dominant modes of subjectivity with their tangential, dissonant forms of identification born of their Mediterranean mobility.

Revisiting the multiple forms of violence perpetrated against women and other minoritarian subjects in the process, *N'zid* aims to extricate processes of identity formation from the realm of mystification and alienation. As the novel unfolds, multiple forms of bereavement linked to the spectral space of Algeria are outlined: in Nora's ominous words, "This other death for which Algeria has a knack: disappearance. This definitive absence which gives way to never-ending mourning" (166).[42] This "death without end" (Djebar 81) runs through Nora's life and colors her engagements with the excoriation of the past. Assia Djebar's *Le Blanc de l'Algérie* locates a successful politics of mourning in the critique of excessive models of grieving, either in the guise of FLN-sponsored narratives of martyrdom or overzealous religious rituals. Striving to extricate the singularity of the lost object from the clamor of histrionic mourning rituals, Mokeddem's quest is a response to the memory deficit that Djebar's text identifies (too much memorialization making for inadequate memorialization, a point that intersects with Khanna's critique of a rhetoric of "monumentalization").

One of Nora's allegorical interludes exemplifies the way the novel channels Djebar's dynamics. In the drawing in question the engagement with melancholia is illuminated by the same versatile, palimpsestic figure of the jellyfish ("méduse"), this time resemanticized as a mythological Gorgon. Designating both a jellyfish and the incarnation of the Gorgon Medusa, the polysemic French word *méduse* is to be elucidated through lexical echoes and detours via ancient Greek mythology. Even though she is presented as a panacea in the face of violence, the *méduse* is soon resignified as an embodiment of guilt, the reflection of a moral sin ("une faute" [Mokeddem, *N'zid* 115]). She is the site of pathological mystification and alienation to one's sense of self: "She let snakes feast on her head and mummify her" (115).[43] All that is left of her is "an exaltation . . . a series of falsified images of the self that preclude objectivity, reparation, and therefore healing" (115).[44] The text offers no definite answer as to the origin or location of the sin that the *méduse* reflects. As Nicolas Abraham and Maria Torok have pointed out, the repressed loss at the heart of melancholia is a secret incorporated from previous generations; as such it lies beyond the subject's understanding. Accordingly it soon becomes clear that this original guilt is to be construed in relation to Nora's mother's attempts to leave behind the strictures of the Algerian nation. It is with a similar feeling of "culpabilité" (guilt) that the mother's exile to France is depicted—guilt for abandoning her family but also for not participating in the birth of the Algerian nation. As Nora presciently puts it, "One does not emerge unscathed from a tribe's moral code" (139).[45] After meeting her father and giving birth to her, Nora's mother, Aïcha, returned to Algeria and abandoned the pair to their fate. Forced by her family to marry an Algerian man who would regularly impregnate her, she found refuge in aphasia, unquestioningly embracing her subaltern condition as a woman whose sole social function is to produce heirs to the tribe. Reflecting her self-silencing, a core of blankness comes to shroud her evocation. Investing the realm of tragedy as the original *mater dolorosa* presiding over the course of the story, Aïcha will pay dearly for her desire for independence, which is in many ways her tragic flaw: "[Such is the] frailty and fury of those who lack the means to achieve their aspirations. . . . In 1952, women could not escape. Not in those days. . . . The situation breeds guilt" (139).[46]

Through her incarnation as a supple *méduse*, Nora thus reflects and channels the "monstrous deformations" of her mother's psyche. For if her mother inhabits the space of deformation, it is Nora who mediates her guilt and desire for independence. Self-exclusion from the lines of tribal affiliation shrouds the figure of the mother in a condition of spectrality, the aftermath of absolute violence (in the text the multiple annihilating rapes she suffered, which lead to her mental and ultimately physical obliteration). As she allows her mother's mute specter to penetrate her and speak through her voice, Nora herself is made coextensive with her silence, with the blankness she embodies. Nora's haunting thus performs a two-pronged melancholic reading: a restitution of her mother's right to representation and visibility but also, and maybe more important, a nostalgic quest for the inscrutable core of a hollowed-out Algeria. Through her subconscious drawings Nora embraces the deformity of the *méduse* as a memorialization of her mother's repressed alternative engagement with the nation. By coming to terms with her mother's erasure from the community and moving beyond allegorical representation to the figurative, critical genre of caricature (204), Nora releases the *longue durée* of family trauma from the realm of oblique suggestion to that of memory and analysis. With this gesture she is ultimately able to excavate what lay beneath thirty-five years of silence. Through the haunting performed, memory is released and confronted—including Nora's as she urges herself to "retrace [her] steps immediately. In full awareness. Without erasing anything this time . . . without disowning anything" (146).[47]

The original sin at the core of mind-numbing, unprocessed guilt seems to be located somewhere in the tumultuous relation the subject weaves with a questionable nation: "Three Gorgonas: Ireland, Algeria, and France. All that is left to do is to uncover the sin" (Mokeddem, *N'zid* 115).[48] Nora's attempts to negotiate the tumultuous space between the three poles of her identity testify to her desire to work out the multiple tensions and fault lines of her complex heritage. This effort signals a need for an alternative mode of signification respectful of heterogeneous subjective engagements with history. The constitutive haunting at the heart of her mourning produces its own mode of remembrance, effectively attending to the specters of the past. In amnesia Nora is said to have been "erased. She is like a ghost who forgot to unearth her story. She has nothing left to haunt" (17).[49] In this deceptively secure numbness, the anxieties of the unknown abound. They cast Algeria as the core of this black hole, as a devouring ogress of its own—the very Ghoula that Nora's performative acts had been so keen to reclaim and annihilate. Its "definitive absence which gives way to never-ending mourning" precludes a possible working through of trauma. This amnesia only repeats the cycle of disempowerment and victimhood for the perceiving subject; no form of collective memorialization can be attained, no closure enacted. In contrast the working through performed by her mother's haunting can ultimately be reclaimed as a political gesture imbued with ethical undertones. It implies attending to the specters of the past with the firm objective of uncovering and resolving them. Ultimately, moving beyond the medusa identification and the stigma of sin that it carries allows Nora to process melancholia and the deformed self-perception that feeds it.

As Nora untangles the intricacies of her mother's life decisions, it is her own appeased relationship to Algeria that she performs. Her identification with the haunting figure offers a blueprint for her own life. It provides the material for her drawing rhetoric to unfold, as well as a justification for her own wandering. Through its parallel with her mother's political gesture, the haunting lends her a certain legitimacy and purpose with regard to Algeria, and the novel ends on her determination to pay a delayed visit to her mother's homeland. In this juxtaposition of their lives both women are thus endowed with an epic character at cross-purposes with the usual reading of Mediterranean femininity in terms of tragedy.[50] They regain agency and individuation through the process. *N'zid* places women's individuation and social definition at the center of its preoccupations. Distancing itself from postcolonial narratives of female victimization, the novel stages Nora's acceptance of her history and her resolve to move forward from, if not fully beyond, the moment of trauma. Redrawing the space of female subjectivity away from the realm of the interdict (*haram*), Nora's attempt to bring her mother's story to completion is intimately tied in to the struggle over cultural and social territory. Aïcha's radical choice is to be commemorated to complicate narratives of national identity and to restitute gender as one of many plural dimensions fallen through the cracks of nationalist rhetoric. Through the appropriation and subversive acting out of her mother's life story, Nora's heuristic quest traces the contours of female abjection anew, questioning women's depiction as disempowered subjects condemned to embrace their status as willful victims.

Planting the seeds of citizen responsibility, Nora adumbrates another Algeria enriched from its contact with its Mediterranean borders. Reiterated by Nora's nautical peregrinations throughout the many lands bordering the sea, her mother's life-altering choice to leave her country for France brings much-needed perspective to the vision of Algeria. Perturbing the historical incarnation of Algerian identity under the double mark of Islam and nationalism, *N'zid* brings the focus back to the question of citizenship. Debunking the mandate of a univocal attachment to one's national language (or rather, in Algeria's case, to the language of nationalism), an impossible occurrence due to her multiple concurrent affiliations, Nora substitutes for any exclusive identification a "water voice between languages" (113).[51] The homophony between the *voix d'eau* (water voice) and the *voie d'eau* (waterway), which served as a title for one of her early sketches of the Mediterranean, is paramount. Whether *voie d'eau* as amniotic water and space of protection, or *voix d'eau* as the voice of Mediterranean haunting precluding the tyranny of restrictive national narratives, the novel proposes another form of *algérianité* marked by relationality and incorporation of its margins. Implementing the commemoration and restitution of the country's plural past in the direction of a brighter future, this process has the potential to effectively put an end to binary identity narratives emphasizing irreconcilability. After all, as Nora reminds us, "a jellyfish is only a little water" (64).[52]

Nora's allegorical sketches founder when scrutinized in the light of their potential for a postidentitarian quest, but their unfolding still facilitates the deciphering of recurrent symbols and the elucidation of the novel's overarching message. Allegory points simultaneously to the referentiality of the blank slate of the post-traumatic present and to the echoing significance of the past that transpires through it. It becomes the conduit eventually enabling the subject to perform her melancholic deciphering of individual identity in its fraught relationship to the collective. It enables the acknowledgment of trauma in a way that facilitates its incorporation into the subject's memory and its release from the realm of the repressed. The fluctuations of allegorical meaning open the way for considerations of singular-plural interactions; they facilitate the elaboration of a cogent model of social interactions based on the preservation of labile, non-coextensive experiences. This construct is crucial to the elaboration of a public space tolerant of the rich history of the Algerian nation and of the right of its people to formulate multiple concurrent allegiances that take to task reductive formulaic narratives of identity, foremost among them Sheikh Abdelhamid Ben Badis's famous formulation "Islam is my religion, Arabic is my language, and Algeria is my country," also touted at independence.

The search for a more inclusive version of *algérianité* certainly finds its mark in this fertile ground. In *The Coming Community*, Giorgio Agamben offers a compelling characterization of the example as an empty conceptual site where all cases pertaining to the same logic are fitted as representative (i.e., exemplary) of that logic. Neither truly singular nor quite universal, the example inhabits the loaded space of contact between multiple "singularities [that] communicate without being tied to any common property, by any identity" (10–11). This notion of exemplarity reverberates with the inherent functioning of allegory as mediation. In this ghostly space of hauntings and phantasmatic echoings, a distended thread can be woven between the subject and the collective, in which "singularities com[e] together [heralding] a non-identificatory community-to-come" (Khanna 55). This "community-to-come" shares significant semantic territory with the alternative model of social relations suggested by Mokeddem's text. Forgoing the quest for a precisely delimited, identifiable Algerian identity and questioning the possibility of a unified Algerian experience, *N'zid* reclaims the right to citizenship through the fluid detour granted by nomadism. Mokeddem's Mediterranean-inspired take on national identity arises from genuine transnational mobility and intercultural contact. It performs more inclusive forms of dialogue, not least through her use of nonverbal spaces of expression. Against the grain of a strict inscription into the terrain of Algeria and of the danger of linguistic aporia that it spells, *N'zid* embodies the experimental quest for alternative modes of representation less amenable to recuperation by rigid rhetorical machines. Agar-Mendousse's argument on Mokeddem's desert nomadism construed the "sédentaire" pole of the dichotomy between rooted and nomadic subjects as the core constituency of belonging, rightly emphasizing the overlap between nomadism and marginality ("Counterviolence" 186). In contrast, by laying claim to the subject's right to a nation despite the mobility it advocates, Mokeddem's nomadism of the sea applies a new Mediterranean ethos to the novel's mappings of Algerian citizenship.

In an earlier text, *Des Rêves et des assassins* (1995), composed at the height of the Black Decade, Mokeddem portrayed the space of the sea as a buffer separating the narrator from the brutality tearing her country asunder. The Mediterranean figured a space not to be directly engaged. Nora's model of memorialization of Algeria's complex past in *N'zid* performs a singularity cognizant of the irreducible plurality of the Algerian nation and of its heritage of conflicts, frictions, and concealments. In this context the Mediterranean acts as an interpretive grid, a model for negotiating same and other, the singular in the plural. More important, it suggests a possible outward trajectory of subjective projection into the world. Eschewing the "sense of despair with regard to the relocation of [Algeria's] identity" that has plagued women's writing from Algeria (Hiddleston, *Assia Djebar* 5), *N'zid* attempts to locate this identity by exploring the full nexus of connectivity tying Algeria to other Mediterranean sites. Bringing these insights to the Mediterranean region implies recognizing its political potential for the redefinition of national community. It also requires reintroducing the principle of reciprocity undergirding the novel at the core of the subject's engagement with the community. This approach invigorates alternative local modes of connectivity, also opening them up onto the world. If we are to read the postcolonial as inherently political and tending toward the determination of more equitable forms of collective destiny, performing a more inclusive vision of national community is an indispensable first step.

CHAPTER 4

Strait Talk

Crossing (and) the Rihla *Tradition of Travel Writing*

We are denied existence, but at the same time we are forbidden to leave.

—Salim Jay, *Tu ne traverseras pas le Détroit* (Thou Shalt Not Cross the Strait)

The Arabs have become clandestine, hidden in the Spaniards' consciousness, in their unconscious.

—Abdelkébir Khatibi, "Au-delà du trauma" (Beyond Trauma)

Mokeddem's *N'zid* enacts a logic of contact.[1] Freeing the space of Algeria from narrow nationalist logics and identitarian politics, the constant mobility enacted by her main protagonists implements an inclusive relational framework that opens the Maghrebi world to its European neighbors. In this configuration the Mediterranean is not at the center of a staunch opposition between North and South, Europe and Africa. Rather it figures a point of convergence from which a great relational ensemble is deployed by cross-continental models and transnational frames of contact. Within the space of the novel this partnership is predicated on a relation of equality and near interchangeability between the contiguous spaces along the sea and, by extension, between the subject positions they foster. Thus the secondary character Jean Rolland, a French national enamored with postcolonial Algeria, is marked as both Algerian and French without much regard for the loaded distinction between the two identities. As his affiliations shift in keeping with his changing personal interests, national loyalties are reduced to no more than the fluctuating whims of a rebel personality. His vision of fluid identities is utopian and reveals a casual engagement with borders and fault lines, which the harsh realities of other forms of trans-Mediterranean crossings belie. Despite its eventual politicized deployment, the novel's aestheticization of the Mediterranean figures a romanticized perspective on mobility. In this respect it is oblivious to the material realities of other modes of maritime displacement—most notably *hrig* or *hijra*, the Mediterranean passage of clandestine migration from North Africa to Europe.

To be exactly fair the novel does not completely ignore the life-threatening journey undertaken by clandestine migrants across the sea. Yet it conflates *hrig* with the voluntary, elitist *cabotage* of Nora's boat. In this regard two seemingly innocuous episodes puncture the felicitous logic of exchangeability that the novel sets up. In the first one, *harragas* (clandestine migrants) are portrayed as "les fuyards de Gibraltar" (Gibraltar's runaways), a group the narration soon dissolves into a long list of hopelessly romantic lovers of the sea, in which Nora figures prominently (Mokeddem, *N'zid* 69).[2] The second occurrence depicts them as scrawny figures floating about on rafts, in a nudge to other histories of maritime mass exodus caused by the many famines that bled Ireland, the land of Nora's father (Mokeddem, *N'zid* 72). In both cases the novel attempts to minimize the act of migrating, going as far as to question the legitimacy of departure: as the dictionary Littré attests, the term *fuyard* itself reverberates with the stigma of betrayal, being mostly used pejoratively in the nominal form to designate deserting troops. Positioning the *harragas* alongside hedonistic modern-day drifters and a long history of traumatic departures obscures the specificity and resonance of their gesture, and it would be a fair assessment to say that the treatment of the question of *hrig* may constitute the most salient limitation to the novel's productive engagement with the Mediterranean. The notion of a borderless Mediterranean is certainly tempting, yet for a vast majority of North Africans the sea represents fracture and confinement. Although, as I showed in the previous chapter, the transnational frame of Mokeddem's writing productively stretches relational identities to reframe Algerian diversity, it fails to adequately engage the reality of trans-Mediterranean clandestine migration from (North) Africa to Europe. Between the lines of Nora's recollection and very much in the guise of a return of Europe's and Algeria's repressed, the contours of another Mediterranean glisten, one where estrangement is not the product of disaffection toward one's community of origin but is a forced frame of existence both life-threatening and arbitrary. In encounters with those who cannot escape this geography of material deprivation and want, another conception of mobility erupts, characterized by drowning and exclusion.[3]

If colonial structures of power erected marginality into the inescapable fate of colonized spaces, their disappearance in the wake of decolonization did not put an end to the dynamics of segregation they implemented. As Salim Jay's epigraph to this chapter suggests, new forms of hierarchization and exclusion took their place and relegated migrants from the South (*harragas*) to a position of abjection, duplicating the process of subaltern obliteration honed in a colonial context. In a Mediterranean setting the mobilizing of legal institutions within the European Union constructed an exclusive juridical status of citizenship and associated rights that ensured the negation of any form of alterity. Paradoxically it is in the very act of enunciation that brands him as illegal that the *harraga* first gains visibility. Reluctantly inscribed and concurrently proscribed, the clandestine migrant comes into existence through the prohibitive language of the interdict. One could advance the argument that Mokeddem's *N'zid* fails most conspicuously in its inability to recognize the unshakable power of national authority over subjective aspirations. As it hypothesizes subject positions free from any coercion and geographic restriction, the novel is oblivious to the harsh fact that most subjects from the Global South are ultimately bound to the incontestable framework of the nation, which simultaneously entraps them and excludes them. Exposing the postcolonial nation-state's failure to live up to the promise of independence, the existence of the aspiring *harraga* and its irrepressible desire for the European shore sheds light on the subject's alienation and disenfranchisement within the postcolony. In Katarzyna Pieprzak's ominous words, the experience of these migrants "ha[s] created visible geographies of desperation that force an examination of the relationship of the state to its subjects" (104). The phenomenon of *hrig* can thus be read as a marker of the nation-state's failure to protect and provide for its citizens. Through it another map of belonging is deployed, tracing the contours of modernity's dark side and spelling the many failures of independence.

The liminal, fractured nature of the subaltern migrant reaches its full potential in the act of burning—burning the distance between the two continents in an attempt to force one's way across the dividing line between prosperity and affliction, but also burning one's identity papers, the material proof of unambiguous belonging to an all-encompassing postcolonial nation-state. Underscoring the etymological connection between the Arabic term *hrig* and the triconsonantal Arabic root referring to the act of burning (Ha-ra-qaf), Hakim

Abderrezak explains that "'brûler' ('to burn') translates more accurately the common practice of burning identification documents before undertaking the sea crossing in order to avoid repatriation, and the figurative act of 'burning the road' (in this case, the sea), and of illegally 'burning up' kilometers in one fell swoop" (Abderrezak, "Burning the Sea" 463). Reaffirming exclusion from the postcolonial social contract, the act of burning kilometers or one's ID needn't be physically carried out to complete the subject's exclusion from social life. Voluntarily leaving behind his marginalized position within postcolonial society, the *harraga*'s mere aspiration to departure consummates his withdrawal, relegating him to the heterotopic space of the beach where he awaits passage. There his existence becomes coextensive with his one objective: *partir*.[4] By renouncing a legible inscription into the ordering logic of the postcolony, the migrant slips into a space of a different nature. Without identity papers the migrant refuses a possible return; he irrevocably renounces any rooted sense of identity, becoming "a stateless individual [who] can never return home" (Orlando, *Francophone Voices* 166), perhaps the truest incarnation of Deleuze and Guattari's nomad. Localized in the interstices of the Global South (here the Maghreb and, farther away, Africa), the *harraga*'s existence contradicts the stability of embodied forms of power. It effects a surreptitious denunciation of the porosity of concepts of sovereignty and borders, of the fiction of clearly demarcated identity constructs and stable community outlines. His discrepant position exposes the fundamental weaknesses of the hegemonic state, thereby complicating the authority of the regimes of knowledge that underpin it.

As a possible avenue into these complex considerations, I consider the ways *hrig* begets alternative modes of writing the collective that force us to rethink our reading practices. In an effort to critically engage this reality I explore the relation tying these modes of expression of the clandestine to other, long-established ways of writing mobility across the space of the Mediterranean—namely, the classical Arabic travel narrative, or *rihla*, a term designating both the knowledge-seeking journey underpinning the development of Arab modernity from the days of al-Andalus and the account produced in its wake. I do not attempt to defuse the very real idiosyncrasies of *hrig* writing by assimilating it to centuries of travel narratives and to the authors they have established. The surreptitious nature of *hrig* mobility is a function of its disruptive potential, and no criticism of clandestine crossings could without much loss deny the unique nature of the type of writing they inaugurate. Yet it is my argument that a juxtaposition of *hrig* to the illustrious Arabic travel writing tradition, a connection of which the texts under scrutiny readily avail themselves, can productively help us investigate an otherwise elusive corpus, whose power of resistance rests precisely in its interstitial, intangible character. I read *hrig* and its concluding shipwreck as the negative mirror image of *rihla*. Bidirectional by nature, as it always implied a return home, *rihla* envisioned displacement as an accumulative endeavor leading to institutional and societal reforms in the wake of the journey. In contrast *hrig* emerges as a journey of loss, often ending in shipwreck and death. Through this comparison I directly engage the resonance of clandestine crossings of the Strait of Gibraltar in the making and unmaking of knowledge paradigms within the Moroccan postcolony, offering a new lens through which to examine the postcolonial subject's relation to the nation and its claims to authority.

Lying at the confluence of Atlantic and Mediterranean, Europe and Africa, Christianity and Islam, the Strait of Gibraltar is a key geopolitical space for the analysis of clandestinity. Strategically situated at the junction of Spain and Morocco, the area has been at the forefront of issues of migration. The Moroccan Mediterranean coastline is also infamous for having long held the record for the highest number of clandestine crossings to Europe in all of the Maghreb. For that reason I explore contemporary literary engagements with the phenomenon of *hrig* produced on either side of the fertile contact zone of the Strait in French, Spanish, and Arabic. As a point of departure I read Tahar Ben Jelloun's canonical early configurations of Tangier as Morocco's epicenter of subversive displacement as the lingering intertext against which subsequent contrapuntal renderings of the Strait zone unfold. Two such incarnations, *Al-Hijra al-Sirriyya* (Clandestine Migration), the collection of stories by the Tangerine author and journalist Muhammad al-Baqqash, and the poetic anthology, significantly entitled *Rihla*, by the Spanish-language Gibraltarian poet Trino Cruz illuminate the epistemic shifts surrounding any attempt at expatriation. The choice of these two little-known texts is significant in several ways. Through their congruent interest in *rihla*, which they mobilize to address contemporary crossings, both authors productively turn their back on the dominant paradigm of Orientalist travelogues composed in European languages and reinscribe the space of

Tangier in an Arab literary geography. Through it these texts harken back to the days of Islamic expansion and northbound Mediterranean crossing. This dynamic is most conspicuously recorded in allusions to the mythicized space of medieval al-Andalus, as the Khatibi quotation used as epigraph to this chapter shows.[5] Moreover these narratives rely on a literary model entangled with the development of the Arab *nahda*—the linguistic, cultural, and political renaissance born of growing encounters with Europe beginning in the late nineteenth century. Through this connection these authors pose the question of the Moroccan nation and its contemporary state after the far-reaching ideological crisis that swept through the Arab world following the 1967 Six-Day War and Gamal Abdel Nasser's defeat by Israel. The plurilingualism of my corpus, extending far beyond the absolute ascendancy of French, is a testament to the transnational nature of the issue of *hrig* both culturally and politically, as well as an incentive to consider alternative geographies of the Maghreb that bypass the dominance of paradigms inherited from French colonization. Admittedly, circumventing the predominance of France does not mean doing away with the persistence of empire as an ordering category. After all, the northern part of Morocco was as powerfully bound to the exclusive structure of the Spanish protectorate as the portion of the land that was under French authority was to the French Empire. Yet shifting the focus to this other colonialism productively complicates the usual mapping of Morocco as a former French protectorate, decentering French domination as the one overdetermining event to reveal other histories and entanglements.[6] Furthermore Cruz's very circumstances as a subject of the British Crown in Gibraltar (an overseas British territory lying on a three-mile-long isthmus at the extreme southern end of the Iberian peninsula) kept him at a fecund distance from the storyline of Spanish ambitions in North Africa, further blurring the supposedly dichotomous lines tying Morocco to its former colonial powers. Emerging from this sedimented landscape, the contact zone of the Strait reverberates with myriad echoes of spectral encounters, both anchored in this complex, multifarious history of crossings and receptive to the new models of mobility that the consideration of *hrig* helps to bring to the fore. In the interplay between Spanish, Arabic, and the silenced echoes of the Riffian dialects spoken by al-Baqqash's exiled protagonists, another topography of Mediterranean Morocco surfaces, whose coordinates hardly coincide with those of its colonial history—or postcolonial models of governance.

LOCAL TOPOGRAPHIES OF DISSENT: THE SUBVERSIVE POWER OF "LA PAROLE"

Picture Tangier, a former international zone of contact and mixing, the gateway to Africa for forlorn Westerners yearning for an immutable Orient of debauchery and experimentation, but also, and more crucially perhaps, the gateway to Europe for thousands of African migrants ready to risk it all for a remote chance at the European dream. Tangier—port of call, home to the key economic hub of the Tangier Free Zone and the thriving Tanger-Med port complex. Tangier—port of departure, the city from which Ibn Battuta set off in the fourteenth century for his legendary eastward journey to China, the epitome of a Golden Age of travel and knowledge-seeking that has left its indelible mark on one of the most revered pages of Arab intellectual history. Tangier—Mediterranean city, lying a mere fourteen kilometers across the Strait of Gibraltar from Spain, its iconic coordinates inextricably linking it to the tragic stories of the *harragas*, gazing upon the coast of Tarifa, Spain, waiting to attempt their perilous crossing. From deep within these embedded configurations of the city, an aura of deception and violence surfaces, permeating the pages of its best-known narratives. From the sexual transgressions of Mohamed Choukri's *For Bread Alone* to Jean Genet's licentious experiences of the city in *The Thief's Journal*, Tangier's sulfurous reputation has steeped it in the realm of excess and debauchery. Inscribed into the Moroccan nation as a marginalized, decadent space, the city lies at the intersection of a local geography of destitution (the northern regions of Morocco are historically among the poorest in the country) and the projected fantasies of its Western visitors. In Ahmed Idrissi Alami's words, "Tangier serves as an arena where indigenous trajectories of desire encounter the returned gaze of the Western (gay) male, the ex-colonizer/surrogate father" (6). But most of all the city's ambivalent nature has made it an un-co-optable space of dissidence and rebellion, a hotbed for resistance to the authoritarian form of power that came to life in Morocco in the wake of independence.

Speaking to the omnipresence of Genet's tutelary figure in his play *Beckett et Genet, un thé à Tanger* (Beckett and Genet, Tea in Tangiers, 2010) and in *Jean Genet, menteur sublime* (Jean Genet, Sublime Liar, 2010), the Moroccan Tahar Ben Jelloun, a Goncourt Prize laureate, has certainly intended to situate his own Tangerine writing in dialogue with the eminent genealogy. The first translator of

Mohamed Choukri into French (for Gallimard in 1984), Ben Jelloun has set out to revisit some of the city's most iconic texts, stretching the porous limits of Tangier's symbolic literary capital to encompass more destabilizing narratives exceeding sexualized Orientalized stereotypes. Beyond the possible capitalization that comes from association with this illustrious intertext, Ben Jelloun's Tangerine texts have carved out a specific space for the liminal city around which his literary imaginary revolves. From his first novel, *Harrouda* (1973), onward, the cityscape of Tangier has haunted his narrative production, so much so that it could be argued that it has been his oeuvre's one recurrent and most formidable character.[7] But to understand the valence and attraction of Tangier in his work, one needs to reinscribe it in the symbolic geography of Morocco, reading it through its fundamental opposition to the prestigious city of Fez, Ben Jelloun's birthplace. Morocco's holiest city, home to the Karaouine Mosque, the second largest in the Maghreb after Kairouan, to the sacred music festival every June, but also the heart and soul of the Moroccan artisan class, Fez can be considered the cultural, intellectual, and spiritual capital of Morocco. For Ben Jelloun the tension between his native city and his city of adoption reveals a deeper fracture, a split inaugurated by French colonialism, which loosened the weave of society by rewarding an ever more self-serving elite in exchange for its allegiance. In this respect *Harrouda* provides unprecedented insight into the interplay between Fez/"Fass," the space of colonial co-optation, and Tangiers/"Tanger-la-trahison" (Tangier betrayal, a phrase borrowed from Genet), not least because it presciently speaks to the valence of mobility and the issue of the Arab nation that Muhammad al-Baqqash would revisit some thirty years later in the same context of Tangier.

Ben Jelloun's *Harrouda* obliquely traces these questions to two foundational moments: Emir Abd El Krim's staunch resistance to Spanish penetration into the Rif region after World War I and Hassan II's ruthless repression during the Lead Years (from the late 1960s to the late 1980s), the latter having emerged in many ways as the litmus test for the figure of the Arab intellectual in the context of the Moroccan postcolonial nation. In the crosshairs of this renewed dialectic of power and defiance, Tangier emerges as a space of clandestine dissent, the site of resistance to entrenched forms of authority embodied in the power structure of the Moroccan "deep-state" apparatus, also known as the *makhzan*.[8] The realm of the "in-Tangi-ble" ("l'écriture intangible," intangible writing, commemorative of Tangier's layered past [116]), the city's sedimented history from its nebulous origins to the Vandal conquest bears the mark of immateriality. None of the many invasions from beyond the sea has succeeded in subjugating the region, which, in the manner of Amrouche's eternal Jugurtha, remained impervious to various histories of penetration hailing from the North. The city endures as "Tingi" in Ben Jelloun's prose, rife with the echo of its pre-Roman name. In the background the murmur of the sea perdures, the only form of continuity in which every Tangerine can commune, oblivious to the petty disagreements about the interpretation of its complex history.

Interestingly touting a local bedrock of identity (the ancient heritage being by far the predominant one) does not exclude reinscribing the city in Arab history. Fez is rescripted as "Fass . . . the Arabic transcription of Fez" (*Harrouda* 48), the French transliteration harkening back to colonial times and linguistically incarnating the very palimpsestic identity described in the text.[9] Likewise the migration out of corrupt Fez, which underlines the novel's diegetic progression, eventuates in the North, "where they say a warm wind blows from the East, cleansing bodies and purifying memories" (117).[10] The text brings no clear elucidation of the origin or the significance of this wind. Nevertheless the avowed desire to cleanse the memory of the subjugation from the North redraws local coordinates away from any southbound axis of European penetration. It recasts the rejuvenating flow along a horizontal axis sweeping the northern shore of Africa from the confines of the Middle East to the extreme western limit of Morocco (*al-Maghreb*, literally "the West" in Arabic). Reinvigorated by this breath of new life, a new desirable identity process springs, associated with the direct invocation of Harrouda. The novel's interstitial, subversive female character, she functions as a principle of wild femininity and disruptive verbal inventiveness standing in sharp opposition to ossified structures of authority. A "veiled celebration of the elusiveness and subversion of poetic invention decolonized" (Aresu, *Tahar Ben Jelloun* 16), this "writing of the original migrations" (Ben Jelloun, *Harrouda* 115) opens up the space of writing to the power of dissident femininity as antidote to the loss of authenticizing memory.[11] This form of writing lays claim to the suggestive betrayal underpinning the construct of "Tanger-la-trahison" and to its upending of fixed, corrupt forms of memorialization. In this respect the city lies at the opposite end from Fez, the latter mired in the venality and self-interest of its elite; Fez is reconfigured as "the capital of the wound to come," the hiatus between "hand and thought" (82), that is, between the intellectual, Westernized elite and the artisan class that refused to succumb to the temptations of greater material rewards under the thumb of colonial power.[12] Tangier indeed—the reclaimed fertile terrain for a reactivation of Morocco's true national identity far from the seductions of empire and its multiple violations.

The wind is said to come "alternatively from the East and the West" (Ben Jelloun, *Harrouda* 123) in a transverse, fluid direction that stretches Morocco's symbolic geography to encapsulate the territories lying east of the country—that is, if one were to couch it in geopolitical terms, the Arab nation, a reading supported by the subsequent discussion of Emir Abd El Krim's engagement with Arab nationalism.[13] This East-West axis thus also brings to mind the westward winds of change that swept through Morocco in the form of smuggled outlawed periodicals disseminated from the nevralgic center of Egypt in the days of colonial domination. Yet it also duplicates another line of contact running along the same direction: the Moroccan Mediterranean coastline facing the southern edge of the European continent. Taken as interface with the other shore, whose promise is never quite fulfilled, this second line reverses the geography of conquest ingrained into the landscape of the region. In this new logic invasion is rescripted as a northbound aspiration from Morocco and evokes previous Arab crossings in a Golden Age of territorial conquest and intellectual expansion (the Muslim empires of al-Andalus). It thus brings the focus back to the African shore as the sole point of origin and authority: "We came to stretch out our arm, to cheat the Strait's fog, to point to the other shore without naming it" (Ben Jelloun, *Harrouda* 113).[14] A space of abandon, the sea figures openness and fluidity in opposition to the obliterating movement of the land ("the land has crushed their hope"), a space of oblivion from which a different kind of memory can surface: "the waves and the foam reconciled on the edge of a sun-saved memory" (115).[15]

The ploy of contrasting the abundance and mutability of the maritime space with the strictures of landed forms of rootedness is familiar in Mediterranean-inspired Maghrebi literature. What Ben Jelloun's text brings to the equation, however, is the superimposition of the Mediterranean geography of Morocco with the East-West axis of pan-Arabism, potentially intimating that this sea-inspired form of contestation may in fact operate as the true implementation of the

Arab national ideal. The heritage reclaimed through the trope of the sea is once more al-Andalus, this time conceived not as a principle of cohabitation but as a metonym for the Golden Age of Arab hegemony and empire. The sea provides a desirable perspective, a refuge against the many forms of betrayal experienced in the grounded space of the labyrinthine city: "The sea protects them. They know that it is a parable gushing forth through multiple sources" (Ben Jelloun, *Harrouda* 153).[16] Echoing the notes of an Andalusian song wafting up in the night, another *écriture* is offered, "the writing of the waves," contiguous to the desirable body of "the blue Andalusian queen / the lover from the sands, her back resting against desire's bow" (114).[17] It deploys an alternative language that cuts through the fog of deception shrouding the city in its tight embrace, "the spoken word [*parole*] . . . to discover the itinerary of the sea" (150).[18] A new type of crossing occurs as the fertilizing encounter with the sea comes to fruition—the return to another signification lying beyond the codification of *l'écrit*, the privilege of Fass. This other form of expression gains momentum in the vivacity of orality, in the improvisation of the *parole* of the sea or the coffee house, the last refuges against pervasive deception: "The written word born of the sea returns to the signs of the wave/woman/child. . . . Arabic verbs turn a nomadic blue, they depose fate" (116).[19] Evoked by the image of Arabic verbs turned blue, this other type of crossing, the intersecting of sacralized written Arabic and Mediterranean instability, undoes the inviolable authority of the word of God. Released into liquid immanence and resounding in the figure of the guiding female periodically materializing from the sea to deliver prophecies, the language of the sea mediates another rendition of the Arabic language and of the nationalist project it historically underpinned. Collecting in the foam churned up by the waves, this maritime idiom is reminiscent of the intangible writing of Tangier's palimpsestic past. This mixing preserves a layered form of remembrance at "the crossroads of wandering memories" (123), which functions as a reinforcement of the transverse direction of the wind.[20] This other history, bordering on the insubstantial, is the domain of the alternative expression of the purifying wind, "the writing of the original migrations" (115) based on the emancipatory power of a free-roaming *parole*. The freedom of this new signifying configuration stems from the confluence of the two complementary and inseparable currents of the Mediterranean Sea and the Arab Orient in the crucible of the Mediterranean shoreline. This complementarity casts a shadow over the omnipotence of restrictive definitions of the Moroccan nation and of the regime's confiscation of the nationalist impetus. In this common matrix lies an unadulterated Morocco, intact and unrealized, ready to be revealed by insightful *parole.*

Portentously posing the question of the validity and characteristics of the Arab nation in an era of increased authoritarianism, Ben Jelloun's novel paves the way for a thorough consideration of the nature of the social compact at work in the Moroccan postcolony in 1973, at the onset of one of the bloodiest periods of repression known to history. The Lead Years, as they would come to be known, was a twenty-year-long period of intense *makhzan*-led repression during which political dissidents were subjected to forcible disappearance, torture, and possible death at the hand of the police or in secret prisons. One such site of secret violence is the infamous Tazmamart camp in the Atlas Mountains, which Ben Jelloun evokes in *Cette aveuglante absence de lumière* (*This Blinding Absence of Light*), his controversial rendering of the testimony of a former prisoner, Aziz Binebine.[21] Ben Jelloun himself was no stranger to such brutal crackdowns. Suspected of being involved in the organization of the Casablanca students' demonstrations against the regime in 1965, he was sentenced to a disciplinary camp, where he stayed for over a year, a bitter episode that may be seen resurfacing in *Harrouda* in the metaphor of the octopus eating children in a scene of rare violence and chaos (Aresu, *Tahar Ben Jelloun* 15).[22]

In contrast to the pettiness of an ever stricter regime, the text poetically mobilizes iconic moments of triumphant Arab history in an effort to supplement alternative models of heroism to those supplied by the postcolonial state. A striking example of this dynamic can be found in the narrative of Tariq Ibn Zayn's heroic invasion of Andalusia, which inaugurated centuries of Muslim rule over Spain and southern Europe. In Ben Jelloun's account, Tariq supplants the Greek hero Hercules, who is said to wither away in the popular Tangerine cave bearing his name, cursed for separating Kalpé from Abyla, the illustrious pillars on either side of the Strait. Whether functioning as a principle of intellectual collaboration or alluding to the iconic reign of a lofty Arab civilization, the Andalusian reference fruitfully disengages the course of Moroccan history from the exiguous perspective of Hassan II's power. This echo simultaneously recasts heroism as a function of a seafaring Arabo-Islamic genealogy revisited in a Mediterranean perspective, although it could be argued that

Tariq himself was of Amazigh descent. The same conflation of origins under an imagined Arab identity is visible in the text's characterization of the messianic figure of Emir Abd El Krim El Khattabi, another Amazigh hero of Moroccan resistance to Spanish colonial penetration.[23] Touted as the quintessential Moroccan hero, Abd El Krim clearly embodies the providential leader that is supposed to emerge every one hundred years to wake the Arab world from its stupor.[24] Yet his stated genealogy nevertheless obscures his true origins: "We are from Ajdir; we belong to the Béni Ouriaghe tribe, from the Rif. We are directly descended from the Oulad Si Mohammad Ben Abd El Krim, originally from the Hedjaz . . . on the Red Sea. Our ancestor was named Zarra de Yambo. My family settled in Morocco around the third century of the *hijra*. Thus, for more than a thousand years, the land stretching between the Alhuceimas Bay and Targuist has been our homeland" (*Harrouda* 127).[25] Mostly inspired by Abd El Krim's own words (per J. Roger-Mathieu's testimony in his 1927 *Mémoires d'Abd-el-krim*, cited in Tahtah 36), this long lineage boasts a perfect blend of ancient Arab ancestry and local legitimacy with emphasis on the family's long-standing presence in the Rif region of Morocco. However, his Rifan identity is compacted in a series of geographical markers along the Mediterranean coast. This elision could be construed as a mode of resistance against the opposition between the Amazigh, the so-called Berbers of colonial anthropology, and the Arabs that the colonial regime was intent on establishing.[26] Through this resistance the novel reduces Moroccan identity to its affiliation with a halcyon Arab past, refusing the predominance of colonial visions of identity. But this recentering on the heritage of Arabism could also be read as an effort to set the stage for a thorough discussion of conflicting visions of national identity in the development of Moroccan nationalism.

The nationalist project born of the Arab *nahda* (renaissance) in the Middle East hinged on the recuperation of the Arabic language as the basis for a collective identity common to all. The point of convergence of both secular and Islamist visions of nationalism, the Arabic language catalyzed all anticolonial, nationalist energies (Suleiman; Tibi). Within this geography of revolt Morocco was something of an exception as early forms of decolonial thought sooner capitalized on the country's historical Islamic heritage as a vector of national unity than on a strong attachment to the Arabic language, a preference that can be explained in part by Morocco's distinctive linguistic and ethnic diversity. Mohammed Chekroun explains that Arabism was at times resisted for being anti-Islamic (55). The theorization of statehood abutted the persistence of a tension between the concept of a secular governing body and that of the *umma*, the national community unified by Islam and connected to other national communities throughout the Arab world. According to Chekroun, pre-independence Istiqlal nationalists, such as Allal El Fassi and, especially, Abdelkrim Ghallab, located political sovereignty in the Muslim *umma* as a whole, privileging democracy as the political regime of choice (57–58). It is through *ijma'* (consensus) that this sovereignty is expressed.[27] This vision, inspired by Islamic tradition, rests on the existence of a discrete form of popular power autonomous from the sphere of the monarchy. Both El Fassi and Ghallab emphasize that authority should not belong to one person but to the Muslim *umma* in its entirety, a principle in sharp opposition to the constitutional characterization of the Moroccan monarch as *amir al-mu'minin* (commander of the faithful). In contradistinction to the absolute power of the king, the nationalists of *istiqlal* envisioned an *umma* incorporated into the nation-state in a dynamic aiming to bridge the gap between a faith-based community and the demands of governance. In Chekroun's words, "The political construction of *umma* is restricted to the *umma wataniyya*, the Nation-State which is increasingly becoming the most tangible political and cultural reality" (61). This concept of a nationalized *umma* and its corollary, the sacralized nation (la "nation sacralisée"), performs a "conceptual and political maneuver . . . to reconcile the fundamentally contradictory concepts of the sacred *umma* and the secular Nation-State" (Ellis-House, "Al-Andalus" 103). In this light the top-down model of governance enacted by the *makhzan* is delegitimized as the core values of the nationalist project are disengaged from its incarnation of power, free to be reclaimed by new models of political practice.

Echoing the narrator's exile from corrupt Fez, the mention of "l'hégire" (*hijra*) in Abd El Krim's genealogy aligns his trajectory with Prophet Muhammad's journey.[28] Recasting himself as a late incarnation of Abd El Krim's spirit and the vector of fulfillment of his parting promise ("I will come back to this land. I will come back in veiled form" [Ben Jelloun, *Harrouda* 134]) in a double gesture of preservation and partial resurrection, the narrative voice thus conflates its displaced, minoritarian position with that of the exiled Emir.[29] Abd El Krim is presented as "the Emir without ideology. The exiled Emir"

(129), and yet the first and only legitimate champion of the modern Moroccan nation: "I wanted to . . . win the recognition of those who despised us, to establish us as a modern nation" (131).[30] Abd El Krim's exile on the liner *Abda*, sailing toward the Island of Réunion via Marseille, would last until his last hour in Cairo in 1963. As a temporary victor against the forces of colonialism, during the ephemeral days of his Rif Republic, his historical capital will soon drift into the realm of the symbolic, substituting the logic of myth for that of documented facts. Yet it is precisely his lack of temporal power due to his exile that guarantees his legendary status in the genealogy of Arab nationalism. Based in Cairo, Nasser's capital of pan-Arabism, his resistance invests the realm of *parole* through media communication, conjointly endowing his words with the authority and fluidity of pan-Arab anticolonial rhetoric: "Even since I came to Cairo, I have been vocal [je pratique la parole]; I have called . . . for independence . . . for our liberation . . . for the people's emancipation" (131).[31] Mixed with the frustration of physical confinement outside the nation, the authority of unrestrained political expression surges. Entwined with the evocation of the powerful radio program *Sawt al-ʿArab*, broadcast to the whole Arab world from Cairo, it suggests that true discursive authority is not correlative to a hegemonic status.[32] Surreptitious modes of *parole* are highlighted to show that true adherence to a more fluid Arab nation is to be found underground, in the space of the clandestine that alone can articulate a position of legitimacy. Disincarnated through the metonym of his voice, Emir Abd El Krim is reconfigured as a free-floating principle of nationalism detached from any identity politics or localized instantiation. Although the case is made in the context of anticolonial activism against protectorate regimes, an analogy can be drawn to the later context of postcolonial state-sponsored repression: "The daily use of violence against a whole people makes words [*parole*] rare and pointless. . . . Words . . . are in fact incapable of containing the other kind of violence, the one growing growing growing until one day it erupts in the street under the peaceful sky" (149).[33] Just as Abd El Krim's resistance must be organized into surreptitious channels, so opposition to authoritarian rule must harness the power of the clandestine in the hope of bringing about one such outburst.

If a consistent, substantial intellectual figure is ultimately lacking in Ben Jelloun's framework, *Harrouda* nevertheless calls for the emergence of a messianic guide reminiscent of the providential figure of Arab tradition. In the context of the Lead Years, only the ethereal specter of the mermaid, another avatar of Harrouda, can aspire to temporarily fulfill that role: "The camel confessed to me that another mermaid will come and defy the legend. She will lead the procession of the children/birds and will settle nude on the shore" (120).[34] Yet even she eventually recedes into the distance, forever elusive, whereas the narrator's final dissolution into the poetic communal voice of *la parole* precludes any effective praxis on his end. The space of disagreement is to remain unclaimed, a collective privilege to be seized by all. As the other shore of the sea is ultimately presented as unattainable ("We watch [the shore] receding in the distance there is sand between us" [113]), in anticipation of the sense of bereavement pervading the space of *hrig* narratives, the shore is scripted as a site in stasis and suspension, a nonspace thriving on its limitrophe marginality—the space of resistance par excellence.[35] Sea-inspired *parole* can flourish in it, formulating critical revisions of the nation tinted by the hue of border-zone subversive immateriality. If Tanger incarnates a principle of *trahison*, its discrepancy with the rest of the Moroccan nation enables its marking as a site free from the mire of dominant corruption. It is a space of unadulterated dissent, even though this dissent is confined to the realm of the poetic and the mythical. Through the defamiliarization and disengagement mediated by their common experience of exile, the evasive narrator and his alter ego, Abd El Krim, gain a discerning perspective on what constitutes the desirable foundation for the Moroccan nation—a foundation resting on the kind of genealogy offered by the disincarnate *parole* of *Sawt al-ʿArab* and the Emir's echoing voice. Even though neither one of them can successfully become the embodiment of the intellectual guidance adumbrated in the novel, the enlarged perspective purveyed by the horizon of the Strait provides the distance necessary to draw alternative contours of the nation. Such is the configuration that al-Baqqash's stories will engage some thirty years later, with the notable addition of an engaged query into the power of the Arab intellectual and her ability to exploit the Tangerine space of dissent with significant practical objectives in mind.

FROM RIHLA TO FAILED HIJRA: AL-BAQQASH'S SECOND NAHDA (INTERRUPTED)

Rooted in the complex reality of North-South exploitation and antagonism, al-Baqqash's narratives align the symbolic outlines of contemporary Tangier with the transnational East-West geography that Ben Jelloun's reclaims. His 1998 collection of stories, *Clandestine Migration (Al-Hijra al-Sirriyya)*, stages nine life stories running the gamut of dispossession and forced uprooting in the Strait of Gibraltar contact zone. The collection depicts the respective crossings of nine protagonists, presenting in the process an all-encompassing social fresco of Moroccan hopelessness and destitution. Somewhere in the maritime space of the Euro-African strait, his characters come to life only to be dissolved in the riptide of the sea, their integrity damaged beyond salvation. I propose to investigate the ways al-Baqqash's narratives of clandestine migration reveal submerged substrates of social and intellectual dissent within hegemonic representations of the Moroccan nation. Katarzyna Pieprzak and Ieme van der Poel ("Le Drame des harragas") have shown the extent to which the phenomenon of *hrig* is enmeshed with issues of governance and sovereignty on the part of the Moroccan state and, beyond, its incarnation of the Arab national ideal in the wake of independence. Peeling away the many layers of the characters' social existence, I look beneath the surface of postcolonial processes of social integration, at the forms of intrinsic clandestinity that undercut them. The Moroccan state's eagerness to discount the very real phenomenon of clandestine migration as an insignificant smudge vitiating the picture of a well-functioning, modern state machine points to the deep political ramifications of the issue for the postcolonial regime. Just as the palimpsestic space of Tangier reverberates with the many hues of its conflicting past, so the monolith of the Moroccan state is undercut by spaces of dissidence, where the equation of power, religion, and social affiliation is brought into question.

In this context the corpus of "illiterature," as delineated and defined by Hakim Abderrezak to designate the texts taking *hrig* as their subject, strategically engages with the power of clandestine expression.[36] The Moroccan state-sponsored discourse on the clandestine passage, born of the government's official anti-*hrig* line and disseminated through major media outlets (e.g., Al Alam, RTM), effects a criminalization of *hrig* (Abderrezak, "Burning the Sea" 466), making the relationship between the state and the *harragas* one of violence and attempted erasure. Since the "official suppression of the discourse of the clandestine" in Morocco denies openly voicing the *harraga*'s experience and the multiple causes that trigger the desperate escape of thousands of nationals, this clandestine geography of alienation remains necessarily concealed: "the voice of the State" works only to "reinforce . . . the voicelessness of the clandestine" (Pieprzak 107). In turn, engaging with the complex phenomenon of *hrig* implies seeking a literary practice "framed within the trajectories of social justice and human understanding" (Mehta, *Dissident Writings* 109), a practice at cross-purposes with dominant narratives. Refusing the obliteration performed by legal codifications and discourse, *hrig* writers aim to reclaim the migrants' subjectivity and visibility through compassionate storytelling centered on the personal experiences of the *harraga*, attempting a "rehumanizing [of] the de-humanized" (Abderrezak, "Burning the Sea" 467). The raison d'être of illiterature lies in its ability to write the clandestine into being, to "resist the burial of unsatisfied lives in a quick-sand of state-sponsored amnesia and encourage . . . the bodies and their stories to be metaphorically dug up" (Pieprzak 110). Running counter to the widespread discourses of criminalization and racial segregation that make up the bulk of engagements with illegality both in the European and the Maghrebi public spheres, illiterature attempts to offer an "alternative to monolithic narratives in mass media and politics concerning clandestine migration" (Abderrezak, "Burning the Sea" 462).

While positing clandestinity as his main preoccupation, I argue that al-Baqqash's corpus of illiterature redraws the map of community and nationality in the postcolony and sheds new light on the incorporation of *hrig* into a rhetoric of resistance and belonging. His emphasis on Mediterranean crossing as the spatial enactment of the clandestinity experienced by the intellectual within the nation sets the stage for a provocative consideration of the forms of knowledge purveyed by the thinking in exile that it generates. The phenomenon of *hrig* has provided a sobering counterpoint to the Mediterranean connectivity evinced throughout history. Yet despite the unavoidable reality that northbound Mediterranean crossings today are mostly construed in terms of illegality and sanctions, coextensive patterns of mobility were once associated with the *rihla* that has historically galvanized the development of Arab modernity. As Roxanne Euben has argued, the genre marks "an occasion to map complex connections among travel, theory, and knowledge" (13). Al-Baqqash's notable parallel between the golden era of *rihla* and that of *hrig* in the days of the postcolonial, globalized Moroccan nation forces a reassessment of stable forms of knowledge production underpinning an unwavering, if at times complex sense of national belonging. With its focus on the human toll of illegal migration, al-Baqqash's prose illuminates a subversive level of experience and exposes the deep-rooted crisis of intellectual values and genealogical filiation breaking apart the seemingly smooth structure of the Moroccan nation. In this respect his texts reveal submerged layers of reality rooted in alternative histories and itineraries that run counter to the grand narratives of national identity and community belonging in Morocco.

The Arabic word for "journey," *rihla* as a literary genre denotes a type of foreign travel undertaken chiefly as a quest for knowledge and spiritual advancement. Ian R. Netton fittingly characterizes *rihla* as a search "for the shrine and/or its circumambient religious geography; for knowledge; for recognition and/or power; and for the satisfaction of a basic wanderlust" (x). Many *rihlas* were undertaken for religious purposes, such as the *hajj*, the pilgrimage to Mecca that is one of the five pillars of Islam. The practice commanded such respect that travelogues immortalizing the journey flourished, lending additional significance to the term *rihla*, which soon came to designate a new literary genre altogether, inextricably associated with the long-standing tradition of travel literature. *Rihla* as a genre counts many illustrious examples in the history of Arabic literature, a history in which Morocco stands out. Ibn Battuta's narrative, often titled "The Rihla of Ibn Battuta," recounts the fourteenth-century Moroccan scholar's journey from Tangier to Asia, Africa, the Middle East, and various locations in the Mediterranean; many believe it marks the apogee of a genre that was to persist well into the modern period, with later incarnations, such as Muhammad al-Saffar's *rihla* to Paris in 1845.

Other examples of *rihlas* abound in the modern period across the Arab world, bringing with them complex cultural and social ramifications. Of note among them, the narrative of the Egyptian scholar Rifaʿa al-Tahtawi's journey to Paris under the aegis of Muhammad Ali played a key role in promoting cross-cultural translation and literary circulation between the Arabic world and Europe in the late nineteenth century. The account published in the wake of his stay in France in 1834 tremendously influenced the development of the Egyptian *nahda* (Arab Renaissance), notably through the translation of seminal historical and legal materials, an effort that did much to spark a series of modernization reforms in various domains of Egyptian social and cultural life.[37] Embedded in this circulatory dynamic, *rihla* functioned as an arena of encounters between a colonial, Orientalist Europe purveying a purportedly universal form of modernity and Arab travelers, each uniquely involved in the intellectual life and nascent reformist ethos permeating his respective society. Charting the course of the Arab world's accession to the time-space of modernity, the renaissance born of these exchanges very much emerged as a long-term political project deployed in national and transnational actions.[38] Bearing the mark of ambivalent transcultural conciliation, the translation the *nahda* effected attempted to balance the impulse toward modernity with the negotiation of local narratives of authenticity in what Shaden Tageldin has named a politics of translational seduction. Emphasizing reciprocity, equivalence, and commensurability between the two cultures in the face of the increasing estrangement and polarization brought about by the violence of the imperial conquest, the *nahda* remained inextricably bound up in a dialectic of concurrent complicity and resistance to the enticing sway of Western modernity.

If the genre of the *rihla* marks "an occasion to map complex connections among travel, theory, and knowledge," as Euben suggests (13), its multiple declensions spur on a variegated critical approach to the trope of displacement and the knowledge systems that it made accessible. In classical instances of *rihla,* as al-Tahtawi's experience exemplifies, the traveler's newfound cosmopolitanism serves as the foundation on which new forms of knowledge production are articulated back home. Bearing the mark of the hybridity resulting from the encounter between the traveler's society and the cultures he discovered, these forms interrogate "the complex, permeable, and constantly shifting contours of membership and community within and beyond the *Dar al-Islam* (Abode of Islam) across history" (Euben 14).[39] Yet it is precisely in relation to a postulated stable referent of Dar al-Islam that these narratives function, if only to dismantle it. In contrast more recent experimentations with the genre via the novel form have foregrounded the ultimate duplicity and indeterminacy of any quest for well-demarcated, stable forms of knowledge. A salient example can be found in *Rihlat Ibn Fattuma* (*The Journey of Ibn Fattouma*) by the Egyptian novelist Najib Mahfuz, a Nobel Prize winner. The novel can be read as an allegorical rewriting of the *rihla* trope as a journey through idealized sites in a moral search for the ideal system of social and political governance. A critique of the nation-state as the end of modernity in the Arab world, the novel comes to an ambiguous ending when the last chapter, significantly titled "The Beginning," fails to bring a clear conclusion to the journey in terms of either failure or success, calling into question the didactic fulfillment of the *rihla* as the protagonist refrains from transmitting knowledge (al-Musawi, *Islam on the Street* 202). Mahfuz writes, "It is Satan who is controlling us, not the Revolution" (4), taking to task the rhetoric of nationalism at the core of the Arab nation-state; the perfect model of social harmony sought by the character remains an asymptotic goal. The end of the protagonist's meandering journey is perpetually delayed, making knowledge and belonging ever elusive. Mahfuz's complex, ateleological instantiation of the trope of the journey thus disrupts the configuration of knowledge foregrounded in the classical tradition, unhinging the *rihla* from its ethos of accumulation and transmission to highlight the uncertainty and fluctuation of any sense of a self-contained, self-sufficient community. Mahfuz enacts disenchanted *rihla*, bearing the brunt of intellectual detachment from the certainties of a stable sense of Arab identity, its political incarnations included.

Such is the context within which al-Baqqash's story "Ma'sat adiba" (A Female Writer's Tragedy) has meaning. Probably the most cogent illustration of the mechanism of clandestine dissent in the collection, the tale recounts the life events that lead an impoverished young girl, Zeinab, to attempt to flee the country in search of a more tolerant homeland. For lack of an alternative to a life of destitution in a home bereft of humanism, she dedicates her youth to the service of a philosopher, who supplies her with numerous lessons and books in addition to a meager income. By the time of his death, the pupil has outdone the master, and the dying philosopher bestows upon her the task of pursuing and disseminating their research: "Zeinab preserved what she inherited from her teacher and chose a way to disseminate it" (n.p.).[40] Arrested on account of her notoriety at home and abroad (the text consistently stresses the international impact of her writing on feminism), Zeinab will be incarcerated for close to ten gruesome years, during which she will keep producing clandestine essays attacking the social and political status quo. Once released she decides that the freedom of expression the state still begrudges her is a right worthy of exile and proceeds to procure a counterfeit passport and alter her physical features before embarking on a ship headed to Europe. The Moroccan police, however, arrest her before departure, and she is executed for her crime. The storyline is in many ways a familiar one: a young educated Moroccan who is unable to cope with the discriminatory regime of her homeland attempts to escape, is stopped in her tracks, and is ultimately sentenced for her insubordination and dissidence. Nor is it a surprise that the actual crossing never happens. It is rarely completed in illiterature; only twice in al-Baqqash's collection do protagonists reach the other shore, and both times the arrival in Spain is soon punctuated by some tragedy that costs the *harraga* his life. But the narrative is deployed around one particular focal point: the clandestine forms of affiliation that the two thinkers construct against a hegemonic nation-state. Reactivating a dormant sense of intellectual community one subject at a time, this alternative collective disputes the omnipotence of the Arab nation-state through its actions and reach. The power derived from this marginalization is stressed throughout the story and develops through an alternative humanist genealogy both desired and reclaimed—the only subject position to which Zeinab will be able to lay claim.

The subaltern character leading the story acquires symbolic capital through the construction of a substitute model of civic and intellectual affiliation running against the grain of the national community defined by the strictures of the postcolonial state. Arrogating to herself the entwined heritage of dissent and concealment, Zeinab explores the power of language to foster the clandestine. Her education is indebted to the elderly man's personal teachings, not to the state's educational system, rekindling a more traditional learning template: the *murshid-murid*/master-disciple relationship at the heart of Sufi learning, here redeployed in a more secular mode under the leadership of a philosopher. Zeinab inhabits the space of subalternity within postcolonial Morocco; prior to her encounter with the philosopher, she is illiterate and subsists mostly thanks to a parallel economy that falls outside the purview of more regulated money exchanges. With her scholarly learning Zeinab will be able to succeed the deceased philosopher at the helm of several intellectual projects and to capitalize on his inheritance, earning a living from the dissemination of her ideas. Gaining prominence through her intellectual activities, she will enter mainstream Moroccan society until the weight of censorship forces her back into clandestinity, relegating her once more to a marginal, disenfranchised position.

Throughout the story a number of echoes and mirroring effects tie the language of clandestinity as physical displacement (*hrig* or, in al-Baqqash's lexicon, *hijra*, a term resonating with the lingering echo of Prophet Muhammad's original journey) to a more subdued, sedimented kind of secrecy. This clandestinity highlights the surreptitious power of literary language, a construct redolent of Ben Jelloun's *parole*, to weave an alternative reality and foster dissidence in the face of rational systems of oppression. The title of the collection, *Al-Hijra al-Sirriyya*, builds on the empowering concealment that the feminine adjective *sirriyya* (secret, hidden) evokes. The word appears only once in the story, in the phrase "al-kitaba al-sirriyya" (secret writing), in a move that seemingly associates Zeinab's scholarly work in prison with a kind of clandestine passage or a cutting across precisely demarcated boundaries. Zeinab's writing is carried out surreptitiously after pen and paper have been procured illegally, in the belly of hollowed-out bread loaves brought to the prison where she has been incarcerated. The bread is brought by her disciple Said, one of the young people she teaches, in a reiteration of the same *murshid-murid* relationship that presided over her own apprenticeship. Designated by the lexeme *al-shabab*, which is also one of the terms used to designate the younger fringe of candidates for clandestine migration, this group of students stands in between the two poles of *al-nas* (the people whose diegetic collective existence materializes in their anger toward their government) and *al-dawla* (the state), two poles that the narrative describes as growing increasingly at odds. Through the overlap between Zeinab's following and the reference to *hrig*, al-Baqqash's Arabic lexicon therefore attempts to construct coterminous networks where intellectuals and migrants are reconciled in a similar dynamic—that of a clandestinity that can meet no other outcome than exile.

In this context displacement can be read as the necessary consequence of the disenfranchisement and exclusion of the nation's youth by corrupt, iniquitous systems of governance. The trilateral root Ha-ra-qaf, which also lies at the core of the word *hrig*, is used in the text in its literal sense of "burning" to depict the fate reserved to any and all unorthodox intellectual production. Via a detour through al-Andalus, which remains one of the ghostly presences at work in al-Baqqash's intellectual palimpsest, Ibn Rushd's legacy—his books—are said to have been burned to ashes by his detractors ("ahraqu"). From the burning of the books to the philosopher's forced exile out of Cordoba following conflicts with the orthodox Muslim clergy, the same dynamic is at play; discord with the powers that be leads to alienation, exclusion, and eventually symbolic (or physical) disintegration, much like that experienced by *harragas*. In other words, Zeinab's *hrig* can be construed as a second burning following the first symbolic auto-da-fé of her works through a chilling parallel with the fate of the Arab philosopher. The Tunisian poet Tahar Bekri's engagement with Muslim intellectuals' exodus from Cordoba in *Les Chapelets d'attache* further testifies to the symbolic power of al-Andalus as the trope of a Golden Age of Arab intellectualism standing in sharp opposition to bigoted forms of temporal power across history.[41] Interestingly the term used to evoke the philosopher's legacy, *turath*, is also the term mobilized in relation to Ibn Rushd's writings, extending the illustrious Andalusian humanist genealogy to the contemporary period and aligning both thinkers along a common history of subversion and incrimination. One final incarnation of this Andalusian humanist ideal is to be found in the figure of Socrates, metonymically embodying the Greek philosophical tradition that Andalusian men of science resurrected and made available to a benighted European world through translation.

As the distinct subject positions of the intellectual and the potential *harraga* are blurred, a rhetoric of secrecy and erasure emerges in the interstices of the state's structures of dominance—a rhetoric that keeps the appearance of legality and that Zeinab's effort to procure a fake passport continues to reinforce. Under the identifiable contours of state-issued identity papers, a different identity is cloaked that can be fulfilled only by the subject's maritime wandering. The Mediterranean crossing therefore becomes a correlative for the repressed intellectual journey, an extension that carves out a space for this alternative reality lying beneath the surface of legality but still fitting within its structures. How, then, does the narrative arrive at the imperative of *hrig*? What is the status of this migration within the symbolic economy of the story?

Whereas classical *rihlas* have been known to foster far-reaching institutional and societal reforms (as in the case of Egypt in the wake of al-Tahtawi's voyage, for instance), al-Baqqash's alignment with contemporary rewritings of *rihla* precludes the possibility of change and the implementation of reform back home. The crossing his fiction stages can only unfold interstitially before fulfilling its destiny of material and philosophical shipwreck. It is not surprising, then, that his collection of stories should be called *hijra sirriyya*, replacing the forward-reaching and accumulating paradigm of *rihla* with the unidirectional term for exile bereft of a possible return home (*hijra*, in a religious context). Deriving from the Arabic etymon for "migrating," but also colored with the sedimented meaning of "breaking ties with someone" and "abandoning," *hijra* refers to the mass exodus of

Muslims from Mecca to Medina in ad 622. Actualized by the start of a new calendar in the Islamic world, this fundamental mobility is reenacted in al-Baqqash's story in the guise of Zeinab's attempt at "political asylum" ("al-luju' al-siyasi") in a land where human rights enjoy widespread support and where intellectual activity is promoted and valued. Yet this displacement also marks a rupture with the land and way of life left behind. While the subject's nation collapses as a stable point of reference in her imaginary, the anticipated integration into the host society allows the migrant to foster a new community, a rippling effect also present in the original *hijra*. Muhammad Khalid Masud reports that after the *hijra* out of Mecca, all blood ties were severed with Muslims who had purposely stayed behind. Instead "a new bond of brotherhood (*mu'akhat*) between *muhajirs* (migrants) and *ansars* (inhabitants of Medina . . .) was established, which entitled them even to inherit from one another" (31). Seeping into the right of inheritance usually restricted to the realm of family ties within Islam, this new form of brotherhood temporarily favored the new alliances necessary to the sustainability of a vulnerable Muslim community over well-established family lineages. Even if traditional injunctions regarding family rights were eventually restored, this parenthesis illustrates the might of the Muslim community's desire to assimilate into their new surroundings, highlighting the strategic nature of alliances and community formation in the early days of Islam. The recourse to *hijra* symbolically opens the door to tactical reformulations of community belonging in the contemporary period in relation to new contexts, such as the Moroccan postcolony.

Rife with the ethos surrounding these early forms of *hijra* and of the new forms of collectivity that they instigated, al-Baqqash's story traces the contours of other social formations. Extricated from any ossified notion of national sentiment, loyalty is recast as a function of intersubjective interaction, which is individually crafted in the privileged arena of intellectual dissemination along the *murshid-murid* axis that Zeinab has extended through her own teachings. She is said to have "remained faithful to the heritage of the philosopher," acting out of "her duty to her master" (n.p.).[42] Another community emerges from this exclusive bond, issuing new patterns of memorialization beyond nation and family. Two oppositional heritages soon materialize on the issue of preservation (*hifz*), which demarcates official commemoration at the hands of the state from Zeinab's sacralizing dissemination of her master's teachings. "Zeinab preserved what she inherited from her teacher" (n.p.); in so doing she merely follows in the footsteps of Socrates and his devotees, whereas the officials imposing their iron rule over her intellectual activity are presented as conservatives (*muhafizin*), the preservers of the ruling order, both terms deriving from the same trilateral root, Ha-fa-Dha.[43] Through lexical mirroring two visions of cultural legacy are pitched against each other, delineating two irreconcilable collectives in their wake: *al-dawla* (the state), historically the incarnation of the national impetus that guided anticolonial activism, which has since devolved into a state of endemic iniquity and corruption, and *al-umma*, the Muslim nation, a term also present in the *umma wataniyya* (the national community), central to the early nationalists' project as the site of all legitimate popular will and political sovereignty in the face of the *makhzan*.

By arrogating to Zeinab's disciples the status of *umma* (the only mention of the word occurs in relation to her followers: "Each one of them was an umma" [n.p.]), the story ambitions to reclaim the true spirit of a popular Moroccan nationalism congruent with Islamic principles in opposition to actualized forms of political power in the postcolony, in an reaffirmation of Abdelkrim Ghallab's early nationalist concept of *ijma'* (consensus).[44] Through this literary and philosophical legacy each person becomes an *umma* unto himself, multiplying the corrosive power of thought in the face of institutionalized structures of oppression. Whereas the authority of the *dawla* is anchored in the regulated space of the country's capital (it is to the capital that Zeinab is sent after her arrest), Tangier emerges once again as the space of dissent par excellence, capitalizing on its rich literary intertext. Presiding over all Arab and Maghrebi cities, the port city resonates with the experience of overlapping political geographies running the gamut from local Moroccan statehood to the pan-Arab nation.[45] Through the multiple scales of dissent it fosters, the city lays claim to a humanist heritage, gaining inscription into a long tradition of dissident thinking whose echo resounds through time: "For that [the philosopher's] was a human heritage and not a selfish or individual one"; "her teacher wrote for [both] the private and the public" (n.p.).[46]

A secondary etymology of *hijra* brings further semantic weight to al-Baqqash's project. Qur'anic uses of the term emphasize the notion of distance that it encapsulates. Meaning "to reject" or "to shun," the term enacts "a distancing—physical or otherwise—usually from evil and disbelief" (Masud 32). Bringing to mind the ominous echo of Mahfuz's resounding judgment on the nation-state in *Rihlat Ibn Fattuma* ("It is Satan who is controlling us, not the Revolution" [4]), this lexical link underpins the construal of *hijra* as a moral duty when practical measures need to be taken against deficient temporal incarnations of power. Reinforced by Masud's analysis of the conjoined use of the verbs *hajaru* (they migrated) and *jahadu* (they waged war) throughout the Qur'an (32), this perspective assimilates exile to a necessary act of resistance and adumbrates the kind of dissenting, humanist migration embraced by Zeinab. In this context the word *jihad* is to be taken literally as "striving," its semantic resonance extending far beyond its usual narrow characterization as a holy war. *Jihad* thus denotes a struggle aiming for the implementation of a greater good in the service of God and the people, which does not necessarily point to the perpetration of violence (Cook; Mirbagheri). In this case *jihad* in the service of the people's moral preservation is to be realized through migration rather than direct violent action against the powers in place, and such is the religious model retained and openly developed by al-Baqqash in his tale. In this recoding the original knowledge-seeking goal of *rihla* is undercut by more pressing realities; the journey renounces the aspiration to knowledge acquisition and reform implementation back in the homeland to embrace more modest objectives: the preservation and cultivation of existing forms of knowledge away from the perpetually renewed risk of obliteration in an adverse environment. *Hijra* therefore becomes the extension of the reign of clandestinity qua clandestinity at play within the nation, the sanctioning of ambivalence and resistance that cannot be co-opted—but also, *a contrario*, one that cannot prevail. In what nevertheless remains a problematic gesture, al-Baqqash's story ultimately presents "the riding of the sea" as the ultimate mark of intellectual independence and maturity, the sole resolution to the dilemma of repression and epistemic violence through inclusion into an international intellectual community that would be united by its promotion of universal principles.

Lying at the conjunction of Islamic principles and philosophical humanism, al-Baqqash's redefinition of the nation (*al-watan*) partakes of the same reading. In its only occurrence the term refers to an idealized, purely utopian vision of the national entity in utter isolation from any sense of identity anchored in the physical confines of the postcolony traced at independence. In Zeinab's parting words to her disciples, the alternative community galvanized by her teachings, her philosophy is made clear: "Our religion is worldly [all over the world] and our nation is the world wherever our ideal reigns" (n.p.),[47] in an echo of the Qur'anic sura al-Nisa' 4.97: "Was not the earth of Allah spacious enough for you to emigrate therein?" Her decision to leave her country is couched in a language tinged in places with the resonance of religious fervor (she speaks of "salvation"). In her own words, she "[is not] leaving for fear of trouble, but to work there in an environment open to contradictions for the sake of enlightenment and to attract supporters of the truth there" (n.p.).[48] With her departure the text anticipates a renaissance, a second *nahda* of sorts.[49] Al-Baqqash suggests that the seeking of political asylum may be the truest form of national struggle, again associating *hijra* and *jihad* while problematically raising escapism to the level of political praxis. Yet the text soon seems to crumbles under its own weight as the polysemy intrinsic to the core lexeme in Zeinab's parting promise lends limited credence to her words. The verb of which she makes use, *sada* (to reign), derives from the same trilateral root (sin-waw-dal) as the verb *sawwada* (to blacken, a lexeme whose use stretches to include denigration as well as the blackening of paper in the process of writing). Although the two are separate verbs with discrete meanings, the etymological resonance linking *sada* and *sawwada*, if considered in its own right, might limit the purview of Zeinab's claims by destabilizing the idea of successful nation-building. If undercut by the tinge of denigration, one of the core meanings of *sawwada*, the integration of the community's ideal and the tolerant land that Zeinab postulates comes undone. Through yet another etymological haunting it could also even be argued that a true nation can be created only by the act of tentative and incomplete writing (*sawwada* as writing, understood more as the process of drafting than its polished result), belying the promise of a natural incorporation into the hospitable land to which Zeinab lays claim.

Investing the differential space between both verbs, the political concept of *watan* wanes short of actualization. The unshakeable restrictions imposed by the Moroccan nation-state curtail the potential of *hijra*, dooming the crossing to intangibility. Since Zeinab is unable to leave, her obliteration from the diegetic machine presiding over the course of the story becomes inevitable (she is arrested as her boat prepares to leave Morocco). In retrospect it could be argued that her inexorable failure may even have overdetermined the very formulation of her desired emigration, nullifying it at the very moment of its utterance. If unsuitable to embody the incarnation of the true *watan*, the Moroccan postcolony nevertheless remains the only perspective, restricting Zeinab's aspirations to the realm of clandestinity and surreptitious resistance never to be realized. Her alternative nation will therefore lie in the preservation of knowledge (*hifz*) against the totalitarian power of the conservatives (*muhafizin*). Drawing from its deep imaginative insertion into the genealogy of a humanism born of multiple translations and transmissions between Europe and the Islamic world throughout the Golden Age of al-Andalus, this mode of inscription into history, albeit utopian, forms anew the kind of ties that reconnect the Moroccan intellectual to the world. This worldly sensibility revives the pursuit of knowledge as an act endowed with the religious aura it possessed in the age of *rihla*, even if no implementation of reform can ever materialize at home.

Deploying the protagonists' illegal crossings of the Mediterranean in relation to the *rihla* tradition thus emphasizes the discrepancy between a real Golden Age of early modern Mediterranean relations, when travelers were welcome to cross borders, and the current dehumanizing circumstances that accompany the journey across the sea. The rewriting of *rihla* in a negative mode (a *rihla* severed from its power to mold the nation), *hijra* thus comes to express both one's hope for a revised community partaking of a universal humanism and the subsequent disillusion in the face of bleak reminders of the omnipotence of the regimes of repression. By reconfiguring the coordinates of *rihla* as *hijra*, al-Baqqash rewrites the medieval Mediterranean of contact and interaction into a fractured space bearing the mark of failed yet resurgent nationalisms and their attendant claustrophobic affiliations. In a world of solidified borders, the fresh start that his protagonists hope for appears frustratingly unattainable. Their existence remains necessarily bounded by the strictures of nationalism, their critical potential limited to the lacunar spaces of dissent they have managed to excavate within the national construct. They remain as illicit as the sheets of paper smuggled into Zeinab's cell in the hollowed-out belly of a bread loaf she would blacken with her writing, the only possible materialization of the other nation to be built. As the mirage of political asylum dissipates in the distance, clandestinity therefore seems to be a fate that cannot be altered. Behind the progression from *rihla* to *hijra* to failed *hijra* the shadow of a totalitarian state lurks, inextricably binding the characters to its intractable logic. Significantly al-Baqqash's choice of the term *shakhsiyya* (character, as both disposition and protagonist) to designate the disciples making up this alternative *umma* brings into question their very existence outside the confines of the text. The avowed power of clandestinity therefore seems to come undone as the impossibility of a landing across the sea makes the space being traveled not one of finite, knowable regimes of knowledge, as in *rihla*, but one incommensurable to them. The desire for an inscription into another legible system of governance, a democratic one accompanied by the benefits of full citizenship, is eventually overpowered by the *harragas*' inescapable reality: entrapment in the subaltern position bestowed by the nation-state.

ESPEJISMOS (MIRRORINGS)

From across the Strait, the Gibraltarian poet Trino Cruz's take on the issue of clandestinity provides a compelling response to al-Baqqash's configuration of *hrig* in light of its anticipated destination—in other words, as the vector of a transmaritime *mise en relation* under the aegis of an enlightened universal community respectful of philosophical truths and supportive of intellectual discernment. Cruz's rather sparse poetic output, collected in his suggestively titled *Rihla*, is remarkable for its complex, fine-tuned structure. An *opera aperta* engaged in the refinement and rewriting of a few key concepts illuminating his vision of identity formation and cultural visibility, Cruz's poetic creations give voice to overlapping fields of experience marking the hybrid, liminal character of his border writing.[50] He delineates a vital space of exchange that provides a unique localization for his poetic persona, whose concern with the universal human condition is crisscrossed with renderings of specific, localized experiences of the global. For Cruz's poetry is first and foremost an ontological effort through which the poet uncovers the complexities of his own Gibraltarian identity: "Writing is for me a means to confront myself, a way to investigate my own identity" (qtd. in El Bouanani and Abdelouahab n.p.). And indeed his inclusion in the poems of an interlocutor in relation to whom the poetic voice is articulated sheds light on the dialectic relation that his persona maintains with his other.

The latter part of *Rihla*, which is my focus, stages an evolution from the earlier poems, involved in the issue of representation and the power of the metaphor as a vector of engagement with reality, to a cluster of texts more directly entangled with the ontological and cognitive experience of the *polizón* (*harraga*) ensuing from the event of his crossing. Trapped in his disenfranchised position and hopelessly rooted in the Global South, the migrant that emerges from the verse maelstrom remains inescapably other, resisting Cruz's desired identification. Cruz's *harraga* is irremediably tied to the space of subalternity, bringing to mind al-Baqqash's protagonist in several instances. Like Zeinab, the *polizón* remains indebted to a black market economy ("unreal dollars obtained on some black Market" [*Rihla* 48]); like hers, his emigration plans make use of existing northbound maritime routes and rely on physical concealment ("You embarked on a cargo boat . . . and you hid" [48]).[51] Yet Cruz's theoretical engagement with the ultimate nature and purpose of the crossing reveals incommensurable perspectives between the two authors, abutting on the issue of the *harraga*'s assimilation into society on the other shore. For if ensnarement in the fateful straitjacket of national affiliation ultimately unravels Zeinab's dream of European assimilation, al-Baqqash's text still postulates the existence of a cosmopolitan intellectual caste nurtured in a culture of humanism and characterized by its hospitality toward foreigners. Whereas his story debunks the attempted crossing, the reality of the community is never questioned, hypothesizing a global universalist position to which intellectuals from all over the world could possibly lay claim. In this outlook the space of the sea is reduced to the pure connectivity afforded by its limitrophe coastline, in a reading that flattens out the complex conjunctions materializing under the seemingly placid surface of the sea. Existing merely as the transitory space to be crossed on the way to inclusion into this transnational community, the sea loses its function of obstruction to the project of migration. (Zeinab's project flounders after she is arrested by the police, not because the sea eventually regains its rights over her crossing.) However, where al-Baqqash's prose postulates a possible national community marking the end of Zeinab's *hijra*, Cruz's poetic anthology remains determinedly circumscribed to the elemental space of the sea itself and, in tune with much of illiterature, ultimately conveys the utter disintegration of the *harraga* figure.

Anchoring his verse in modes of belonging lying outside the territoriality of the nation, Cruz situates the poetic voice in circumstances of exile. He reconfigures critical, revised transnationalism as the only adequate corrective to discriminatory configurations of identity inspired from the fractured geography of modernity. Offering a fractal perspective informed by a cultural identity lying somewhere in maritime space, Cruz proposes a vision of Euro-Mediterranean relations that displaces the framing of the sea along the lines of cultural division between North and South. By positing a subject position born of the drifting currents, his poetic persona vibrates with the echoes of his own double family heritage, implanted in both the space of Gibraltar and the northern shore of Morocco (Tangier, but also Tetuan) and replete with connections to the Sephardi community. Himself a resident of both shores, albeit with the privilege of British citizenship, Cruz models identity on the intrinsic principle of mobility, which operates as the common denominator between the poetic voice and his hypothesized *harraga* alter ego. The synecdochic relationship embedding the two figures is but a reverberation of the long history of entanglement embracing the two spaces from the days of al-Andalus. From 1969 to 1985, the years of the Gibraltar-Spanish border closure in the wake of yet another showdown between Spain and Britain regarding the fate of the city, Gibraltar was more indebted to the other shore of the Strait than it was to the Franquist nation. When the territory lost its Spanish labor force overnight, the border closure prompted the migration of Moroccan migrant workers to take the place left vacant by the day laborers hailing from Spain. With Gibraltar's dependence on the ascendant, food imports not supplied by Britain flowed in from Morocco, while Tangiers became the usual port of call for anyone jetting for Spain as all direct transport links with Spain were severed (Alvarez; Vallejo; Archer). Reinvigorating the territory's historical legacy as a space of refuge for all Mediterranean wanderers fleeing violence and persecution, the border closure shed new light on Gibraltar's insertion into a pan-Mediterranean topography of tolerance and openness, making it a possibly paradigmatic end to Zeinab's postulated quest.

Capitalizing on this variegated heritage, Cruz's poetry redraws the coordinates of Zeinab's hypothesized encounter with her humanist community on the dialogical mode, as an ontological reconciliation with an ever elusive *harraga*. In contrast to Zeinab's romantic notion of intellectual ecumenism as the cement of trans-Mediterranean scholarly fellowship, Cruz revises universalist claims to knowledge, restricting the possibility of contact to the fundamental dyad that he forms with his phantasmatic double. Returning Zeinab's gaze and perspective from its position of entitlement, the poetic voice erases any clear identity marker proceeding from geography, crafting in its stead a polychromatic maritime affiliation uniting disparate subject positions from either shore of the Strait. Cruz's poetry thrives on the retrieval of common preoccupations—what he envisions as a mediating position joining all Mediterranean subjects in defiance of modernity. As both intimacy and rupture inform relations between southern Europe and North Africa, Cruz's social imaginary builds on the familiar postcolonial tropes of exile and fracture, tropes experienced not as physical displacement but as the ontological loss of one's double without whom the self cannot be complete. (Of his journeys Cruz has said, "I lived in different places, but my cosmopolitanism is intellectual. I do not presume to have traveled much" [qtd. in El Bouanani and Abdelouahab n.p.]). If subjects along the shores of the sea are united in a common history, as Cruz's poetry suggests, true solidarity can come to fruition only by thinking beyond the artificiality of politically imposed borders. As Cruz's poetry aims to reinscribe his North African alter ego in the central position that is rightly its own, the figure of the clandestine migrant comes to haunt the dialectical process of identity formation to which the poet subjects himself.

Rife with echoes of his alternative hermeneutics into the nature of reality, the consideration of the *polizón* partakes of the same aesthetic of *espejismo* (mirroring) that undergirds Cruz's poetic excoriation of the real. Starting from the premise that all knowledge is by nature subjective and contingent, despite the claim to universal truth constitutive of modern epistemological models, Cruz provides a mode of relation to reality (and relation *of* reality) that questions the boundaries of knowledge and its recourse to reason as a guarantee of its supposed universalism. The cycle of poems, "como la mirada que ha de pervertir este espejo o las imágenes como fuente de conocimiento" (like the gaze that has to pervert this mirror, or images as the source of knowledge), delineates the contours of this alternative epistemology. The symbolisms of the tide and of the mirror (*espejo*) become entwined to form a new, complex genealogy of meaning. Language is reconfigured as elastic. (Cruz talks about pulling language to its limits, "tensar el lenguaje.") It is conceived as a mirror on the fluctuating surface of which representations of reality are formed following a principle of deformation. Cruz acknowledges the potentiality of the mirror, that is, its reflecting surface cognate to the surface of the sea, but "not the reflection that forms on it" (*Rihla* 40).[52] Rather it is on a journey rendered as a *buceo* (diving) through the surface of representation that the world can be construed, always in conjunction with parallel readings by others, as it is only "when we share the same *espejismo* [that] we can call it reality" (40).[53] The reverberating surface remains indeterminate, full of possibilities, as it opens the door to another level of experience not directly perceptible to the eye. This experience is tributary to concomitant readings construed as the basis for the kind of complementarity between poet and migrant advocated throughout the anthology. The mirror's unorthodox approach to reality is relished for its mendacity, for its creation of mirages and illusions, which alone have the power to transcend the deceitful appearance of things. The mirror therefore becomes a "limbo," an in-between space from which Cruz can develop his alternative approach to reality, or, more literally, a space where he can "invent . . . a location from which to launch those images" (40).[54]

Diving through the surface of the mirror allows the poet to plumb the depth of oblivion, the *abismo* (abyss), replacing the horizontal fault lines running along the main routes of capitalism and illegal itineraries with vertical probes of the sea's density. Redoubled through the concurrent readings of its reflection by both figures, the dual perspective purveyed by the mirror fancies itself as a rewriting of stable origins, an embrace of the polyvocality of metaphorical perception. After the detonation of poetical language has consummated detachment from semantic stability, only the poet's alter ego remains, both infinitely intimate and painfully incommensurable, clasped in an imperfect embrace generative of entropy and darkness. A measure of the system's disorder, this energy loss washes away obsolescent forms of signification, clearing the path for a reconstruction of another form of memory born of repressed symbolisms and haunting absences. Treasured for its fruitful fluidity, this instability is the "limbo" suggested by the poetic voice, the meeting point for both subjectivities, for "between one way of thinking and another / there is a limbo in which I breathe and don't breathe / in which I stumble against discarded image" (*Rihla* 41).[55] In this semantic alluvium a new narrative of origins is coined from the union between word and idea: "We are the bridge that unites matter to metaphor" (42).[56] The bridge (*puente*), an echo of the Greek etymon *pontos*, charged with a double semantic acceptation as bridge and sea, traces a direct connection between the act of mediating and the mirroring surface of the sea. Reconfigured as an ontological space of self-discovery and encounters with others, the sea performs a return to true origins beyond the codification of complacent genealogies narratives. Such is the defining characteristic that Cruz envisions as the bedrock of an authentic

Gibraltarian form of expression conveying a pan-Mediterranean sensibility and generating a more encompassing form of memory ("El bilingüismo gibraltareño").

Yet the persistent emphasis on the drowning *harraga* portrays another reality. Upon reaching the shore, the poetic persona momentarily turned *polizón* is said to expectorate "weak, bitter mirrors," a scourge marking the death of creativity ("I was emptied of all images," *Rihla* 45).[57] In the last tableau, or rather "mirror" ("en este último espejo"), as utter disenchantment sets in, the poet acknowledges the inevitable disaster of his cognitive undertaking, the objective correlative of the journey at sea: "I failed precisely as I was supposed to" (*Rihla* 46).[58] Yet this is a fruitful failure in all respects as it is from the confrontation with the gaping chasm threatening the integrity of the poetic voice that unanticipated sightings can occur, that language can stage its own form of resistance to annihilation, continuously "perfecting the void, circling it without suspecting it" (46).[59] A far cry from the *rihla* paradigm of accumulation and abundance to which the anthology lays claim through its titular affiliation, the poems included in the self-proclaimed "Tríptico" resonate with the aura of betrayal characteristic of Ben Jelloun's Tangier: "The sea, like language, is at times the refuge that betrays us, a traitor that gives us shelter" (49).[60] As the *harraga*'s shipwrecked destiny looms larger, flotsam starts floating in, bringing along clues used to reconstruct the meaning gleaned during the crossing. With each fragment a fundamental ambiguity assails the poetic voice left in charge of the semantic reconstruction of the sinking: rife with "espejismos," this time of the perplexing kind, the ebb and flow of the wreckage leaves few pointers as to the purpose of it all. As memory threatens to disintegrate along with each nail and splinter of the hull (the rutting anchor of Bekri's ode to Ibn Hazm comes to mind), the poet's vertigo surges to record the *harraga*'s metaphorical acumen gained during his failed journey of initiation. Construing the space of the exile's wait as yet another form of doubling or *espejismo* (between physical presence and projection toward destination), this epistemology of mobility ascertains the contours of memory, of the traces it has left on what is now the appearance of reality.

Reviving the *harraga*'s drowning, the poet lyrically dives into the chasm of the shipwreck to restore the complexity of history. As the flotsam lends itself to deciphering, the lines that surface from the poet's ontological excursion into the depth of the abyss lend insight into the nature of things. In this resurgent poetry born of the diving into the depth of the sea and of the partial resurfacing that follows, the journey of the *harraga* is enshrined, his physical eradication memorialized. The poet becomes the depository of this new intellectual archive through his progressive transfiguration into his complementary double. Coextensive with the migrant, the poetic voice plays on the ambiguity of the last lines that announce the eventual emergence of a *polizón* from the pages relating the wreckage—a *polizón* who reaches the shore in possession of a new sort of accumulated knowledge gleaned from the darkness of the abyss, acquired by circling its voracious annihilating core: "You'll see how [these pages] sink, how the *polizón* that they carry inside / escapes / gets to the shore / and reaches you" (*Rihla* 54).[61] This new clandestine figure is but a reincarnation of the poet endowed with demiurgic power, as indicated by the denomination of the following poem, "El vértigo del polizón (apuntes para un autorretrato)" (The Stowaway's Vertigo [Notes for an Autoportrait]) (55). His survival and remembrance warranted by the very poetry composed in his name, the *harraga* is absorbed into the poetic voice that allows him to continue his clandestine voyage through the appearance of things: "You frequently live inside me, possess me, pick me as a vessel for some journey" (51).[62] The excavation promised by the poems is completed by the superimposition of the two gazes, leaving both explorers to a threatening disintegration: "If I am your only trace / when the tide washes me away . . . who will bring back to me the body that disobeys the vertigo?" (68).[63]

This obliteration raises the question of the status of this *rihla*, as disappearance into the maelstrom of the sea is revealed as the sine qua non for knowledge. The last eponymous poem, "Rihla (aproximaciones a cero)" (Rihla [Approximation to Zero]), offers a more optimistic perspective resting in the excavation of palimpsestic forms of memory, akin to the kind of sedimentation intrinsic to Ben Jelloun's take on Tingi. The poet's opening judgment leaves no room for ambiguity: "Finally / fecundation will come" (*Rihla* 70).[64] From the movement of approximation, here to be understood in its Latin etymology as a movement of convergence and proximity, the emphasis is placed on the asymptotic mode of contact with this void. Tending toward the abyss, the poem makes most of its eventual distantiation, of the productive hiatus between its grounded full possession and the utter devastation entailed by the journey. Revisiting *rihla* as intellectual perambulation through the multiple layers of reality, Cruz aligns his dual heuristic figure of the *polizón*-poet with al-Baqqash's protagonist and her search for a transmaritime form of solidarity. The *rihla* performed by Cruz's verse similarly postulates the interconnectedness of the figures of the poet and the *polizón* as the preliminary condition for the dissemination of the poems' philosophy. Conjoining the southern migrant's intrepid intellectual gesture enacted by his perilous journey and the lyrical mastery of the northern poet's expression, the verse marked with the seal of their collaborative *rihla* reflects the desired universalist position at the putative end of Zeinab's quest. The requirement to delve into the rich sediment of memory to retrieve meaning at the risk of losing oneself is offset by the (relative) stability offered by the mediation of the poetic voice. Through a collaboration between the two, poetry transpires: if the *harraga* is pulverized, his message can expect to find its way back to the surface of the verse through the poet's mediation. The *aproximaciones a cero* postulated in the poem therefore mark the safeguarding enacted by the lyrical voice with regard to the process of excoriation staged by the voyage. If dissolution impends, its grip loosens in the face of these overlapping positionalities born of the commensurate geography of the Strait region.

A conjoined reading of the final *rihla* piece in light of Cruz's deliberations on the (lack of) a specifically Gibraltarian form of literary expression in "El bilingüismo gibraltareño: Aproximación a una literature que se resiste a nacer" (Gibraltarian Bilingualism: Approximations to a Literature Resisting Its Own Birth) divulges yet another facet of the approximation to disappearance reclaimed in the piece. Another abyss delineated by the poet's discerning gaze, the concept of Gibraltarian literature—another "zero" of sorts—necessitates immersion in the entangled memories of the Mediterranean: "To make literature is to give shape and depth to what we are" (n.p.).[65] Laying claim to a lexicon reminiscent of the terminology underpinning the poem's *buceo*, Cruz's text emphasizes the necessity to resist any smooth inscription into the adverse order of modernity catalyzed between Hercules's pillars: "If we don't reinvent ourselves, we will be submerged without leaving a trail in the mud. . . . After all is done, who will come near the shore to come across our flotsam?" (n.p.).[66] The struggle for one's specificity against the dissolving undercurrent of modernity proposes to restitute the specificity of the Mediterranean itself against the reductionism of global dynamics. Restoring the emphasis to the space of the sea thus constitutes a political gesture of confrontation against the global order of power. In the realm of literary existence the undertaking assumes delineating the contours of a specifically Gibraltarian imaginary tributary to other influences but resisting obliterating forms of allegiance. Only by reappropriating its expressive self-determination can this literature find its place on the global map, bringing with it the acknowledgment of another form of transnational identity generative of political inclusion, an identity nurturing the kind of layered memory summoned by the poet: a "memory [that] becomes visible through its weaving with the very substance of the abyss" (n.p.).[67]

Addressing the reality of trans-Mediterranean crossings in our extreme contemporary period implies embedding the Mediterranean in a global perspective, consecrating the ineluctable shift away from utopian understandings of the region as a space of happy hybridity and felicitous encounters to reveal the darker nature of the sea in our global time. To bring this chapter to its conclusion, I return to Mokeddem's novel, with which it started. Keeping in mind the complex coordinates of *hrig* permits the reevaluation of Mokeddem's paradigm: a subjective quest unfolding under the enthralling spell of a "return" to Algeria. By charting the itinerary as a journey of no return (and, in some cases, of no departure), the corpus of illiterature significantly complicates narratives of national belonging, revealing heterotopic spaces within the fabric of state hegemony and global flows. Out of the purview of history the inscrutable space of the clandestine is thus imbued with disruptive potential and resilience to decipherment and representation. Its existence on the margins of the nation disrupts official mappings of national identity and belonging and underscores the entropic forces chipping away at the integrity of the nation-state. In this context the power of illiterature is paramount; it facilitates the task of the writer to hack away at the silencing forced upon these discordant experiences of crisis. However, al-Baqqash's model leaves one wondering whether, in the context of *hrig*, illiterature as a literary genre can ever aspire to transcend the limitations of clandestinity and promote an alternative social model that stands the chance of being actualized. Do *hrig* narratives always contain the seeds of their own obliteration? In other words, does literature even in its most global, seemingly nomadic instantiations ever succeed in escaping the straitjacket of its national limitations?

The observable inability to extricate *hrig* from the marginalized, repressed space of subalternity carries with it additional considerations linked to the obliteration of the *harraga* figure. Its disappearance in the wake of the planned crossing calls into question the possibility of alternative collective affiliation. The shipwreck to which the *harraga* is destined points out his utter unassimilability. In other words, there is no ecumenical intellectual community for him to join. His position remains frustratingly peripheral as he is ensconced in subaltern difference while his dream of citizenship and belonging remains forever out of reach. As Cruz's verse has shown, it is only through total absorption into a northern Mediterranean voice that his message can survive, to the detriment of his own integrity. Rehearsing Spivak's well-known "ventriloquism of the speaking subaltern" (255), it seems that, in the context of *hrig*, only physical disintegration can pave the way for subaltern expression. As the hope of recuperation into alternative networks founders, another form of inscription, maritime this time, surges. This ontological affiliation with the Mediterranean, often a purveyor of death, reveals a new Mediterranean space marked by dystopia. This new valence of the Mediterranean as a voracious abyss sets the stage for a consideration of the forms of epistemic violence intrinsic to the region and productively complicates readings of the space of the sea as a site of cultural mediation and collaboration inspired by the enduring ideal of Andalusian *convivencia*.

Epilogue

Plumbing the Transcontinental Mediterranean

Therefore, to think the Mediterranean, one needs
to play both games: the one that acknowledges
difference and the one that narrows inequalities;
the one that opens to the other and the one
that preserves communal relationships of solidarity.

—Franco Cassano, *Southern Thought and Other Essays on the Mediterranean*

Suppose the Mediterranean doesn't exist. Suppose the term itself only designates its lack of realization, spelling aporia rather than indisputable existence. Suppose that it is no more than "our trembling questioning as to its reality" (Stétié n.p.). Whether incarnated as a fading historical category defeated by the rise of nationalism (Ben-Yehoyada) or as a utopian identification mediating unrealizable projects of countermodernity, the concept has historically developed at loggerheads with politically engaged planes of action. Yet if it arises as a stubbornly apolitical construct, the multiple forms of Mediterranean identity claims that mobilize it are, in turn, eminently political. If the Mediterranean exists only as a result of its conceptual enunciation, what does it mean to *choose* to be Mediterranean? What is it a proxy for?

As is often true in other cases, the intrinsic modularity of the term impedes clear elucidation. Depending on the geographic location from which one may be speaking or the social context of the utterance, the designation *Mediterranean* can refer to a vast array of judgments hinging primarily on whether the label is imposed or self-attributed. For police work and official identification purposes in France, a "Mediterranean type" may be a euphemism to designate someone of North African heritage in a paradigmatic example of the "othering" uses to which the concept may be put. In contrast the appropriations of a Mediterranean identity that this book discusses need to be construed as deliberate identity claims, antidotes to claustrophobic identity discourses throughout the Mediterranean world.[1] A transcontinental Mediterranean is eminently connected, relational, and contiguous. It forms an extension of the space of the Maghreb to which it is bound through the presence of other cultural idioms born of the region's interactive history. Whether its poetic configuration echoes national tensions regarding diversity or seeks to obliterate them through a vertigo of translations and detours, the Mediterranean surges as a plane of connectivity. It is a continent—one that contains, holds together, places within the same inclusive space the many shores of the sea. Through this coextensivity it emphasizes both tensions and conjunctions, rifts and continuities. New Mediterranean models need to be devised that do not simply rehearse the to-and-fro movement from ex-colony to ex-metropole. In the quest for a paradigm of choice in the context of the modern Mediterranean, Assia Djebar's "trans-Mediterranean *navette*," shuttling between shores and texts, languages and geographies, is a particularly suitable candidate (MacDonald)—that is, a fully deployed *navette* that extends through plurilingualism beyond the conventional model of Maghrebi bilingualism crystallized around French and Arabic.

Building on Sharon Kinoshita's concept of a "heuristic device" and gesturing to Stétié's "trembling questioning as to its reality," the transcontinental trope is distinct from essentialist readings of Mediterranean identity. As each writer invents his or her own Mediterranean, the sea morphs into a reflecting surface on which to project and sometimes resolve conflicting claims to modernity. Zygmunt Bauman has emphasized the fundamental fluidity of our global moment with his concept of "liquid modernity," a configuration that harkens back to the dynamic of fluctuation and modularity of the Mediterranean critical construct. In a corrective to the increasing policing of borders and boundary lines along the shore, the material manifestation of the sea deploys its fraught history as mediating surface. Yet it also endures as an unpassable checkpoint. After twenty years of vivid representations of tumefied illegal bodies washing up on the shores of Europe, the sea's incarnation of the unbridgeable rift separating entitled, nomadic subjects and abjected, disenfranchised migrants has become an irrefutable reality. The vast discrepancy separating Mokeddem's nomadic framework from the *hrig* depicted by al-Baqqash or Cruz is testimony to this ever-increasing fracture. At this juncture the Mediterranean maritime model of connectivity takes on darker hues. This notable evolution serves as a powerful reminder of the inescapable limits of the models of contact and openness that our critical moment so eagerly strives to apply to cultural exchanges. The brutal reality of clandestine migration calls attention to the fact that national restrictions often inflict their unrelenting violence on the world's least desirable populations. If elite subjectivities can happily be formed by rootless *cabotage* to the multiple centers of the Global North, the promise of mobility rings significantly hollower for the thousands of disenfranchised African migrants attempting to clandestinely escape a future of destitution at the risk of their lives. For these global subjects the strictures of the nation are an inescapable reality, whose very tangible aftermath cannot simply be theorized away. The weight of these dystopian trans-Mediterranean patterns of migration certainly goes a long way to complicate our epistemologies. They bring a nuanced corrective to our valorization of frameworks reverberating with a postnational promise.

Considerations of the Mediterranean often wrap themselves in the shroud of postideological, apolitical models. These readings hail from all shores. In the context of Israeli cultural politics, where the dealings with the region's de facto multiconfessionalism remain a key issue for national politics, David Ohana poses the hypothesis of a "new" Israeli identity defined as a "*non-ideological* Mediterranean melting-pot blending together immigrants from east and west, from the Christian countries and the Muslim countries . . . constructed out of geography and culture" (Ohana, foreword xvi, my emphasis). As he argues in "Israel and the Mediterranean Option," Israeli *yam tikhoniut* (Mediterraneanism) performs the shift "from Oslo to Barcelona," that is, from the failed political promise of the Oslo peace process to possible inclusion in the Euro-Mediterranean partnership born of the 1995 Barcelona Declaration (Hochberg 41). Attempting to set Israel on an inclusive "European trajectory," *yam tikhoniut* develops as a counterpoint to hostile Middle Eastern politics (43). Reactivating mythicized renderings of the past dating back to the 1940s, this vision emphasizes Hebrew contributions to the history of the sea alongside Roman and Greek influences by aligning the biblical people of Israel with other Mediterranean civilizations (Shavit, "The Mediterranean World" 106).[2] This incorporation into the Mediterranean portrays Israel as a plural society favoring dialogue over warfare and plurality over chauvinism. Similar preoccupations animate broader visions of the Mediterranean as an anti–clash-of-civilizations paradigm (Barbé), a framework that advocates for collaboration and cross-cultural understanding. Emerging in the form of a rejection of rigid nationalism, either as an aspiration during the colonial period or as an alternative model of governance after independence, these Mediterranean affiliations propose to eschew the dangers of ethnic exclusion and sectarian strife. In their stead they favor "vital dialogue" (Ohana, "Israel and the Mediterranean Option," n.p.) and openness to the world in a humanistic gesture. In the context of the war-torn Middle East or in the authoritarian Maghreb, the proposition is certainly enticing (Bouraoui; Dugas, *Algérie*).

Yet the issue of the nonideological nature of this transnational move remains fraught with complexities. Questioning the naturalized "geo-cultural affinity" theorized by Ohana in the Israeli case, Gil Hochberg suggests that Mediterraneanist arguments have had the effect of deepening the fracture between a transnationally redeployed Israel and a postcolonial Arab Muslim Middle East (46). For, as she argues, if Israel joins Italy, Greece, and the mythical space of turn-of-the-century cosmopolitan Alexandria as the paragon of cultural diversity, tolerance, and hospitality, it does so in opposition to its Arab neighbors, which the comparison indirectly relegates to the quicksand of conservatism and rigidity. In contrast to Ohana's reading, she thus concludes with Sharon Rothbard that "Mediterraneanism in an ideology" (57). In a discrepant reading of the concept, Alexandra Nocke suggests instead that this Mediterranean form of identification is "link[ed] to a stratum in the Israeli leftist peace camp, which seeks to find a peaceful solution to the Arab-Israeli conflict . . . [as it] seek[s] to enhance rapprochement and peaceful coexistence between Israelis and Palestinians" (242). Regardless of how one may ultimately construe this Mediterranean strategy, its entanglements with the complex web of Middle Eastern politics are undeniable, as Nocke herself recognizes despite subscribing to Ohana's assertion of the concept's nonideological nature.[3] In the context of the Maghreb, Mediterranean affiliations have often refused to consider a possible contribution of Arab nationalism to a suitable revised model of Maghrebi identity.[4] In its stead these alternative Maghrebi affiliations have leaned toward the universalism that postcolonial subjects mired in the oppositional identitarian models born of independence have too often been begrudged. Yet the very choice of universalism is in itself an eminently partisan move, and its supposedly nonideological stance remains an elusive ideal. Elusive too is Nadia Khouri-Dager's recent paradigm of a Nouvelle Andalousie (New Andalusia) of exchanges, translations, freely elected affiliations, nomadism, and, most important, fully reclaimed plurality, which appropriates the palimpsestic history of the Arab world in a utopian effort to reach universalism. "The Andalusian spirit," she asserts, "is another translation of the word *métissage*," a judgment remarkable for its obliviousness to the complex political resonance of al-Andalus on both sides of the Strait of Gibraltar (n.p.).[5]

What these would-be nonideological readings lack is an acknowledgment of the political thrust of Mediterranean tropes. Khatibi's other-thought, under whose auspices this book has developed, is resolutely averse to the strictures of totalizing systems of thought. Yet it does not amount to political irrelevance. It is necessarily a "concrete thought of difference" ("Pensée-Autre" 15) anchored in the postcolonial realities of the Maghreb. As Khatibi emphasizes, the specific critique born of the Maghreb's colonial history requires a degree of politicization that will necessarily differ from the subversive models at work in the former colonial centers. As such it is as removed from inherited thought systems as it is from the preoccupations animating Blanchot's or Derrida's thoughts of difference, which need to be adapted to better fit the kind of struggles animating Maghrebi subjectivities. Claudia Esposito rightly sees this position as a rejection of uncritical multiculturalism, of a "simple assertion of the plurality of monolithic cultural forms" (xiv). The revolutionizing potential of other-thought runs deeper. As Khatibi's paradigm materializes as "minoritarian, marginal, fragmentary, and incomplete" ("Pensée-Autre" 13), it concurrently asserts the need for politically imbued relationality.[6] His other-thought is first and foremost a marginal mode of thinking refusing to reject alterity. It abjures a position of self-reliance rid of the need for others (what Khatibi calls "autosuffisance" in its most exclusive sense). Undermining any hegemonic desire within specific cultural forms (local entities aspiring to universality), this "concrete thought of difference" supposes a linkage to other marginal, subdued, minor positions in a common cartography of rebellion: "We are trying to move toward a planetary and plural thought" (25).[7]

Denouncing "the lie of the assimilationist model that has turned difference into a phantom" (Khanna 166), this model concurrently resists its own erasure. Its deployment works against the grain of the assimilation enacted through the process of nation formation. Ranjana Khanna has argued that Renan-inspired national amnesia relegates difference to a space of silence and invisibility. In this context the need for a radical articulation of plurality surges anew. An attentive Mediterranean reading practice needs to consistently emphasize the connective networks afforded by a maritime frame of action. Through it self-aware plurality works to restore the memory of a more distant past in a process Khanna has called melancholic. This mechanism turns the deep sense of loss resulting from the violent erasure of difference into an effusive "lived political memory" (166)—a source of praxis. Revealing the deep mechanisms lying behind its obliteration in a national context, this retrieved difference reaches far beyond a mere oppositional consciousness. It shapes a courageous reflection on identity that chips away at the metaphysical and material conditions of its alienation in the manner postulated by Khatibi's other-thought (here against the forces of nationalist assimilation and neocolonialism; in Khatibi's context against the Maghreb's alienating colonial and theological legacies). With its articulation in melancholic modes of remembrance, this reflection rehabilitates the rich sedimented history of the Maghreb, pressing for alternative and more democratic politics. This is not merely a perfunctory politics of multiculturalism, the "simple assertion of the plurality of monolithic cultural forms" that Esposito rightly indicts. It is a forward-thinking mode of action, distrustful of nostalgia for the politically fallow elite cosmopolitanism bred by empire—the cosmopolitanism that Ben-Yehoyada identifies as a prominent force of countermodernity. This Mediterranean is agentive, deliberately chosen, forcefully staking claims to the political. It is not a capitulation to the throbbing wound of a loss, nor is it an escapist paradigm whereby depoliticized nomadism can be freely relished without any imperative to collective thinking or political activism.

Situating the Maghreb in the fertile context of Mediterranean studies does not induce neglect for the kind of considerations that inform cultural analysis in a national context. The transcontinental makes it possible to track and propose resolutions to issues pertinent to both national and transnational contexts—and to all other scales postulated in between and around those two poles. It thus resists surrendering the political arena to fundamentalist forces, in either religious or nationalist garb. Tackling depoliticized paradigms of deterritorialization is essential to constructing alternative transnational patterns that would be attentive to the urgency of engaging totalitarian claims to the nation (whether Islamist or "nationalitarian" in Béji's words). As this book comes to a close, the recent terrorist threats to a budding democracy in Tunisia by the Bardo and Sousse attacks are testimony enough of the enduring relevance of the national as a battlefield yet to be reclaimed. And indeed the postrevolutionary parliamentary discussions around the possible mention of Tunisia's historical inclusion in a Mediterranean civilization in the 2014 Constitution show that Mediterranean claims have a key role to play in national debates when the time comes to seek effective ways to promote democracy.[8] A thorough examination of the Mediterranean sheds light on some unresolved issues burdening the Maghreb: identity issues (coexistence among communities, ethnicities, religions), but also the working through of colonial trauma. Eschewing the "neocolonial" desire for a cosmopolitan past enmeshed with the order of colonialism identified by Dobie (403), this heuristic line forms a sustained effort to bring the detours afforded by the Mediterranean to bear on the Maghrebi subject's engagement with a national construct still to be realized. It colors efforts to inflect this heritage and redefine it along more democratic lines through the melancholic reclaiming of more inclusive historical narratives. It is therefore crucial to hint at these other alignments through which southern Europe and North Africa, or conflicting confessional spaces, can be recast as belonging to the same cultural logic. Developing the insights cited as epigraph, Franco Cassano has suggested that "fundamentalism is not the expression of the essence of Islamic culture but is the option that prevails after the defeat of nationalism [to bring about equality with the West]" (*Southern Thought* 146). In light of the exponential rise of jihadist movements as an appealing model of action today, developing alternative political narratives rooted in more tolerant readings of identity may be our best chance to promote an appeased relation to modernity.

ACKNOWLEDGMENTS

A book is an itinerary, a journey, a story of growth. It is polyphonic, textured—resonating with the voices and words of those whose insights served to shape it. Along the way I gained perspective from the most unexpected, often anonymous interlocutors in chance encounters on the streets of the Mediterranean or in fleeting conversations in the hallways of American conference centers. To all of you not acknowledged by name below, my sincerest thanks for indelibly leaving your mark.

This book started as a work on alternative modernities in the Mediterranean in the Department of Literature at the University of California, San Diego. Although the original thesis has little in common with these pages, the guidance and support I received during those formative years have encouraged me to plot a new course I may not have dared to chart on my own. I owe a debt of gratitude and esteem to Winifred Woodhull, as well as Michael Davidson, Hasan Kayali, Lisa Lowe, the much regretted Rosemary Marangoly George, who with her customary intuition was the first to orient me toward Mediterranean studies, and Oumelbanine Zhiri, whose support and friendship endured far beyond my time at UCSD. Among early supporters I want to recognize Elisabeth Manivel, David Harvey, and Román de la Campa. None of this would have been possible without them.

I have been fortunate to be surrounded by many congenial colleagues and students. My gratitude goes first to Tulane University for providing me with the space and peace of mind necessary for this budding project to mature and materialize. Many thanks to the faculty, staff, and students of the Department of French and Italian at Tulane for fostering such a collegial atmosphere and lavishing friendship and support when I needed it. I want to extend my appreciation to Jean

Bidima, Khedidja Boudaba, Linda Carroll, Elena Daniele, Bouchaib Gadir, Marky Jean-Pierre, Charles Mignot, Roberto Nicosia, Kristin Okoli, Vaheed Ramazani, Alexandra Reuber, Oana Sabo, Annette Sojic, Teresa Villa-Ignacio, Toby Wikström, Jeanny Keck, and Darnell Pierce. I owe a special debt of gratitude to Felicia McCarren for her generous, ever insightful guidance and for always caring about my personal and professional well-being. My heartfelt thanks go to Michael Syrimis, Beth Poe, Fayçal Falaky, and Thomas Klingler for volunteering their time, for mentoring lunches, and for always making themselves available to me. Beyond the department I am especially indebted to the Morocco Group, the Newcomb College Institute, my Faculty Writing Retreat cohort, and many colleagues from the School of Liberal Arts for their incisive questions and comments; Elio Brancaforte, Jean Dangler, Elisabeth McMahon, Esra Özcan, Yigit Akin, and Ferruh Yilmaz were particularly helpful. I want to express my thanks to Dean Carole Haber, Tara Hamburg, and the Dean's Office for their support of my research and of this book. It is a true privilege to be a part of the Tulane community. At Yale many thanks to Sonia Arias, Ora Avni, Emily Bakermeier and the Office of the Provost, Agnès Bolton, Kamari Clarke, Edwin Duval, Moira Fradinger, Inderpal Grewal, Marcia Inhorn, Alice Kaplan, Lilia Labidi, Nadia Marzouki, Christopher L. Miller, Maurice Samuels, Françoise Schneider, Julia Titus, and Yue Zhuo. I had the privilege of teaching and advising brilliant Ph.D. students both at Tulane and at Yale; among them Nathalie Batraville, Nicole Horne, Ryan Joyce, Mary Anne Lewis, Anne-Marie McManus, Sarah Piazza, and Aaron Schlosser have enriched me in more ways than I can tell. A special mention goes to Anne-Marie McManus and Yasser Elhariry for their help navigating the meanders of Arabic transliteration and, over the years, for their help with Arabic, to Hakim Abderrezak, Fayçal Falaky, and Bouchaib Gadir. Whatever inaccuracies remain are mine. I am beholden to the library staff at Tulane University (especially Joshua Lupkin and Sean Knowlton), Yale University, the Fonds Roblès-Patrimoine Méditerranéen at the Université Paul Valéry in Montpellier (Guy Dugas and Florence Chaudoreille), the Archives Nationales d'Outre-Mer, the Biblioteca Nacional de España, the Archives Nationales de Tunisie, and the Centre d'Études Diocésain–Les Glycines in Algiers (Guillaume Michel).

Christopher L. Miller, mentor and friend, consistent model of integrity and kindheartedness, guided the first steps of this project with his customary intellectual rigor and insight. I owe the breadth of my argument to two of his many provocative questions that have resonated with me throughout the writing of this book. I thank him for consistently challenging me to think beyond my comfort zone and to probe what makes this Mediterranean trope truly unique. Alec Hargreaves and Marta Segarra have been two staunch supporters of my work. I regard them as the kind of accomplished and dedicated academics that I hope to become. This project would certainly have taken a very different turn if not for the stimulating discussions and insightful feedback from which I benefited in several stages of the writing. For their encouragements and invigorating comments, my gratitude goes to Yasser Elhariry, tireless interlocutor and flowing source of inspiration, Claudia Esposito for her abiding friendship and dazzling mind, as well as Hakim Abderrezak, David Álvarez, Safoi Babana-Hampton, Ziad Bentahar, Tahar Bekri, Maya Boutaghou, Norbert Bugeja, Carla Calargé, Brian Catlos, Carole Fadda-Conrey, Patrick Crowley, David Damrosch, Alfonso de Toro, Madeleine Dobie, Anne Donadey, Seth Graebner, Alexandra Gueydan, Olivia Harrison, Jason Herbeck, Samia Kassab, Sharon Kinoshita, Anouar Majid, Elizabeth Marcus, Felicia McCarren, Anne-Marie McManus, Jean-Marc Moura, Martin Munro, Mohamed-Salah Omri, Oana Panaïté, Graziella Parati, Laura Reeck, Alison Rice, Mireille Rosello, Cristián Ricci, Adelaide Russo, Debarati Sanyal, Ronnie Scharfman, Shaden Tageldin, Dominic Thomas, Corbin Treacy, Sevinç Turkkan, Ieme Van Der Poel, Teresa Villa-Ignacio, Rebecca Walkowitz, Richard Watts, and Mark Wollaeger. In Tunisia thanks to the Kassab-Charfi family for giving me a home away from home; to Samia Kassab, Ahmed Mahfoudh, the School of Doctoral Studies at the University of Tunis, and all the wonderful graduate students that I had the privilege of teaching there; to Rafik Ben Salah, Tahar Ben Guiza, Nadia Ghrandi, and Alia Mabrouk for their hospitality and wonderful company. In Algiers I am indebted to Les Glycines and Guillaume Michel; to David Álvarez and Si Kamel, my indefatigable travel companions; to Azzedine Fergui for sharing his love of the casbah; to Naima Bayhou for her friendship; and to Najet Khadda for her patience and her kind authorization to reproduce Mohammed Khadda's *Méditerranée*.

My research was facilitated by the generous support of the UCSD Center for the Humanities, the Columbia University Center for European Studies in partnership with the Andrew W. Mellon Foundation, the Northeast Modern Language Association, the Office of the

Provost and the Whitney Humanities Center at Yale University, and the School of Liberal Arts at Tulane University. The publication of this book was made possible through a publishing grant from the School of Liberal Arts at Tulane. At Fordham University Press my gratitude goes to Thomas Lay for his unflagging support and expert guidance throughout the publishing process, as well as to the press's competent and dedicated staff, among them Kathy Sweeney, Kate O'Brien-Nicholson, and Will Cerbone. Thanks to the Modern Language Initiative managing editor Tim Roberts and copyeditor Judith Hoover for their kindness and professionalism. I am grateful to the press's two anonymous readers for their invaluable suggestions and kind words of support.

As for all of you, scattered over three continents, those closest to the heart—only your selflessness and unconditional love made this project possible and worthwhile. This book is also for you.

Parts of the introduction were previously published as "The Languages of Translocality: What Plurilingualism Means in a Maghrebi Context," *Expressions maghrébines* 11.2 (2012): 9–26. Reprinted with permission. Parts of chapter 1 were previously published as "Between Nostalgia and Desire: *L'Ecole d'Alger*'s Transnational Identifications and the Case for a Mediterranean *Relation*," *International Journal of Francophone Studies* 10.3 (2007): 359–76.

NOTES

INTRODUCTION: THE TRANSCONTINENTAL MAGHREB

1. For the epigraph: "Sur la place d'El Boramar / Tes yeux / La nuit aux chants du condor / Scrutent la traversée du silence / Flûte de Pan Lune levant l'ancre / C'est la fête des amarres Appel des Andes."

2. "'El Boramar' (Bord de mer) est une petite place dans la ville catalane, Collioure, où se trouve une tour ancienne construite par les Arabes."

3. A more complete history can be found on the Fort Saint Elme website: http://www.fortsaintelme.fr/index.php/fr/fort.

4. One could also add to the list ancillary regional initiatives, such as the 1995 Euro-Mediterranean partnership, redesigned in 2008 as the Union for the Mediterranean, whose façade of trans-Mediterranean collaboration conceals a more opportunistic strategic alliance in priority areas such as free trade and migration management. On the Barcelona Process, see Thomas, *Africa and France*; Wolff, "Border Management" and *The Mediterranean Dimension.*

5. According to Cyril Aslanov, the evidence of a dominant lingua franca in the Levant is more tenuous.

6. For a more thorough discussion of *pataouète*, see chapter 1.

7. On Mediterranean migrations in the age of European empires, see Clancy-Smith; Andrea Smith; Liauzu, *Histoire des migrations.*

8. See Esposito et al.; Ricci, *Hay moros en la costa, Letras marruecas*, and *Literatura periférica*; Abderrezak, *Ex-centric Migrations*; Parati; Thomas, *Afroeuropean Cartographies.*

9. Notable additional examples of this corpus, which remains woefully understudied, include Larbi El-Harti, *Después de Tánger* (After Tangier), winner of the 2002 Sial Prize for fiction; Najat El Hachmi, *Jo també soc catalana* (I Am Catalan Too); Leila Karrouch, *De Nador a Vic* (From Nador to Vic), winner of the 2004 Columna Jove Prize; Mohsen Melliti, *Pantanella*; and Rachida Lamrabet, *Vrouwland* (Woman's Land) and *Een kind van God* (A Child of God), which won the 2008 BNG New Literature Prize. To this budding corpus of texts we can add hispanophone

writing from northern Morocco, such as Ahmed Ararou's "Rickiem" and Mohamed Sibari's *Cuentos de Larache* (Tales of Larache). For a critical discussion of these texts, see Esposito et al.; Ricci, *Letras marruecas* and *Literatura periférica*; Segarra, "Migrant Literature"; Bueno Alonso; Van der Poel, "Unlike(ly) Home(s)."

10. For a broader contextualization of Khatibi's thought, see Rice, "Translating Plurality"; Hiddleston, *Understanding Postcolonialism*; Lionnet, "Counterpoint and Double Critique"; Qader.

11. "Une pensée-autre, une pensée peut-être inouïe de la différence."

12. "Maghreb, ici, désigne le nom de cet écart, de ce non-retour au modèle de sa religion et de sa théologie (si déguisées soient-elles sous des idéologies révolutionnaires) . . . d'autre part le nom 'arabe' désigne une guerre de nominations et d'idéologies qui mettent au jour la pluralité active du monde arabe [une pluralité comprenant] ses marges spécifiques (berbères, coptes, kurdes . . . et marge des marges: le féminin)."

13. "Un droit à la différence, qui se contente de répéter sa revendication, sans se mettre en question et sans travailler sur les lieux actif et réactifs de son insurrection."

14. "L'Occident habite notre être intime, non point comme une extériorité absolue et dévastatrice, mais bel et bien comme une différence, un conglomérat de différences à poser en tant que tel dans toute pensée de la différence."

15. "La condition d'une responsabilité qui reste encore à prendre en charge."

16. "Domination exogène et endogène."

17. Abdelwahab Meddeb's *Pari de civilisation* resurrects the history of scientific, philological, and philosophical interactions between Arab and Greek scholarships.

18. "Traduction en arabe du monothéisme abrahamique."

19. "Il faudrait penser le Maghreb tel qu'il *est*, site topographique entre l'Orient, l'Occident et l'Afrique, et tel qu'il puisse se mondialiser pour son propre compte."

20. "Résonne dans sa pluralité (linguistique, culturelle, politique) . . . [un Maghreb] repensé, décentré, subverti."

21. See also Silverstein; Dine.

22. Other attempts to postulate a Mediterranean unity gave in to polarizing essentialist readings. The work on exogamy by the ethnologist Germaine Tillion, which had the unintended effect of casting the region as a space of belatedness and stagnation, is a case in point (see Dobie 393).

23. Less generous readings of their work have rightly emphasized their downplaying of "not only the role of cultural representations . . . [but also] the social role of representations, not to mention the representational meaning-production of the social sciences, including historiography" (Fogu 4). Their configuration thus seems to have "truly missed the boat that Braudel set on the course of a self-conscious and critical historiography of mentalities and civilizations" (4). In addition, as Naor

Ben-Yehoyada and others have consistently emphasized, their decision to ascribe the end of Mediterranean history to the onset of the modern period had the unfortunate effect of impeding scholarly investigations of the modern Mediterranean as a unified object of study.

24. A cognate form of maritime criticism has emerged in studies of the novel, such as Cesare Casarino's *Modernity at Sea* and Margaret Cohen's *The Novel and the Sea*, which focus on the sea as a space to be charted and explored.

25. Jacques Stephen Alexis and Derek Walcott pursue the same analytical line in their own writing. See Dash.

26. On Africa-Maghreb connections, I would like to point out Hélène Tissières's *Transmigrational Writings between the Maghreb and Sub-Saharan Africa* and Ziad Bentahar's "Continental Drift: The Disjunction of North and Sub-Saharan Africa."

27. For a theorization of other forms of non-Francocentric Maghrebi transcolonialism, see Olivia C. Harrison's work on Maghrebi-Palestinian networks.

28. Exemplary in this respect is the "transversal" work of the Centre de recherches francophones at the University of Leipzig in Germany (see De Toro). For Arabic, I am referring more particularly to Muhsin Al-Musawi ("Engaging Globalization"), who proposes to read modern Arabic literature in relation to the contemporary global order and its conflicting cultural claims, and to Hosam Aboul Ela, who calls for its critical incorporation into the transnational category of the Global South, of which it is part.

29. Ben Yehoyada makes this argument in relation to Ottoman port cities from1870 to 1920, but a similar case may be made about Maghrebi port cities on the eve of independence.

30. Other examples of Camus-based scholarship include Rencontres Méditerranéennes Albert Camus; Toumi.

31. On Djebar, see Gueydan; on Bey, see Rosello, "Comment s'inventer"; Rice, *Polygraphies*.

32. For a thorough analysis of the evolutions of allegory through time, see Machosky; Copeland and Struck.

33. The reference to "impossible mourning" is obviously borrowed from Derrida's reflections on the aporia of mourning in "Mnemosyne": "Is the most distressing, or even the most deadly infidelity that of a *possible mourning* which would interiorize within us the image, idol, or ideal of the other who is dead and lives only in us? Or is it that of the impossible mourning, which, leaving the other his alterity, respecting thus his infinite remove, either refuses to take or is incapable of taking the other within one self, as in the tomb or the vault of some narcissism?" (6). As chapter 3 demonstrates, Mokeddem's staging of melancholic incorporation somewhat complicates this tension.

CHAPTER 1. HYBRIDIZING THE MYTH, ALLEGORIZING ALGERIA

1. Seth Graebner identifies Ahmed Bouri's possibly unfinished *Musulmans et chrétiennes* (Muslim Men and Christian Women, 1912), published in serial form in the Oran weekly newspaper *El Hack*, as the first of these Algerian novels decades before the fight for independence (*History's Place* 126). Other so-called *roman indigènes* include works by Mohammed Ben Cherif, Khodja Chukri, Hadj Hamou Abdelkader, and Mohammed Ould Cheikh. Their position at the heart of a complex web of assimilationist politics, linguistic mimicry, and colonial censorship tinges their elaboration of a counterdiscourse with the hue of unresolved ambiguity. See also Déjeux, *Maghreb littératures*; Dunwoodie, *Francophone Writing*.

2. As I will argue, the same denunciation of national mystification can in fact be found in Kateb: "It was then that we should have turned a blind eye to the mirage, refused the promises, broken with the illusion of belated reform, sparked off rebellion [C'était là qu'il fallait fermer les yeux sous le mirage, refuser les promesses, rompre avec l'illusion des réformes tardives, mettre le feu aux poudres]" ("Une étoile de sang noir" [A Star of Black Blood] 201).

3. "Dramatique amoureuse de l'Algérie."

4. "Le même pays."

5. "Je pensais alors que 'du même pays' voulait dire splendeur côtière, immensité de paysages . . . et il m'apparut que toutes les explications des déchirements et désastres et luttes historiques de l'Algérie avaient été grevées d'un grand oubli."

6. Valéry himself is a paradigmatic example of the colonial period's fluctuating engagements with the Mediterranean. Whereas his "Mediterranean Inspirations" sheds light on the sea's hybrid nature, an earlier text, "La Crise de l'esprit" churns up the usual stereotypical dichotomy between a dormant South and an industrious, modern North (Dobie 393–94).

7. "Ce grand oubli . . . seuls certains textes d'Albert Camus l'ont exprimé."

8. Significantly Edward Said associated Camus's choice of a realist aesthetic with the enactment of his colonialist affect: "Camus' writing is informed by an extraordinarily belated, in some ways incapacitated colonial sensibility, which enacts an imperial gesture within and by means of a form, the realistic novel, well past its greatest achievements" (*Culture and Imperialism* 176).

9. "Le passage d'une réalité allégorique à une allégorie devenue réalité."

10. It is nevertheless important to point out that Kateb himself reiterated this oppositional reading between colonial and native authorship in a 1975 interview, where he contrasted what he perceived as the lukewarm reception of his and Mohammed Dib's work in the metropole to Camus's emphatic success (Corpet et al. 60).

11. L'Association des écrivains algériens (Algerian Writers Association) was founded in 1921, together with Le Grand Prix Littéraire de l'Algérie (Great Literary Prize of Algeria) and, in 1924, an Algérianiste literary journal, *Afrique*. For further discussion of the genealogy and evolution of the Algérianiste movement see Siblot, "Pères spirituels"; Dunwoodie, *Writing French Algeria* chapter 4; Graebner, *History's Place* chapter 2.

12. "L'Afrique du nord . . . n'est, en somme, que l'ancienne province romaine d'Afrique."

13. "En d'autres termes, l'Afrique française d'aujourd'hui, c'est l'Afrique romaine qui continue à vivre, qui n'a jamais cessé de vivre, même aux époques les plus troubles et les plus barbares. Les archéologues connaissaient parfaitement cette Afrique du passé." However, romanization was never the smooth, all-inclusive process claimed by Bertrand (Cailler 52–53). In Graebner's words, "Bertrand does not so much discover Roman ruins as build them; on the already fading memories of heroic French Algeria, he fabricates vestiges worthy of Empire" (*History's Place* 49).

14. "L'essentiel, c'est le vieil héritage de la Berbérie romanisée." "Le berbère est convertissable qui a été autrefois chrétien et latin." I use the self-chosen term *Amazigh* to designate what colonial historiography has usually identified as "Berber" populations. Bertrand identifies this enduring Latin heritage in the community's "dress, jewelry, baths, buildings, universities, mosques [costume, les bijoux, les bains, les bâtisses, les universités, les mosquées]," concluding, "All this is still inspired by the old Latin ways [Tout cela continue à suivre le vieux modèle latin]" (*Les Villes* 24). On rebarbarization, see Lorcin, "Decadence."

15. "Je pensais . . . que la France, fatiguée par des siècles de civilisation, pouvait se rajeunir au contact de cette apparente et vigoureuse barbarie."

16. "D'énergie et quelquefois d'héroïsme, de régénération physique, intellectuelle, nationale et sociale."

17. "On bâtissait l'Alger moderne."

18. "J'ai écarté le décor islamique et pseudo-arabe qui fascinait des regards superficiels, et j'ai montré . . . une Afrique vivante qui se différencie à peine des autres pays latins de la Méditerranée."

19. The creation of Auguste Maurice Victor Robinet (better known by his pen name, Musette), the adventures of Cagayous were first published in the satirical journal *Le Turco*. From there, these stories were compiled into small weekly bulletins, which would sell within a few hours. The first book-length collection of stories, *Cagayous, pochades algériennes*, came out in 1896. It was followed by over twenty volumes. The character reached such popularity that he became ubiquitous in colonial popular culture, participating directly in the mythology of French Algeria (Prochaska, "History as Literature"). See also Siblot, "Cagayous anti-juif"; Dunwoodie, *Writing French Algeria* 140–43. On *patatouète*, see Bacri; Audisio, introduction to Cagayous; Brua, *Fables* and *La Parodie*.

20. "Mais, au fond, les autres les méprisaient à cause de leur sang mélangé et de leur ressemblance avec les Maures et les Juifs."

21. For additional discussion of the specificities of Maltese identity, see Andrea Smith; Mallette.

22. Gobineau's ideals held great sway over Bertrand's vision of race as a spiritual entity that cannot withstand mixing (*Sur les routes* 218). Anti-Semitism was another chief feature of Bertrand's writings, as has been widely argued in reference to the "Death to Jews!" episode in *Le Sang des races* (see, for instance, Dunwoodie, *Writing French Algeria* 86; Graebner, *History's*

Place 38). Anti-Semitism flared up throughout Algeria in the years leading up to and following *l'affaire Dreyfus* in France; of note are the rise of newspapers like *L'Antijuif* in Algiers, a city under the mayoralty of Max Régis, the leader of the Ligue antijuive (anti-Jewish movement), and the pogroms in major Algerian cities in 1898, the same year that saw the publication of the disquieting volume *Cagayous antijuif* (Cagayous Anti-Jew).

23. The natives' increased political visibility found its most direct expression in the publication of numerous texts dealing with the failure of colonial assimilation in *Afrique* (Graebner, *History's Place* 71–88; Dunwoodie, *Writing French Algeria* 148–74; Haddour 10–16).

24. Although predominant in criticism, the name L'École d'Alger (also known as École Nord-Africaine des Lettres, the North African School of Letters) does not designate a unified literary movement; it was, in fact, refuted by Camus and Roblès. I use the designation to refer to the set of writers who coalesced around Charlot and who extended the Algérianistes' reflection on colonial hybridity and postulated a non-Latin Mediterranean form of identity.

25. Kateb himself published one of his earlier texts, the poem "Bonjour," in *Forge* in 1947. Furthermore a study of his correspondence reveals that he owed the acceptance of two of his manuscripts at the NRF to the same Camus whom he was so prompt to deride (Corpet et al. 23). Kateb and other native writers owed much of their early career to the support of individual members of L'École. Thus Mohammed Dib reports that his vocation as a novelist came to light in the wake of the 1948 Sidi Madani literary retreat that gathered European writers from L'École and their native consorts. The retreat led Dib to Jean Cayrol, who would later introduce him to the Éditions du Seuil, where his first novel, *La Grande Maison* (The Great House), would be published as the inaugural volume in Roblès's new collection "Méditerranée" ("Letter from Dib to Roblès," qtd. in Dugas, "Les Amitiés").

26. "Continent liquide aux contours solidifiés." "Pour les peuples de cette mer, il n'y a qu'une vraie patrie, cette mer elle-même . . . je dis: la patrie 'méditerranée,' en redonnant à ce qualificatif la force centripète que 'méditerranéenne' a complètement perdue."

27. "Son propre rassemblement."

28. "Je ne crois pas aux races pures . . . 'mon peuple,' a de multiples visages comme tout ce qui vit, et son authenticité repose, comme toutes les vérités, sur un amalgame d'antécédents suspects."

29. "Naturelle confusion des sangs." "Chaudron où mijote 'le sang des races,' avec une sauce assez piquante en vérité."

30. "Ce je ne sais quoi de juif et peut-être de nègre."

31. "Des jeunes, pour de jeunes, par des jeunes."

32. "L'Orient sémitique . . . de la mystique juive."

33. "Sous la domination romaine, la latinité n'y change presque rien."

34. "Constantes . . . de l'homme méditerranéen."

35. "L'Afrique du Nord, et spécialement l'Algérie, se présente à nous comme une image réduite, un véritable microcosme de tout le monde méditerranéen."

36. "L'amalgame de ces divers éléments est resté superficiel, plus apparent que réel . . . la communauté algérienne n'existe pas."

37. "L'Algérie *conquise* . . . [et] l'Algérie *colonisée.*"

38. Thus Emily Apter writes of "the idealized proto-Braudelian fantasy of 'Mediterranean man,' a Euro-African subject whose cultural attachments allow him to forget the *Realpolitik* of colonial power imbalance" ("Out of Character" 508). Apter follows a long tradition of critics who read Camus as an unrelenting colonialist whose work justified and further enacted the colonial system plaguing Algeria (Said; O'Brien; Haddour; Lacheraf). A more sympathetic reading of Camus has emphasized the courage of his appeals for a civilian truce in the midst of conflict and his determination to give a voice to the voiceless (Carroll; Esposito; Azza-Bekkat; Toumi; Gonzales; Spiquel).

39. "Édification, dans le cadre régional, d'une culture [méditerranéenne]."

40. "Cette odeur ou ce parfum qu'il est inutile d'exprimer: nous le sentons tous avec notre peau."

41. "Ici, je laisse à d'autres l'ordre et la mesure. C'est le grand libertinage de la nature et de la mer qui m'accapare tout entier. Dans ce mariage des ruines et du printemps, les ruines sont redevenues pierres, et perdant le poli imposé par l'homme, sont rentrées dans la nature. . . . Aujourd'hui enfin leur passé les quitte, et rien ne les distrait de cette force profonde qui les ramène au centre des choses qui tombent."

42. "Rien de ce qui est barbare ne peut nous être étranger."

43. "La Méditerranée est de tous les pays le seul peut-être qui rejoigne les grandes pensées orientales. Car elle n'est pas classique et ordonnée, elle est diffuse et turbulente. . . . Et à ce confluent, il n'y a pas de différence entre la façon dont vit un Espagnol ou un Italien des quais d'Alger, et les Arabes qui les entourent. Ce qu'il y a de plus essentiel dans le génie méditerranéen jaillit peut-être de cette rencontre unique dans l'histoire et la géographie née entre l'Orient et l'Occident."

44. "La race curieuse et forte qui vit sur nos côtes."

45. "[Une] sorte d'île immense, défendue par la mer mouvante au nord et au sud par les flots figés des sables . . . [un] pays sans nom."

46. "L'immense oubli . . . était la patrie définitive des hommes de sa race."

47. The 2010 Caravane Camus literary project, scheduled to move though France and Algeria on the occasion of the fiftieth anniversary of his death, is a recent reminder of Camus's split legacy in the world of Algerian letters. Supported by Yasmina Khadra's Algerian Cultural Center in Paris and a fraction of Algerian intellectuals, it was simultaneously the object of a petition in the name of anticolonialism. The project was finally canceled before its launch. On critiques and appropriations of Camus by Algerian authors, see Azza-Bekkat et al.; Rosello, "Comment s'inventer"; Rice, *Polygraphies*; and recent fiction (Daoud; Bachi; Grine).

48. Taking the argument further, Woodhull suggests that the novel is in fact "a figuration of the revolution's potential failure to ensure social equality for women" (1).

49. This sentiment pervades many literary representations of Constantine in the Algerian corpus. See, for instance, Ahlam Mostaghanemi's *Memory*

in the Flesh: "All the woods and the rocks here enlisted in the ranks of the revolution before you did. Some cities do not choose their destinies. They are sentenced by history and geography not to surrender" (13).

50. Graebner's detailed reading of the city's architecture complicates the assumption that the train station may simply be a symbol of triumphant colonialist modernity: it is rather a "hybrid product of colonial history . . . of the interactions between Algerians and French which made up colonial history and culture" (*History's Place* 267).

51. "[Il s'éteint] dans la bave d'une mer lamentablement vautrée, mère de mauvaise vie et de sang froid qui répand dans la ville un air de maléfice et de torpeur. . . . 'Pays de mendiants et de viveurs, patrie des envahisseurs de tout acabit, pense Mustapha, pays de cagoulardes et de femmes fatales'" (Kateb, *Nedjma* 61). I cite Richard Howard's translation as "*Nedjma* trans." When I cite both the original and the translation, the page number of the translation appears first.

52. "Chevelure fauve" (Kateb, *Nedjma* 61); "pâleur native" (73), "[des] blancheurs de fonderie" (73), "très brune, presque noire" (72).

53. "Une lueur exaspérée d'automne, une cité traquée qui se ferme au désastre" (Kateb, *Nedjma* 173).

54. "Fleuve tari" (Kateb, *Nedjma* 163). "Pseudo-Rachid issu trop tard de la mort paternelle, comme l'oued-el-Kebir ne prolongeant que l'ombre et la sécheresse du Rummel, sans lui restituter sa violence vaincue" (Kateb, *Nedjma* 170).

55. "Vaincu . . . traqué sous le Rocher comme les Maures chassés d'Andalousie . . . évasion sans issue" (Kateb, *Nedjma* 168).

56. "Transform[a]nt en paix la défaite" (Kateb, *Nedjma* 173). "Trop de pères pour naître au grand jour, trop d'ambitieuses races déçues, mêlées, confondues, contraintes de ramper dans les ruines" (Kateb, *Nedjma* 173).

57. "Spectre[s] ennobli[s]" (Kateb, *Nedjma* 165)

58. "Les restes des Romains . . . ce genre de ruines où l'âme des multitudes n'a eu que le temps de se morfondre, en gravant leur adieu dans le roc" (Kateb, *Nedjma* 164).

59. "Les ruines en filigrane de tous les temps" (Kateb, *Nedjma* 164).

60. "Celles que baigne le sang dans nos veines" (Kateb, *Nedjma* 164).

61. "Les inestimables décombres du présent" (Kateb, *Nedjma* 164).

62. "Le lieu [et] l'instant qui conviendrai[en]t pour les voir" (Kateb, *Nedjma* 164).

63. This concept of "building upon" also underlies Graebner's reading of the passage dedicated to the ruins of the present ("les inestimables décombres du présent" [Kateb, *Nedjma* 164]), which he takes rather literally in terms of a vertical directionality. Through it he opposes productive "baroque" ruins, "place[d] . . . on top of the new [cities]" (Graebner, *History's Place* 273) to spurious archaeological arguments typical of the colonial period, which located in the Roman ruins of Algeria the foundation of a new Latin Algeria under the aegis of French colonialism.

64. "Un nom peut-être plus ancient, peut-être byzantin; un nom peut-être plus ancient que Cirta" (Kateb, *Nedjma* 173).

65. "La vieille Numidie où se succèdent les descendants romains" (Kateb, *Nedjma* 165).

66. "Mais les Romains sont remplacés par les Corses; tous Corses, tous gardiens de prison, et nous prenons la succession des esclaves, dans le même bagne, près de la fosse aux lions, et les fils des Romains patrouillent l'arme à la bretelle" (Kateb, *Nedjma* 38).

67. "Ni les Numides ni les Barbaresques n'ont enfanté en paix" (Kateb, *Nedjma* 165).

68. It is interesting to note the parallel with Jean Sénac's discussion of what makes an Algerian author in *Le Soleil sous les armes* (The Sun under Arms, 1957): "*An Algerian writer is any writer who has definitively taken the side of the Algerian nation* . . . whether he writes in French, Arabic, or Berber [*Est écrivain algérien tout écrivain ayant définitivement opté pour la nation algérienne* . . . et celà [*sic*] aussi bien en français qu'en arabe ou en berbère]" 20–21).

69. As Graebner argues, *Nedjma* lent itself particularly well to a discussion of contrasting interpretations of Ibn Khaldun's historiographic model, thereby broaching broader issues regarding the nature of historiographic writing in the Maghreb. In his view the novel tackled "how to write a history of the Maghreb that would mesh with popular myth and collective memory, thereby allowing the colonized to become actors in it, in their own right" ("Kateb Yacine" 140).

70. The date of the Setif and Guelma riots, which were ferociously repressed by colonial troops and which mark a high point in the radicalization of the Algerian nationalists' demands, is 1945. The Algerian War of Independence began with an FLN attack on November 1, 1954.

71. "Dans sa force 'impersonnelle et concrète', la Kasbah d'Alger n'estelle pas un dédale? C'est cette force usurpée qui . . . transforme en exil toute tentative d'évasion. . . . Ali la Pointe et tous les condamnés à mort sont des enfants du polygone. Ils habitent une mort violente, comme j'écris dans une impasse."

72. On the significance of the polygon, see Aresu, *Counter-Hegemonic Discourse*.

73. "Pointant vers l'extérieur des angles offensifs." "Ils habitent une mort violente."

74. "*Gharib*, en arabe, signifie étranger. La *ghorba*, c'est l'exil. Le Maghreb, mot de même racine, était pour les Arabes une terre d'exil. Le même mot, *ghorba* en arabe, *gourbet* en turc, signifie à la fois l'errance du poète et la présence étrange de l'étranger."

75. "Les deux ombres se dissipent sur la route" (Kateb, *Nedjma* 31/245).

76. "Imaginez l'Andalousie, pendant la fin du Moyen-Âge. Imaginez l'apothéose du monde arabe en ce temps-là. Une famille venue du Yémen, établie à Séville et fixée à Tunis, donne le jour à Abou Zeid Abderrahmane Ibn Mohamed. On l'appellera Ibn Khaldoun." The same text appears in slightly altered form in "Nazim Hikmet" (239).

77. "Des Tolbas, des étudiants errants" (Kateb, *Nedjma* 116).

78. "Élu ou adopté en quelque sorte par les natifs qui entrèrent peu à peu dans sa famille, et finirent par en faire le vétéran de la communauté" (Kateb, *Nedjma* 117).

79. On this point see Soraya Tlatli's reading of the text in light of the figure of *atlal* (vestiges) in pre-Islamic poetry.

80. Many critics have commented on this point. See, for instance, Sellin; Bonn, "L'Irrégularité"; Gontard; Aresu, *Counter-Hegemonic Discourse*, among others.

81. Martine Mathieu-Job has emphasized the concordance between the three texts, *Nedjma*, and *Le Polygone étoilé*.

82. "L'Etrangère sans foi ni loi refugiée dans l'île, au temps de la captivité de Babylone; les juifs . . . l'avaient trouvée dans une hutte de branchages, dit-on, tout près de . . . leur quartier."

83. "L'introuvable amnésique de l'île des lotophages."

84. "L'insatiable Française . . . trois fois enlevée . . . une juive" (Kateb, *Nedjma* 97)

85. "Le Soudan unificateur, le soleil de l'avenir et l'ombre de la patrie des morts qui nous revient de la Haute-Égypte et de sa Trinité impersonnelle et concrète."

86. "Car l'histoire de notre tribu n'est écrite nulle part, mais aucun fil n'est jamais rompu pour qui recherche ses origines" (Kateb, *Nedjma* 137). On the symbolic and narrative significance of the figure of Si Mabrouk, see Abdoun.

87. Jacqueline Arnaud sees in this text "an attempt to synthesize Kateb's whole poetic and narrative *œuvre* . . . [which] gives a clearer sense of his *œuvre* in progress" (*Recherches* 439).

88. The name Ghriba (meaning "wondrous, unique") is ubiquitous in North African Judaism. There are no fewer than seven synagogues bearing the name in Libya, Tunisia, and Algeria (Stillman).

89. "[La synagogue] était à l'origine un boudoir de païenne. . . . Elle mourut dans sa hutte et dans son mystère sans jamais révéler sa religion ni ses origines; les fugitifs de Babylone, dit-on, émus du sort de l'Etrangère (ils ne l'appelaient plus qu'ainsi) l'honorèrent d'un temple marquant l'emplacement de la future synagogue."

90. The episode of the Israelites' crossing of the Red Sea is recorded in both the Old Testament (Exodus 14:15–29) and the Qur'an (Sura 26: al-Shuʿara', verses 60–66).

91. On Djerbian Jews, see Udovitch and Valensi; Attal and Sitbon; Salah-Eddine Tlatli.

92. "Israélites bannis après la chute de Ninive, Soudanais affranchis sans l'être . . . musulmans de schismes divers, et tous déviationnistes."

93. "Mémoire collective des enfants d'Abraham."

94. "Jamais le lotophage n'oublie la terre heureuse, le désert verdoyant en la mer du Milieu . . . [des hommes et femmes] hospitaliers dans leur mystère . . . aucune tentation n'en fait des apatrides." Both men and women are mentioned in the original text.

95. "Nos pères . . . des oueds mis à sec au profit de moindres ruisseaux, jusqu'à la confluence, la mer où nulle source ne reconnaît son murmure: l'horreur, la mêlée, le vide—l'océan" (Kateb, *Nedjma* 91).

96. "Alors qu'ils l'ont banni . . . ceux pour qui le Coran fut créé n'en sont même pas au paganisme, ni à l'âge de pierre" (Kateb, *Nedjma* 112).

97. "Ils n'ont pas voulu marcher; il a fallu d'autres peuples, d'autres hommes pour affronter l'espace" (Kateb, *Nedjma* 112).

98. "[Rêve] dissemin[é] au hasard des vents favorable" (Kateb, *Nedjma* 112).

99. "Le désert n'était rien de moins que le paradis ancient. . . . Seule une révolution pouvait le reconquérir" (Kateb, *Nedjma* 112).

100. "Transplanter son rêve" (Kateb, *Nedjma* 112).

101. "Ici, entre l'Égypte et l'Arabie, les pères de Keblout sont passés, ballottés comme nous sur la mer, au lendemain d'une défaite. Ils perdaient un empire. Nous ne perdons qu'une tribu" (Kateb, *Nedjma* 121).

102. "La tribu décimée" (Kateb, *Nedjma* 118).

103. "Le sang des Keblout retrouvera sa chaude, son intime épaisseur . . . mais, sache-le: jamais tu ne l'épouseras" (Kateb, *Nedjma* 121–22).

104. "Cécité parcourue d'ocre et de bleu Outremer clapotant" (Kateb, *Nedjma* 64). "Vastitude, ocre, verte, bleue, blanche, plaine profonde et jaillissante de toutes parts submergée."

105. "La ville décomposée en îles architecturales" (Kateb, *Nedjma* 64).

106. "La brise de terre succéd[e] au vent du large."

107. "Elle s'estompe et se dérobe."

108. "La main caresse des courbes héritées de l'Égypte, de la Grèce antique."

109. "L'île ne conserva jamais le même nom, comme ces amantes polyandres vivant pour chaque époux et chaque amant, le même amour inassouvi de vierges démoniaques, mais en changeant ou en abolissant les . . . points de repère."

110. "C'est là que Si Mabrouk vint négocier les armes. Elles arrivaient à Constantine dans des caisses de poisson."

111. "Elle avait, dit-on, supplié les marins, et tout manigancé elle-même."

112. "Elle lui aurait promis sa main s'il avait le courage de la conduire secrètement à Alger, où elle songeait à réaliser . . . ses rêves de jeune fille 'évoluée'; un enlevement aurait été médité" (Kateb, *Nedjma* 78).

113. "Son fantôme voué à cette pitoyable démarche d'aveugle butant sur le fabuleux passé" (Kateb, *Nedjma* 158).

114. "Que l'expression révolutionnaire rencontre l'expression païenne" (Kateb, *Nedjma* 74).

CHAPTER 2. ANDALUSIA AS TRAUMA: THE LEGACIES OF *CONVIVENCIA*

1. For the epigraph: "L'Afrique commence aux Pyrénées. Voilà pourquoi Roblès est deux fois Algérien, unissant en lui, comme beaucoup d'entre nous, le sang espagnol et l'énergie berbère" (Camus, "Notre ami Roblès" 3).

2. Other members of L'École d'Alger, such as Emmanuel Roblès himself and Jean Sénac, worked more meaningfully on the place of Andalusia in their utopian Mediterranean configurations. See Graebner, *History's Place* chapter 5; Rivas; Dugas, *Emmanuel Roblès*.

3. Although the fate of medieval Andalusia has symbolically eclipsed other geographical locales pertaining to the history of Muslim Europe, due in no small part to the very locational referentiality of its Arabic name, al-Andalus, it is important to remark that the rule of the various North African dynasties over Europe overlay the entirety of the Iberian peninsula, sizable swaths of southern and western France, and a variety of Mediterranean islands (among which were Sicily, Sardinia, Malta, Corsica, and the Balearic Islands) over the course of its eight-century history.

4. I am referring to my analysis of Farès's discussion of myth and mystification in *Un passager de l'Occident* in chapter 1. In contrast to my argument, Bensmaïa associates this "interruption of the myth" with Farès's writing in the 1970s.

5. Numerous scholarly initiatives have flourished with this goal in mind: among them the Spanish–North Africa Project, Al-Andalus-Magreb, and Andalucía y sus relaciones con el Magreb by Sociedad Española de Estudios Árabes (Andalusia and Its Relations to the Maghreb, by the Spanish Society for Arab Studies), with institutional support from the Casa Velázquez in Madrid, the Fondation Temini in Tunis, and the Institut des Études Hispano-Lusophones at the Université Mohammed V in Rabat (Liang et al. 4–5). Also of note, the Fundación Dos Orillas (Two Shores Foundation) in Algeciras, Fundación Tres Culturas (Three Cultures Foundation) in Sevilla, an institutional collaboration between Spain and Morocco, and various nonacademic institutions in the Maghreb, testifying to the relevance and clout of the Andalusian trope in vernacular memory. See, for instance, the recently opened Centre des Cultures Andalouses (Andalusian Studies Center) in Tlemcen, as well as the Music Festival in Fez, which devoted its 2013 edition to the theme "Fès l'andalouse" (Fez the Andalusian; http://www.fesfestival.com/2013/fr/fes.php?id_rub=12).

6. Other notable work on Sephardic Spain includes Gerber; Zohar.

7. The *limpieza de sangre* (purity of blood) laws demarcated purely Christian ancestries from mixed genealogies inclusive of Jewish or Muslim elements. These statutes aimed to palliate the fear of false conversion among the communities of *marranos* (Jewish converts to Christianity) and *moriscos* (their Muslim counterpart).

8. In turn the final expulsion of the converted Muslims, the Moriscos, did not take place until 1609. See García-Arenal and Wiegers; Zhiri, "The Task."

9. On the displacement toward a new Atlantic geography of power, see Mignolo, "The Many Faces"; Dussel. On its connection to the fallen Arab world, see Gana, "In Search"; Chems Nadir.

10. More nuanced accounts include Martin-Márquez; Marín; Rodríguez Mediano.

11. A third historian would add his contribution to this historiographic account. Claudio Sánchez Albornoz followed the deterministic route and construed Spanish character as a constant that endured through the Andalusian interlude.

12. "A fin de . . . exorcizar nuestra consciencia culpable."

13. “Etnocidio purificador.” “Occidentalidad matizada.”
14. “Somos europeos distintos, europeos *en más*.”
15. See Dietz; Rogozen-Soltar.
16. Examples include the journey of the Moroccan ambassador Ahmad al-Kardudi to Spain in 1885 at a time of frequent Arab *rihlas* to Europe, and the Egyptian al-Tahtawi’s and the Moroccan Muhammad al-Saffar’s journeys to Paris; see chapter 4. Interestingly it is also to these journeys and to the benefit of an exterior perspective on the splendor of al-Andalus that Juan Goytisolo ascribes the onset of a Spanish Arabist consciousness dedicated to exploring al-Andalus’s neglected heritage.
17. “The Moors! The Spanish Republicans!”
18. “Vivre, mourir, survivre entre l’Espagne et les Arabes, dans une expérience d’écriture . . . et de pensée.”
19. “La force de l’inoublié entre Arabes et Espagnols.”
20. “Chant de l’inoublié et de l’inoubliable. En ce sens aussi, l’Espagne est un autre nom de la passion de ce souvenir.”
21. “Cette duplicité, ou plutôt cette multiplicité d’histoires, de cultures et de langues . . . secret qui ne se donne qu’à celui qui le déchiffre en l’aimant.”
22. “Cette Espagne historique a appris aux Arabes à se mesurer à l’autre, à le connaître et à le méconnaître dans le même geste d’appropriation et d’expropriation.”
23. “Nous revenons à un passé encore vivant, à une part exilée de nous-mêmes, à l’étrangeté de notre passé.”
24. “Nous réconcilier avec . . . *notre coeur étranger de ce pays*.”
25. “Un chaînon indestructible de filiation symbolique.”
26. “Une écriture de la géopolitique, qui romprait avec la vision folklorique et la complainte mélancolique, une écriture qui rendrait compte de sa profondeur mythologique, qui est à l’arrière-fond de notre être commun, comme si cette rencontre devait se réécrire sur les pages d’un palimpseste—ainsi qu’une lettre en souffrance. ”
27. “Un récit intercontinental et interscripturaire.”
28. “L’Espagne est une question d’écriture . . . l’Espagne ne s’appartient pas, elle n’appartient à personne, elle est cet ailleurs où l’expérience de vivre, de mourir, de survivre au-delà du trauma, nous contraint à entrer dans la mondialisation du récit moderne.”
29. “Nous changeons plus facilement de corps que nous le croyons; refusant de voir que la métempsycose effective à laquelle nous sommes réellement soumis durant la vie nous empêche de croire à l’identité . . . de nos organes vitaux . . . sans lesquels toute vie n’est que pure . . . interrogation.”
30. “L’autre partie de moi-même: morte, supprimée . . . ‘Nous.’ (?) lui et moi (?) perceptibles en même temps, dans le même mouvement de vie, de sensation.”
31. “L’expulsion au-delà de l’être.”
32. “Porté du Vide, dans l’absence de nom.”
33. “Deux mondes donc deux ; parfaitement vus, identifiés, dont l’un (le second) n’est pas le contraire, ni le miroir de l’autre, mais, l’exacte mesure de la séparation . . . sa frustration.”

34. "La chaîne des êtres, et, des cloisonnements."

35. "Cordoue ressemble à un lac, qui, tel un miroir éclaté, aveugle le voyageur. Et c'est ainsi qu'il voit, à son tour, Cordoue, ou, plutôt, qu'il se perd, en elle, en de multiples phrases, qui le nomment, à chaque fois, différemment: en une fragmentation."

36. "L'écran s'ouvre; ouvre l'autre versant du Coeur."

37. "La mort de l'autre." "L'autre—que je croyais: autre—et qui aurait pu être moi: qui a été moi, au moment même où les sentences . . . se mirent à exister."

38. "(Nous étions alors proches, démunis de crainte, ou, d'irréversibilité) (car le risque fut tenu de vivre, dans le monde, la frontière, la marginalité) . . . ici, eut lieu la rupture, le changement."

39. "N'existe qu'une seule erreur que j'ai voulu . . . rectifier."

40. "Une cassure du présent, issue de l'erreur du passé."

41. "'ChezNous,' Mirage de tous les désirs, passés, histoires. 'Nous.' 'Nous.'"

42. "J'ai eu des nouvelles de Pedro, et, de Juana, qui vivent, maintenant (1975: peut-être que tu pourrais aller les voir, et, les inviter à venir ici, chez 'nous'—simplement pour marquer la différence 'n' entre les particuliers 'n' et les nationaux 'N') sur la côte espagnole, à Alicante."

43. "'Nous' qui avons vécu sur les frontières des mondes, et, des différences—acceptés dans les limites étroites, définies, par les hiérarchies sociales, et, leurs indigences."

44. "Il existe plusieurs significations de la nationalité, et du 'nous' contrairement à ce que nous avions pu croire il y a quelques temps: des séparations intérieures, visibles: des exils; des désespoirs; des éloignements."

45. "Un pays sera chargé d'organiser les passages de l'un à l'autre: Jazirat El Maghrib, pays des doux passages de l'étrange!"

46. "Le plaisir de l'interdiction."

47. "La tendre lumière du souvenir. Non pas extase de la loi, mais, simplicité première de l'accueil. . . . Il n'est pas de lumière de soi qui ne prenne assise dans la lumière de l'Autre."

48. "Ustedes no estan [*sic*] de acuerdo conmigo. . . . Pero no importa . . . no importa."

49. "Les Colombes de l'exil."

50. "Le délire du Fondateur."

51. "Toucher l'intérieur de l'idéologie m'a coûté mon équilibre."

52. "L'Andalousie reste ce lieu inachevé."

53. "Étrange rencontre du rêve, et, du 'souvenir': ma venue ici a toutes les apparences d'un voyage connu et déjà fait."

54. "[Le] lieu de retour de Cordouan."

55. "Retour Avenir derrière moi toujours—comme vis re-tour-né: pouvez *régression* vous je culturelle facilement comprendre passé présent avenir: tous pareils."

56. "C'est parce que nous sommes issus—tous deux—de la même tristesse, et, de la même civilisation."

57. "Je pars tôt demain (encore) pour un autre exil."

58. "Ils retournent au monde."

59. "J'aime faire vivre ce point de naissance non pas comme une image de la nostalgie ou d'une terre perdue mais bien comme un point de résistance, une force qui servirait à coudre ensemble et de manière très solide des éclats du réel, qu'ils soient projetés très loin, en exil, éparpillés dans le monde ou au contraire immobiles, blottis à l'intérieur de soi, merveilleusement sédentaires" (Kassab-Charfi, "Entretien" 149).

60. On the distinction between the two, see Samia Kassab-Charfi's argument on the syncretic semiology of Testour, a Morisco village in Tunisia ("Sémiologie").

61. I have written elsewhere of Tahar Bekri's appropriation of the figure of Ibn Hazm (Talbayev, "Mediterranean Criss-Crossings"). Other authors who reclaimed a syncretic fiction of origins include Abdelwahab Meddeb, Chams Nadir, Alia Mabrouk, Turkia Labidi Ben Yahia, and Ahmed Mahfoud, as well as the filmmaker Naceur Khemir. Hédi Bouraoui's *Tunisie plurielle*, Guy Dugas's *Tunisie*, Mildred Mortimer's *Maghrebian Mosaic*, and Alia Bournaz Baccar's collections are some of the main texts to address this diversity from a critical perspective. Hala Halim's work on cosmopolitan Alexandria extends the paradigm to a broader geographical context.

62. I am referring to work by writers such as Fawzi Mellah (*Elissa, reine vagabonde*), Moncef Ghachem (*Cap Africa*), and Leila Ladjimi Sebai (*Elisha*), among others. Bernadette Cailler and Claudia Esposito have discussed the historical reappropriations of Carthage in Tunisian writing.

63. Such is the conclusion of Marie-Therese Ellis-House on the instrumentalizations of al-Andalus as malleable metaphor in 1940s Moroccan periodicals. She identifies two concurrent antithetical uses of the trope: to advocate linguistic homogeneity as the basis for the Moroccan Arab nation in the process of symbolic formation and to defend the suitability of a hybrid idiom of belonging respectful and encouraging of cultural and linguistic diversity ("Al-Andalus").

64. "L'impossibilité d'être quoi que ce soit de précis pour un juif tunisien de culture française."

65. "Une recherche, une interrogation, une invention perpétuelles." On the significance of the "imaginary Jew" construct, see Finkielkraut; Derrida, *Le Dernier des Juifs*.

66. "La désubstantialisation de l'identité du juif assimilé."

67. "Un écrivain se définit d'abord par une incapacité, d'ailleurs nostalgique, à se fondre dans l'anonymat d'une classe ou d'une race."

68. "Tout est là, en transparence. Ma vie et la vôtre. Entre nous deux, la mesure de cent ans et l'histoire de la France."

69. "Toute une population d'objets." "Entrez entrez il y a encore de la place. Angelvin, Meyer, Montelateci, Valentin, Cohen, Bortoli, Disegni, Massuque, Fellous, Fourcade, Rondot, Conti, Verzani, Moulin, Licari, Nuée, Achir, Fescheville, Bugui, Ville, Piperno, Borg, Gagliardo, Sangès, Cattan, Teynier, Viola, Licari, Kloth, d'Amico, Ladislas, Saliba, Galano, Saba, Baccouche, Mariani, Zerafa, Cardoso. Un rôle pour chacun. Un spectacle pris en cours l'année 1893."

70. "Ils ne forment qu'un seul corps, le tissu de ma langue."

71. "Ma mémoire est intacte, elle court sous mes paupières." "Ils bougent tous très lentement sous mes paupières."

72. "Tirer le rideau, faire silence sur tout ce vacarme. Ma prière est ouverte à tous, Arabes, Français, Maltais, Grecs, Italiens, Corses, Berbères, Juifs, Siciliens, Égyptiens, Palestiniens, Portugais, Ouzbeks, Arméniens, Libanais, Chinois, Albanais, Turcs, Afghans, Anglais, Mexicains, Argentins."

73. Of Livornese origin, the *grana* Jewish community acquired privileges unknown to the majority of the native Tunisian Jews (or *twansa*). Paul Sebag reports that a 1846 addition to the 1822 treaty signed by the Great Duke of Tuscany and the Bey of Algiers bestowed upon the newly arrived Livorno Jews a special status as envoys of the European courts ("commerçants des cours d'Europe"), which granted them the protection of the European sovereign (272). The condition of all Tunisian Jews met with significant improvement with the promulgation of the 1857 Fundamental Pact and again with the 1861 Constitution, which established the equality of Jews and Muslims in the eyes of the law and reiterated the commitment to every citizen's safety regardless of religion or origin. On Tunisian Jews and the *dhimma*, see Hagège and Zarca.

74. Of traumatic magnitude, the politically sensitive context of the post-1967 Six-Day War against Israel triggered anti-Jewish riots in Tunis and a subsequent wave of departures.

75. "Cette promenade, je m'y sens bien. Elle ressemble à une prière que j'invente au centre des secondes et qui me fait mieux avancer . . . 1860, 1865,1909, 1913, 1924, 1938, 1943, 1948, 1950."

76. Jewish Maghrebi tradition ties the presence of the first Israelite settlements in North Africa to the time of exile following the destruction of the First Temple. The Jews mostly settled in the big cosmopolitan capitals of the North and, in the case of Tunisia, on the island of Djerba.

77. The Alliance Israélite Universelle opened a boys' school in Tunis in 1878, a girls' school in 1882, and a coeducational institution in 1910 (Sebag 322–23). Sebag records the existence of a Protestant mission school, the London Jews' Society, as well as sundry Catholic schools that counted *twansa* and *grana* Jews among their student pool (274). In later years schools under the purview of the *direction de l'instruction publique* also played a key role (510).

78. The Décret Crémieux of 1870, which endowed the Algerian Jewish community with the privileges of French citizenship, did not extend to Tunisian Jews, who nevertheless were allowed to petition for French naturalization on an individual basis under certain conditions after the 1910 presidential decree (Sebag 325) and, more significantly, the Morinaud law of 1923.

79. "Comme si c'était normal. Normal d'installer un pays au milieu d'un autre, normal de signer des pactes."

80. "La France est alors devenue mon pays. Je n'ai pas eu à réfléchir ni à demander la permission, j'ai juste suivi les consignes."

81. "[La France] m'a invitée à faire partie du voyage, c'est tout."

82. "Votre lieu de naissance, s'il vous plaît? Je dois toujours réfléchir cinq secondes avant de répéter d'un trait: Tunis virgule Tunisie. Tous les lieux d'origine m'agacent, c'est autre chose que je cherche, je le répète, c'est une figure géométrique, un dessin, une arabesque, une ligne de feu, une histoire inscrite dans l'architecture même de la ville. Peut-être une couleur."

83. "J'ai vraiment besoin d'avoir plusieurs appartenances, j'allais dire plusieurs naissances, et je me sens toujours plus vivante lorsque j'entends plusieurs langues autour de moi. Je crois aussi que la modernité se situe précisément là."

84. "Je ne crois pas à la vérité des choses présentes." "Ce sont ces phrases qui les ont poussés à faire le voyage vers ce pays d'opérette."

85. "On n'a pas besoin d'avoir un pays pour exister. On a besoin d'exister, c'est tout, il faut avancer, ne pas tout retenir."

86. "Le monde [qui] nous a été donné [et que] nous devons . . . rendre."

87. "Faire exister [le monde] c'est déjà le rendre. Mais le rendre, c'est aussi disparaître. Et en disparaissant, on le fait apparaître plus clairement, n'est-ce pas?"

88. "Vous avez essayé d'oublier les humiliations, les bastonnades, les incendies, les assassinats. Vous avez préféré retenir l'amitié discrète, la tolérance, la complicité, le goût d'une même culture, d'une même terre, la musique."

89. "Les sauver tous . . . témoigner pour eux . . . rassembler leur histoire, l'éclaircir."

90. "Le monde m'a été donné, je dois le rendre."

91. "Être là donc, au cœur des choses."

92. "Je dis livre, mais je veux parler de la vie . . . les mots s'entendent, se font signe, ils font tous les deux le même travail, l'un prend, l'autre donne, toujours cette loi fatale. Être là donc, au cœur des choses."

93. "Fabriquer ma vie à la main . . . C'est maintenant l'heure de . . . rendre." "Défi impossible des petits derniers."

94. "C'est un cœur qui se met à battre tout à coup, le monde vient de naître, dites-moi s'il vous plaît quelle heure est-il à la Nation?"

95. "Tous les jours au même moment, que je sois à Séville, à Paris, à Rouen, à Tanger, à Palerme, à Florence, à New York, à Samarkand ou à Lisbonne, je cours machinalement rejoindre ces années que je n'ai jamais connues, là-bas, en Tunisie."

96. "En même temps, je le sais, c'est ma prison."

97. "Ils ne savent plus à qui ils s'adressent, si c'est à mon frère ou si c'est à une communauté tout entière."

98. "Merci" or "Voleur."

99. "Tout ce qu'elle n'a jamais pu me dire, ce qu'elle a préféré taire."

100. "Je ne suis plus dans le ventre de ma mère cette fois, je dois fabriquer ma vie à la main, le monde m'a été donné, c'est maintenant l'heure de le rendre . . . j'embrasse le monde qui se fabrique."

101. On this point, see Lia Brozgal's analysis of *Un été à La Goulette.*

102. "Je regarde, je ne trouve aucun mot encore, je suis un enfant qui n'est pas encore né. Je peux voir, mais je ne sais pas parler. Je suis comme les morts."

103. "Ça y est, je reconnais maintenant le visage de Bette Davis. Le nom du film, c'est *L'Intruse*."

104. "Ce jour-là, j'aurais mieux fait de venir en pantoufles et il n'y aurait rien eu de tout ce bazar."

105. "Je reste avec eux, je fais partie de leur histoire, même si je suis étrangère."

106. "Je sais tout faire, même mourir."

107. "Je veux jouer avec [le monde]. Je veux aussi m'éloigner de lui et m'habituer à disparaître."

108. "Entrez, entrez, il y a encore de la place."

CHAPTER 3. TRAUMATIC ALLEGORIES: MEDITERRANEAN NOMADISM AND MELANCHOLIA IN MALIKA MOKEDDEM'S *N'ZID*

1. One of Mokeddem's most famous pronouncements is "Only palm-trees have roots. We are nomads. We have a memory and legs to walk away [Il n'y a que les palmiers qui ont des racines. Nous, on est des nomades. On a une mémoire et des jambes pour marcher]" (qtd. in Chaulet-Achour, "Place d'une littérature migrante" n.p.). The same formula is approximately reproduced in *N'zid* (162).

2. "Il y a trop de traffic, trop d'hélices, hachoirs triomphants qui brisent la mer et la labourent entre les ports du détroit."

3. The outbreak of violence that followed the cancelation of the first multiparty legislative elections in 1992 claimed between 100,000 and 200,000 deaths, mostly of civilians who fell victim to one of the two parties at war—the Islamist militia, or *groupes islamistes armés*, and the armed forces, whose exact role in the bloodshed remains to be ascertained. In addition close to 150,000 intellectuals left the country for fear of being targeted by Islamists despite the initial informal coalition between seculars and Islamists against the all-powerful Front de Libération Nationale. For a thorough discussion of the Black Decade, see Stora; LeSueur.

4. "Plus de passé. Plus de terre. Même plus leur nostalgie . . . avant le plein flot de l'oubli."

5. "Mes parents étaient grecs . . . Étaient? Père copte, mère juive. Je suis née à Paris. Une Franco-gréco-judéo-chrétiéno-arabo-athée pur jus."

6. "Un ghetto. Un purgatoire."

7. "Happée par le néant."

8. "Ce continent liquide est le sien." This anamnesis of the self and its concurrent elaboration of a fluid identity made up of elective affiliations is reminiscent of escapist Mediterranean paradigms dating back to L'École d'Alger. The intertext of Audisio's novel *Héliotrope* is particularly resonant here, most obviously in the intertextual echo of Sauveur's flippant nautical peregrinations: "Nora was sick with the need to be there, to see [the sea] [Nora était malade du besoin d'y être, de la voir]" (Mokeddem, *N'zid* 192).

9. "Ton épiderme a dévoré ton cerveau. Bientôt il va te pousser une fourrure ou des écailles sur la peau."

10. "En voilà un qui met l'écran de la fiction entre lui et le monde."

11. "Tu es comme tes dessins. Des traits. Des formes. Des vibrations sans légende . . . Elle a pensé 'destin' en disant 'dessin.'"

12. Mokeddem's choice of a dual, fractured form of allegory can be construed as the product of Nora's growing realization that, in the Algerian context of state-sponsored violence which underpins the story, language is necessarily caught up between the fictitious self-aggrandizing rhetoric of the FLN on the one hand and Islamist hate-mongering speech on the other. Of verbal expression Nora says: "I don't like words. Especially the ones I utter. They crush and stifle me. I prefer the lightness of drawing . . . it's my way not to choose any of my languages . . . to resist this torture [Je n'aime pas les mots. Surtout dans ma voix. Ils m'écrasent et m'étouffent. Je préfère la légèreté du dessin . . . ma façon de ne choisir aucune de mes langues . . . pour échapper à leur écartèlement]" (Mokeddem, *N'zid* 113).

13. "Le vide de la subjectivité, l'éloignement de l'individu qui devient cet apatride ontologique, intransitif (il n'est pas l'autre *de* quelqu'un), sans corrélat, sans génitif, sans pays d'arrivée. Une personne nouvelle" (Malabou 29).

14. "Un accident vital de mémoire."

15. My introduction and epilogue engage in a more thorough discussion of critical melancholia as a political practice.

16. "Tu ne vas pas t'en tirer comme ça. La mer n'est qu'un sursis."

17. "Qui portent en eux plusieurs terres écartelées . . . qui vivent entre revendications et ruptures."

18. "La mer entière est réduite à une petite méduse rôtie qu'il [le poulpe-soleil] gobe avec délectation."

19. "Pas possible d'habiter le corps d'un autre. Ni de refaire son histoire. . . . Au diable, la mémoire! Tu ne l'as pas perdue, tu t'es évadée de sa prison? N'est-ce pas?"

20. "Des troubles mnésiques, pas une amnésie."

21. "Comme si son bateau et elle n'existaient pas."

22. "Elle se dit que c'est peut-être lui qui n'est qu'une illusion d'optique."

23. "[J'ai] pris du 'je' sous son [Loïc's] regard de mer."

24. "Un Bernard-lhermite? Même eau qu'une méduse, non?"

25. "Plus de Ghoula. Partie avec Bernard Lhermite."

26. "Elle se sent toute chose d'avoir pu dire 'je' et fond sous son regard."

27. "Elle sursaute et s'élance à corps perdu dans le jeu."

28. "Tu n'es pas de nulle part. Tu es un être de frontière. Le nulle part, non-lieu, te condamne au non-être."

29. "Redécouvre [le désert] en elle."

30. "Maintenant, il sillonne le monde pour les besoins de la musique. Maintenant des terres étrangères le rendent à lui-même, au corps vivant de son luth, à ses cordes où se prend la mer. . . . Maintenant la mer est son autre désert."

31. "La langue flamboyante du désert."

32. "Découlent tous trois d'une même essence: la tentative d'apprivoiser tous les sens de l'abandon."

33. "Les dislocations et les désherences."

34. *Déshérence* is the legal term referring to the transfer of an unclaimed estate to the French state whenever the deceased has no heirs. I am here referring to arguments such as Anne-Emmanuelle Berger's masterful reading of the modern Algerian nation through the metaphor of family in *Algeria in Others' Languages*.

35. "Cette filiation qui, sautant la génération sclérosée de ses parents, lui restitue l'identité de ses ancêtres."

36. I am alluding to the murder of the FLN activist Abane Ramdane, the most notorious victim of the internecine violence that tore the FLN apart in the early days of nationalism. In *Le Blanc de l'Algérie*, Assia Djebar reads Ramdane's assassination as the blueprint for the kind of memory abuse that would become idiosyncratic of the FLN. She indicts the FLN-sponsored discourse of national formation for occluding this foundational violation and for depriving younger generations of Algerians of more desirable role models than the junta that was eventually born of independence. Although it does not invoke this particular episode of occluded violence, I read Jamil's accusation "Everything is rigged from the start, especially when it comes to origins [Tout est truqué à l'origine, surtout à l'origine]" in this light (Mokeddem, *N'zid* 206).

37. "La voix qui la reconnaît de cette langue." "Elle fond . . . éperdue de gratitude."

38. "L'a aidée à conquérir sa part manquante, l'Algérie, même si elle n'y a encore jamais mis les pieds . . . Un jour, elle pourra peut-être y accoster."

39. "Sous la pointe de son crayon, une méduse a pour la première fois un visage humain, le sien. Elle danse à la plainte d'un luth."

40. "La musique obsède le dessin . . . court-circuit(e) la menace des mots."

41. "Transforme . . . ce deuil et ceux qui vont suivre en œuvres de virtuose et la mélancolie en volupté."

42. "Ces autres morts dont l'Algérie a le secret: la disparition. L'absence définitive qui installe le deuil sans jamais le laisser s'achever."

43. "Elle s'est laissé bouffer la tête par des serpents et momifier."

44. "Une exaltation . . . une succession d'images falsifiées de soi qui empêchent l'objectivité, la réparation, donc la guérison."

45. "On ne sort pas indemne de la morale d'une tribu."

46. "Fragilité et fureur de ceux qui n'ont pas les moyens de leurs aspirations . . . en 1952, les femmes ne pouvaient pas se sauver. Pas à cette époque-là. . . . C'est le temps libre à la culpabilité."

47. "Refai[re] le même chemin illico. Avec toute ta tête. Sans rien gommer cette fois. . . . Rien renier."

48. "Trois Gorgones: l'Irlande, l'Algérie et la France. Il ne reste plus qu'à trouver la faute."

49. "Effacée. Elle est comme un fantôme qui aurait oublié de déterrer son histoire. Elle n'a plus rien à hanter."

50. "You have tragedy in your eyes. . . . It is one of the reasons why men have always taken to the sea: to escape the *matres dolorosae* [Vous portez la tragédie dans l'oeil. . . . C'est l'une des raisons pour lesquelles les hommes ont toujours pris la mer: fuir les Mater dolorosa (*sic*)]" (77).

51. "Une voix d'eau entre les langues."

52. "Une méduse, c'est seulement un peu d'eau."

CHAPTER 4. STRAIT TALK: CROSSING (AND) THE *RIHLA* TRADITION OF TRAVEL WRITING

1. For the epigraphs: "On nous refuse l'existence, mais dans le même temps on nous interdit de nous en aller" (Jay, *Tu ne traverseras pas* 20); "Les Arabes sont devenus clandestins, cachés dans la conscience des Espagnols et leur inconscient" (Khatibi, "Au-delà du trauma" 129).

2. *Harraga* (burner) is "the neologism used in the Maghreb as well as by French media to refer to individuals who emigrate clandestinely" (Abderrezak, "Burning the Sea" 463). Unlike Abderrezak, I use the Gallicized plural, *harragas*, in keeping with Merzak Allouache's 2009 eponymous film.

3. Yto Barrada's photographic project *Strait* captures the complex geopolitical position of Tangier and the contradictions embedded in a city that she calls "the destination and jumping-off point of a thousand hopes" (qtd. in BabelMed n.p.). On the material aspects of clandestine migration, see Global Detention Project.

4. Tahar Ben Jelloun's 2006 novel on the subject, significantly titled *Partir* (*Leaving Tangier*), addresses the issue in cognate terms, showing in this now canonical dialogue that the act of leaving is by nature intransitive. "Partir" thus becomes an absolute concept, needing no destination:

> *What* do you want to do later on?
> Leave.
> Leave? But that's not a profession!
> Once I leave, I'll have a profession.
> Leave for where?
> Anywhere. (Ben Jelloun, *Leaving Tangier* 92)

> *Que* veux-tu faire plus tard?
> Partir.
> Partir? Mais ce n'est pas un métier!
> Une fois partie, j'aurai un métier.
> Partir où?
> Partir n'importe où. (Ben Jelloun, *Partir* 98)

5. For instance, in his prescient 1992 short story on *hrig*, "Le Clandestin " (The Clandestine Migrant), Ben Jelloun writes of his protagonist, "He remembered being told how his ancestors had conquered Spain some five hundred years earlier and how they had introduced a great and beautiful culture in the country [Il se rappelait qu'on lui avait raconté comment ses ancêtres, il y a cinq cents ans de cela, avaient conquis l'Espagne et comment ils avaient introduit une grande et belle culture dans ce pays]" (96). The

evocation of Arabs crossing into Spain dredges up other more recent episodes of living together: "He also remembered the time when the Spanish used to live in working-class neighborhoods in Tangiers. . . . They didn't seem like rich, powerful colonizers back then; rather like humble, unassuming working people [Il se souvenait aussi de l'époque où les Espagnols vivaient dans des quartiers populaires de Tanger. . . . Ils n'apparaissaient pas alors comme des colons riches et dominateurs, mais comme des gens du peuple modestes et sans prétention]" (96–97). A similar argument will be made in *Partir* (73).

6. On Moroccan-Spanish colonial relations and their representation in cultural production, see Martin-Márquez; Ricci.

7. Ben Jelloun's other novels revolving around Tangier include *Silent Day in Tangier*, *La Nuit de l'erreur*, and more recently, *Leaving Tangier*.

8. In his documentary on the February 20 movement in Morocco, Nadir Bouhmouch defines the *makhzan* as follows: "the governing elite centered around the king and consisting of royal notables, businessmen, wealthy landowners, tribal leaders, top-ranking military personnel, and security service bosses" (1'34"). Although a clear-cut, stable definition has been rather hard to synthesize, in yet another sign of the extraordinary soft power wielded by the group, the origins of the term are well-known. Historically used to name the building where the king's tributes were stored, the word was then used in colonial times as part of the phrase *blad al-makhzan*, to designate the zones where the king's authority was respected, as opposed to *blad al-siba*, which fell outside the purview of the central government (tribal and nomadic zones). Used to coalesce the power of the king and his entourage, the term has functioned after independence as a marker of the resulting system of governance based on clientelism and favoritism.

9. "La transcription arabe de Fès."

10. "Où il souffle, paraît-il, un vent d'Est chaud qui lave les corps et épure les mémoires."

11. "Écriture des migrations premières"

12. "La capitale de la blessure future." "La main et la pensée."

13. "Tantôt de l'Est tantôt de l'Ouest."

14. "Nous sommes venus tendre le bras pour tromper la brume du détroit désigner l'autre rivage sans le nommer."

15. "La terre a englouti leur espoir." "La vague et l'écume réconciliées au seuil d'une mémoire grâciée par le soleil."

16. "La mer les protège. Ils savent qu'elle est parabole qui fuse en sources multiples."

17. "L'écriture des vagues." "La reine bleue d'Andalousie / l'amante des sables adossée à l'étrave du désir."

18. "La parole . . . pour découvrir l'itinéraire de la mer."

19. "L'écrit né de la mer retourne aux signes de la vague/femme/enfant . . . Les verbes arabes virent au bleu nomade, destituent le destin."

20. "La croisée des mémoires vagabondes."

21. Accounts of arbitrary detention and torture lie at the heart of the genre of Moroccan *littérature carcérale* (prison literature) (Orlando, *Screening Morocco*; Benalil). Due to pressure from former prisoners and thanks

in part to the publication of Ahmed Marzouki's *Tazmamart cellule 10*, an account of the author's harrowing years in the infamous camp, Muhammad VI created the Equity and Reconciliation Commission, a forum where victims could tell their stories and demand compensation. Even though the identity of the torturers remained concealed and King Hassan II's name was never mentioned in the subsequent records of abuse that the Commission created, his son acknowledged the regime's responsibility for this dark era and compensated the victims' families in the amount of $200 million (Susan Miller 223). See also Raiss; Oufkir and Fitoussi; Mdidech; Serhane.

22. The 1965 demonstrations started out as student protests. Joined by other discontented lower-class segments of society, students staged a strike that soon morphed into riots. The government's response led to terrible bloodshed that left its indelible mark on the record of human rights violations in the country. For a discussion of the development of Morocco's authoritarianism, see Hammoudi.

23. Abd El Krim established the Rif Republic in 1921, a state independent from colonial powers vying for sovereignty over northern Morocco but also from the *makhzan*'s sphere of influence.

24. In his 2004 chronicle, "Point de vue: Le monde arabe est fatigué" (Perspective: The Arab World Is Exhausted), Ben Jelloun reveals the discrepancy between the long-awaited providential figure whose coming is predicted by Arab legend and current Arab leaders. The sustained hope for a messianic figure reveals a steady belief in the cause of nationalism, a worthy endeavor simply in need of fulfillment.

25. "Nous sommes d'Ajdir; nous appartenons aux Béni Ouriaghel du Rif. Nous sommes les descendants directs des Oulad Si Mohammad Ben Abd El Krim, originaires du Hedjaz . . . sur la mer Rouge. Notre aïeul s'appelait Zarra de Yambo. Ma famille vint s'établir au Maroc vers le IIIe siècle de l'hégire. Ainsi donc, depuis plus de mille ans, la contrée qui s'étend entre la baie d'Alhuceimas et Targuist est bien notre patrie."

26. The rift culminated in the adoption of the colonial Berber *dahir* (decree) that exonerated Amazigh populations from sharia courts and allowed them to maintain their own laws under the control of the authorities, further inscribing the deep disunity between the two communities.

27. Yet this conception of democracy should not be confused with a simple replica of the Western concept. As Chekroun argues, Ghallab insists on the elite nature of the process of consultation lying at the root of popular sovereignty, which was to remain in the hands of the "ahl al-ra'y" (enlightened elite).

28. A word derived from the Arabic *hijra*, *hégire* originally designated the migration of Muhammad and his disciples from Mecca to Medina. *Hijra* is also a ubiquitous synonymous for *hrig*.

29. "Je reviendrai à la terre. Je reviendrai voilé."

30. "L'Emir sans idéologie. L'Emir en exil." "Je voulais . . . nous imposer face à ceux qui nous méprisaient, nous imposer comme nation moderne."

31. "Depuis que je suis au Caire, je pratique la parole; je lance des appels . . . pour l'indépendance . . . pour la libération . . . l'émancipation du peuple."

32. On *Sawt al-'Arab* and anticolonial rhetoric, see Fanon; Mernissi.

33. "La violence faite quotidiennement à tout un peuple rend la parole rare et inutile. . . . Les mots . . . sont en fait incapables de contenir l'autre violence, celle qui accumule accumule accumule jusqu'au jour où elle éclate dans la rue face au ciel paisible."

34. "Le chameau m'a confié qu'une autre sirène viendra défier la légende. Elle viendra à la tête du cortège des enfants/oiseaux et s'installera nue sur le littoral."

35. "Nous . . . regardons [le rivage] s'éloigner le sable nous sépare."

36. Although the corpus is mostly masculine, Brinda Mehta has spotlighted equally interesting accounts by female authors (*Dissident Writings*).

37. For extensive treatments of the *nahda* in literature, see Hafez; Tageldin; El-Ariss; Rastegar.

38. I am referring to the *nahda*'s fortunes as a transnational political imaginary in the days of decolonization. This transnational scale was most evident in the pan-Arabism it inspired, although it was also a key characteristic of its early instantiations. See, for instance, Khuri-Lakdisi; McManus.

39. The concept of Dar al-Islam, literally the Abode of Islam, propagates a transnational faith-based community in a move reminiscent of the concept of *umma* in modern nationalist rhetorics.

40. "Hafizat Zaynab ma warithathu 'an mu'allimiha, ikhtarat tariqan li-idha'atihi."

41. See Talbayev, "Mediterranean Criss-Crossings." In his poems Bekri depicts Ibn Hazm.

42. "Zallat amina 'ala turath al-faylasuf." "Wajibiha nahwa mu'allimiha."

43. "Hafizat Zaynab ma warithathu 'an mu'allimiha."

44. "Kulla wahidin minhum umma."

45. In the original Arabic, "mina' umm al-mudun al-maghribiyya wa-l-'arabiyya."

46. "Bi-haythi kana turathan insaniyyan la ananiyyan aw fardiyyan." "Kana ustadhuha yaktub li-l-khas wa-l-'am."

47. "Dinuna 'alami wa watanuna huwa al- 'alam alladhi yasuduhu mabda'una."

48. "Lastu rahila bi-sabab al-khawf min al-mu'tadin wa innama qasd al-'amal hunak min ajli al-taw'iya fi bi'a maftuha 'ala al-tanaqudat wa injab ansar al-haqq hunak."

49. This second *nahda* should nevertheless be kept distinct from the second *nahda* suggested by the Moroccan poet Abdellatif Laâbi in his introduction to *La Poésie palestinienne de combat* (Palestinian Combat Poetry), a volume that proposed to lay the foundations for a renewed form of Moroccan nationalism held in dialectical tension with the legacy of pan-Arabism in the Mashreq and that reframed Arabism around the Palestinian question.

50. In his introduction to Cruz's *Rihla*, José Manuel Caballero Bonald dubbed Cruz's style a "palabra fronteriza," or "border speech" (5). The poem "Semillas, pecios y paraísos," for instance, was written exclusively from the liminal locations of Tarifa, Gibraltar, and Tangiers (Yborra), a position that accentuates the poet's exploration of a disconnected subject position of

which his relation to the *harraga* is the epitome. In this respect it is interesting to note that the Union of Moroccan Writers has been preparing a Spanish-Arabic edition of a selection of Cruz's poems from 1983–2002 (Ilustre Ayuntamiento de San Roque). See also Fernández Goma.

51. Respectively, "dólares irreales que has conseguido en algún Mercado negro" and "Te has subido a borde de un barco de mercancías . . . y te has escondido."

52. "Pero no el reflejo que en él se configura."

53. "Cuando compartimos un mismo espejismo, podemos llamarlo realidad."

54. "Me invento un lugar desde donde lanzar estas imágenes."

55. "Entre un pensamiento y otro / hay un limbo en el que respiro y no respiro / en el que tropiezo con imágenes desechadas."

56. "Somos el puente que une la materia a la metáfora."

57. "Débiles espejos amargos." "Me he vaciado de imágenes."

58. "Fracas[é] precisamente como debiera."

59. "Ir perfeccionando la nada, ir rondándola si sospecharlo."

60. "El mar como el lenguaje / es a veces el refugio que nos traiciona / un traidor que nos cobija."

61. "Verás cómo [estas páginas] naufragan, cómo el polizón que llevan dentro / se salva / llega a la orilla / y te alcanza."

62. "Con frecuencia me habitas, me posees, me escoges como nave para algún viaje."

63. "Si yo soy tu única huella / cuando me borre la marea . . . ¿Quién me devolverá el cuerpo que desobedece al vértigo?"

64. "Al final / llegará la fecundación."

65. "Hacer literatura es darle forma y profundidad a lo que somos."

66. "Si no nos reinventamos nos hundiremos sin dejar rastro en el barro . . . ¿Después de todo quién se acercará a la orilla para tropezar con nuestros pecios?"

67. "Memoria [que] se transparenta tejiéndose con la misma materia del abismo."

EPILOGUE: PLUMBING THE TRANSCONTINENTAL MEDITERRANEAN

1. Some of them, like the claim to "Mediterraneanism," have embraced some of the fiercest "othering" discourse articulated about the region. Constructed on the model of Edward Said's concept of Orientalism, Mediterraneanism stresses the relevance of enduring stereotypes pervading a "Mediterranean consciousness"—the notorious honor and shame dyad (Peristiany and Pitt-Rivers), but also indolence, political corruption, nepotism, and touchiness, among other such characteristics. Used to assert one's place in relation to a global hierarchy of value, this form of deliberate self-stereotyping does not merely rehearse the caricatural findings of an existing ethnographic archive; it reflects a long-standing model of affiliation that has

been used as a means of resistance to different external hegemonies (by the national center in centralist models of governance, as in France and Greece, or in the context of interregional polarities, as in Italy's opposition between dominant northern and southern regions). See Harris.

2. This is also a main proposition of the Canaanite movement, established in the 1940s. A gathering of intellectuals, the movement rested its vision of identity on the construction of a Hebrew nation (as opposed to the Jewish nation postulated by Zionism) that would stretch across the entire Middle East and exclude exilic elements and traditions (Nocke; Shavit, *The Hebrew Nation*).

3. "Although it is argued here that Yam Tikhoniut is a nonideological frame of reference . . . Yam Tikhoniut is by no means apolitical" (Nocke 242).

4. The rise of Phoenicianism in Lebanon in the 1920s is a fitting parallel. The movement is akin to the Canaanite movement through its association with a mythical ancient past. Supported by Maronite Christians, the ideology became a shorthand for resistance to pan-Arab nationalism, again using a Mediterraneanist ethos to counteract the homogenizing politics of nation-building.

5. "L'esprit andalou est une autre manière de traduire ce mot de métissage."

6. "Minoritaire, marginale, fragmentaire et inachevée."

7. "Nous essayons d'aller vers une pensée planétaire et plurielle."

8. As could have been predicted, an acknowledgment of the Mediterranean character of Tunisia was ultimately kept out of the constitutional definition of national identity, to the benefit of the usual Arabo-Islamic definition. One of the considerations crystallizing resistance was the hypothesis that a Mediterranean inscription would open the door to normalization of relations with Israel, thereby demonstrating the political potential of a Mediterranean trope of relationality.

BIBLIOGRAPHY

Abderrezak, Hakim. "Burning the Sea: Clandestine Migration across the Strait of Gibraltar in Francophone Moroccan 'Illiterature.'" *Contemporary French and Francophone Studies* 13.4 (2009): 461–69.

———. *Ex-centric Migrations: Europe and the Maghreb in Mediterranean Cinema, Literature, and Music*. Bloomington: Indiana University Press, 2016.

Abdoun, Ismaïl. "Quelques remarques sur le mythe des ancêtres chez Kateb Yacine ou comment le Nègre 'providentiel' de *Nedjma* bouleverse la mythologie identitaire." "Pouvoirs du mythe dans les littératures francophones du Maghreb et du Mashrek." Special issue of *Recherches & travaux* 81 (2012). Accessed February 12, 2015. http://recherchestravaux.revues.org/553?lang=en.

Aboul Ela, Hosam. *Other South: Faulkner, Postcoloniality and the Mariátegui Tradition*. Pittsburgh: University of Pittsburgh Press, 2007.

Abraham, Nicolas, and Maria Torok. *The Shell and the Kernel*. Chicago: University of Chicago Press, 1987.

Abulafia, David. "Mediterraneans." In *Rethinking the Mediterranean*. Ed. W. V. Harris. Oxford: Oxford University Press, 2006. 64–93.

Abun-Nasr, Jamil M. *A History of the Maghreb*. Cambridge, UK: Cambridge University Press, 1971.

Agamben, Giorgio. *The Coming Community*. Trans. Michael Hardt. Minneapolis: University of Minnesota Press, 1993.

Agar-Mendousse, Trudy. "Counterviolence and the Ethics of Nomadism: Malika Mokeddem's Reconstruction of Algerian Identity." In *Transnational Spaces and Identities in the Francophone World*. Ed. Hafid Gafaïti, Patricia M. E. Lorcin, and David G. Troyanksy. Lincoln: University of Nebraska Press, 2009. 182–99.

———. *Violence et créativité: De l'écriture algérienne au féminin*. Paris: L'Harmattan, 2006.

Ahmad, Aijaz. "The Politics of Literary Postcoloniality." In *Contemporary Postcolonial Theory: A Reader*. Ed. Padmini Mongia. London: Arnold, 1996. 276–93.

Alami, Ahmed Idrissi. "Dialectics of Desire, Victimhood, and Postcolonial Migrancy in Tahar Ben Jelloun's *Leaving Tangier*." *South Central Review* 30.2 (2013): 1–31.

Al-Baqqash, Muhammad Muhammad. *Al-Hijra al-Sirriyya*. *Syrian Story*, January 2, 2007. Accessed April 26, 2014. http://www.syrianstory.com/bakache.htm.

Allouache, Merzak, director. *Harragas*. Libris films, France 2 Cinéma, Baya films, 2009.

Al-Makkari, Ahmad Ibn Muhammad. *The History of the Mohammedan Dynasties in Spain*. Trans. Pascual de Gayangos. London: W. H. Allen, 1840–43.

Al-Maqqari, Ahmad ibn Muhammad. *Azhar al-Riyad fi Akhbar 'Iyad*. Rabat: Sunduq Ihya' al-Turath al-Islami, 1978.

———. *Nafh al-Tib min Ghusn al-Andalus al-Ratib*. Ed. Ihsan 'Abbas. Beirut: Dar Sadr, 1988.

Al-Musawi, Muhsin J. "Engaging Globalization in Modern Arabic Literature: Appropriation and Resistance." *Modern Language Quarterly* 68.2 (2007): 305–29.

———. *Islam on the Street: Religion in Modern Arabic Literature*. Lanham, MD: Rowan & Littlefield, 2009.

Al-Tahtawi, Rifa'a Rafi'. *Takhlis al-Ibriz ila Talkhis Bariz, aw al-Diwan al-nafis bi-iwan Baris*. Cairo: Dar al-Taqqadum, 1905.

Alvarez, David. "Nation-Making in Gibraltar: From Fortress Colony to Finance Centre." *Canadian Review of Studies in Nationalism* 1–2 (2001): 9–25.

Amrouche, Jean El Mouhoub. "Introduction aux *Chants Berbères de Kabylie*." In *Jean Amrouche: L'Eternel Jugurtha (1906–1962)*. Archives de la Ville de Marseille. Marseille: Palais de Beaux-Arts, 1985. 62–68.

———. "L'Eternel Jugurtha: Propositions sur le Génie Africain." In *Jean Amrouche: L'Eternel Jugurtha (1906–1962)*. Archives de la Ville de Marseille. Marseille: Palais de Beaux-Arts, 1985. 108–11.

Anselin, Jules-René. "Rapport sur Bougie." *Bulletin de la Société d'Anthropologie de Paris* (1860): 155–68.

Apter, Emily. "'Je ne crois pas beaucoup à la littérature comparée': Universal Poetics and Postcolonial Comparatism." In *Comparative Literature in the Age of Globalization*. Ed. Haun Saussy. Baltimore: Johns Hopkins University Press, 2006. 54–62.

———. "Out of Character: Camus's French Algerian Subjects." *Modern Language Notes* 112.4 (1997): 499–516.

Ararou, Ahmed. "Rickiem." *Aljamía* 8 (1996): 75–77.

Archer, Edward G. *Gibraltar, Identity, and Empire.* London: Routledge, 2006.

Aresu, Bernard. "Arcanes algériens entés d'ajouts helléniques: *Le Chien d'Ulysse*, de Salim Bachi." In *Échanges et mutations des modèles littéraires entre Europe et Algérie.* Ed. Charles Bonn. Paris: L'Harmattan, 2004. 177–89.

———. *Counter-Hegemonic Discourse from the Maghreb: The Poetics of Kateb's Fiction.* Tubingen: Gunter Narr Verlag, 1993.

———. *Tahar Ben Jelloun.* New Orleans, LA: CELFAN, 1998.

Armstrong, John A. "Braudel's Mediterranean: *Un Défi Latin.*" *World Politics* 29.4 (1977): 626–36.

Arnaud, Jacqueline. "Les Villes mythiques et le mythe de Nedjma dans le roman de Kateb Yacine." In *Journée Kateb Yacine: Actes du colloque organisé par le Département de francais (5 mai 1984).* Manouba, Tunisia: Publications de la faculté des lettres, 1990. 9–18.

———. *Recherches sur la littérature maghrébine de langue française: Le cas de Kateb Yacine.* Lille: Atelier national Reproduction des thèses, Univer sité Lille III, 1982.

Aslanov, Cyril. "Débat sur l'ouvrage de Jocelyne Dakhlia, Lingua franca: Histoire d'une langue métisse en Méditerranée." *Langage et société* 134 (2010): 103–13.

Attal, Robert, and Claude Sitbon, eds. *Regards sur les Juifs de Tunisie.* Paris: Albin Michel, 1979.

Aubry, Anne. "La Mer Méditerranée: Lieu et non-lieu dans *N'zid* et *Mes Hommes.*" *Carnets: Revue électronique d'études françaises* 1 (2009): 17–32.

Audisio, Gabriel. *Algérie Méditerranée: Feux vivants.* Paris: Rougerie, 1957.

———. *Hannibal.* Paris: Gallimard, 1961.

———. *Héliotrope.* Paris: Gallimard, 1928.

———. "Homère à Alger." *Cahiers Du Sud* 325 (1954): 357–61.

———. Introduction to *Cagayous: Ses meilleures histoires*, by Musette [Auguste Robinet]. Paris: Gallimard, 1931. 7–40.

———. *Jeunesse de la Méditerranée.* Paris: Gallimard, 1935.

———. *La Vie de Haroun-al-Raschid.* Paris: Gallimard, 1930.

———. *Sel de la mer.* Paris: Gallimard, 1936.

Azza-Bekkat, Amina. "Albert Camus et l'Algérie: Le malentendu." In *Albert*

Camus, précurseur: Méditerranée d'hier et aujoud'hui. Ed. Alek Toumi. New York: Peter Lang, 2009. 9–22.

Azza-Bekkat, Amina, Afifa Bererhi, Christiane Chaulet-Achour, and Bouba Mohammedi-Tabti, eds. *Quand les Algériens lisent Camus*. Algiers: Casbah, 2014.

Babelmed. "A Life Full of Holes: The Strait Project." N.d. Accessed September 22, 2012. http://eng. babelmed.net/cultura-e-societa/74-marocco/138-a-life-full-of-holes-the-strait-project.html.

Bachi, Salim. *Le Dernier Été d'un jeune homme*. Paris: Flammarion, 2013.

Bacri, Roland. *Trésors des racines pataouètes*. Paris: Belin, 1983.

Bakhtin, Mikhail M. *The Dialogic Imagination*. Ed. Michael Holquist. Trans. Caryl Emerson and Michael Holquist. Austin: University of Texas Press, 1981.

Balta, Paul, Catherine Dana, and Régine Dhoquois-Cohen, eds. *La Méditerranée des Juifs: Exodes et enracinements*. Paris: L'Harmattan, 2003.

Barbé, Philippe. *L'Anti-Choc des civilisations: Médiations méditerranéennes*. La Tour-d'Aigues: Éditions de l'Aube, 2006.

Barrault, Émile. *Occident et Orient: Études politiques, morales, religieuses pendant 1833–1834 de l'ère chrétienne, 1249–1250 de l'héjire*. Paris: Desessart, 1835.

Barrès, Maurice. *Les Déracinés*. Paris: Gallimard, 1994.

Bauman, Zygmunt. *Liquid Modernity*. Cambridge, UK: Polity Press, 2000.

Béji, Hélé. *Le Désenchantement national*. Paris: Maspéro, 1982.

Bekri, Tahar. *Le Chant du roi errant*. Paris: L'Harmattan, 1985.

———. *Les Chapelets d'attache*. Paris: L'Harmattan, 1994.

Belamri, Rabah. *L'Œuvre de Louis Bertrand: Miroir de l'idéologie colonialiste*. Algiers: Office des Publications Universitaires, 1980.

Belaskri, Yahia. *Une longue nuit d'absence*. Algiers: Éditions Apic, 2013.

Benalil, Mounia, ed. "Écritures carcérales dans les littératures maghrébines." Special issue of *Expressions Maghrébines* 10.2 (2011).

Benjamin, Walter. "Central Park." In *Selected Writings 1938–1940*. Ed. Howard Eiland and Michael W. Jennings. Cambridge, MA: Harvard University Press, 2003. 161–99.

———. *The Origin of German Tragic Drama*. Trans. John Osborne. London: New Left Books, 2003.

Ben Jelloun, Tahar. *Beckett et Genet: Un thé à Tanger*. Paris: Gallimard, 2010.

———. *Harrouda*. Paris: Gallimard, 1988.

———. *Jean Genet, menteur sublime*. Paris: Gallimard, 2010.

———. *La Nuit de l'erreur*. Paris: Seuil, 1997.

———. *Leaving Tangier.* Trans. Linda Coverdale. New York: Penguin Books, 2009.

———. "Le Clandestin." *Libération*, March 22, 1992, 8.

———. *Partir.* Paris: Gallimard, 2006.

———. "Point de vue: Le monde arabe est fatigué." 2004. Accessed July 7, 2014. http://www.taharbenjelloun.org/index.php?id=48&tx_ttnews[tt_news]=161&cHash=4b349873c0172de9ee7036b235673f8b.

———. *Silent Day in Tangier.* Trans. David Lobdell. San Diego, CA: Harcourt Brace Jovanovich, 1991.

———. *This Blinding Absence of Light.* Trans. Linda Coverdale. New York: New Press, 2002.

Bensmaïa, Réda. *Experimental Nations.* Princeton, NJ: Princeton University Press, 2003.

———. "Media-terranean, or between Borders: Nabile Farès's *Un passager de l'Occident.*" In *The Mediterranean Reconsidered: Representations, Emergences, Recompositions.* Ed. Mauro Peressini and Ratiba Hadj-Moussa. Gatineau: Canadian Museum of Civilization, 2005. 109–23.

Bentahar, Ziad. "Continental Drift: The Disjunction of North and Sub-Saharan Africa." *Research in African Literatures* 42.1 (2011): 1–13.

Ben Yahia, Turkia Labidi. *Les Exilés de Valence.* Tunis: Cérès, 1996.

Ben-Yehoyada, Naor. "Mediterranean Modernity?" In *A Companion to Mediterranean History.* Ed. Peregrine Horden and Sharon Kinoshita. Oxford: Wiley Blackwell, 2014. 107–21.

Berger, Anne-Emmanuelle. *Algeria in Others' Languages.* Ed. Anne-Emmanuelle Berger. Ithaca, NY: Cornell University Press, 2002.

Bernal, Martin. *Black Athena: The Afro-Asiatic Roots of Classical Civilization I. The Fabrication of Ancient Greece 1785–1985.* London: Free Association Books and Rutgers University Press, 1987.

Bertrand, Louis. *La Cina.* Paris: Ollendorf, 1901.

———. *Le Sang des races.* Paris: Ollendorf, 1910.

———. *Les Villes d'or.* In *Algérie et Tunisie romaines.* Paris: Arthème Fayard, 1921.

———. *Sur les routes du Sud.* Paris: Arthème Fayard, 1936.

Bevilacqua, Alexander. *The Republic of Arabic Letters: Islam and the European Enlightenment.* Cambridge, MA: Harvard University Press, forthcoming.

Bhabha, Homi. *The Location of Culture.* London: Routledge, 1994.

Boehmer, Elleke. "Minor Transnationalism (Review)." *Journal of Colonialism and Colonial History* 6.3 (2005). Accessed April 14, 2012. https://muse.jhu.edu/article/192166.

Boer, Inge. *Uncertain Territories: Boundaries in Cultural Analysis*. New York: Rodopi, 2006.

Boissier, Gaston. *L'Afrique romaine: Promenades archéologiques en Algérie et en Tunisie*. Paris: Librairie Hachette, 1895.

Boissière, Gustave. *L'Algérie romaine*. 2 vols. Paris: Librairie Hachette, 1883.

Bonn, Charles. *Kateb Yacine:* Nedjma. Paris: Presses Universitaires de France, 1990.

———. "L'Irrégularité de l'écrivain maghrébin francophone: 'Nedjma' de Kateb Yacine dans le contexte des années cinquante." *Revue de l'Institut de Sociologie* (1992): 129–38. http://www.limag.refer.org/Textes/Bonn/IrregulierKateb.htm.

Boudjedra, Rachid. *La Prise de Gibraltar*. Paris: Denoël, 1987.

Boudraa, Nabil, ed. *Hommage à Kateb Yacine*. Paris: L'Harmattan, 2006.

Bouhmouch, Nadir, director. *My Makhzen and Me*. Documentary. Mamfakinch/Seaurchin Productions, 2012.

Bouraoui, Hédi. *Tunisie plurielle: Actes du colloque de l'Université de York*. Tunis: L'Or du Temps, 1997.

Bournaz-Baccar, Alia. *La Méditerranée: Odyssée des cultures*. Tunis: Publications de l'ENS/Les Éditions Sahar, 2008.

Boym, Svetlana. *The Future of Nostalgia*. New York: Basic Books, 2001.

Brahimi, Denise. "N'zid: Quelle naissance?" In *Des femmes et de l'écriture: Le bassin méditerrannéen*. Ed. Carmen Boustani and Edmond Jouve. Paris: Editions Karthala, 2006. 133–43.

Braudel, Fernand. *The Mediterranean and the Mediterranean World in the Age of Philip II*. Vol. 1. Trans. Siân Reynolds. London: Collins, 1972.

Brickell, Katherine, and Ayona Datta. *Translocal Geographies: Spaces, Places, Connections*. Aldershot, UK: Ashgate, 2011.

Brisley, Lucy. "Melancholia and Victimhood in Boualem Sansal's *Le Village de l'Allemand: Ou Le journal des frères Schiller*." *Research in African Literatures* 44.1 (2013): 55–74.

Brozgal, Lia. "When Good Sentiments Make for 'Bad' Cinema: Reconsidering Allegory in *Un été à la Goulette*." *Contemporary French and Francophone Studies* 17.1 (2013): 28–37.

Brua, Edmond. *Fables dites bônoises*. Algiers: Charlot, 1946.

———. *La Parodie du Cid*. Algiers: Andréo, 1942.

Bueno Alonso, Josefina. "Género, exilio y desterritorialidad en *L'últim patriarca* de Najat El Hachmi." In *De Guinea Ecuatorial a las literaturas hispanoafricanas*. Ed. Landry-Wilfrid Miampika and Patricia Arroyo. Madrid: Verbum, 2010. 213–26.

Buresi, Pascal. "La Frontière: Laboratoire des mythes dans la péninsule Ibérique (Xe–XVe siècle)?" *Cahiers de la Mediterranée* 86 (2013): 237–56.

Cacciari, Massimo. *L'Arcipelago*. Milan: Adelphi, 2005.

Cailler, Bernadette. *Carthage ou la flamme du brasier: Mémoires et échos chez Virgile, Senghor, Mellah, Ghachem, Augustin, Ammi, Broch et Glissant*. New York : Rodopi, 2007.

Camus, Albert. *Algerian Chronicles*. Cambridge, MA: Harvard University Press, 2013.

———. "La Culture indigène: La Nouvelle Culture méditerranéenne." In *Œuvres complètes*. Vol. 1: *1931–1944*. Bibliothèque de la Pléiade 161. Paris: Gallimard, 2006. 565–71.

———. *L'Envers et l'endroit*. Paris: Gallimard, 1958.

———. *Le Premier Homme*. Paris: Gallimard, 1994.

———. "Noces à Tipasa." In *Noces, suivi de l'Été*. Paris: Gallimard, 1959. 11–21.

———. *Noces, suivi de l'Été*. Paris: Gallimard, 1959.

———. "Notre ami Roblès." *Simoun* 30 (1959): 3.

———. *The Rebel: An Essay on Man in Revolt*. New York: Vintage, 1956.

———. "*Rivages*: Revue de culture méditerranéenne." In *Œuvres complètes*. Vol. 1: *1931–1944*. Bibliothèque de la Pléiade. Paris: Gallimard, 2006. 869–71.

Carlson, Anne. "Navigation, Intertextuality, and In-between Spaces: Expressions of Identity in Malika Mokeddem's *N'zid*." *Canadian Review of Comparative Literature* 32.3–4 (2005): 343–65.

Carroll, David. *Albert Camus, the Algerian*. New York: Columbia University Press, 2007.

Casarino, Cesare. *Modernity at Sea: Melville, Marx, Conrad in Crisis*. Minneapolis: University of Minnesota Press, 2002.

Cassano, Franco. *Il Pensiero meridiano*. Rome: Laterza, 2005.

———. *Southern Thought and Other Essays on the Mediterranean*. Ed. Norma Bouchard and Valerio Ferme. New York: Fordham University Press, 2012.

Castro, Américo. *España en su historia: Cristianos, moros y judíos*. Buenos Aires: Losada, 1948.

Caygill, Howard. "Walter Benjamin's Concept of Cultural History." In *The Cambridge Companion to Walter Benjamin*. Ed. David S. Ferris. Cambridge, UK: Cambridge University Press, 2004. 73–96.

Chambers, Iain. "A Fluid Archive." N.d. Accessed July 7, 2014. http://www.cidob.org/content/download/38947/603221/file/11-22_IAIN+CHAMBERS.pdf.

———. "Maritime Criticism and Theoretical Shipwreck." *PMLA* 125.3 (2010): 678–84.

———. *Mediterranean Crossings: The Politics of an Interrupted Modernity.* Durham, NC: Duke University Press, 2008.

Chambers, Ross. "The Long Howl: Serial Torture." *Yale French Studies* 118–19 (2010): 39–51.

Chaulet-Achour, Christiane. "Autobiographies d'algériennes sur l'autre rive: Se définir entre mémoire et ruptures." In *Littératures autobiographiques de la francophonie.* Ed. Martine Mathieu. Paris: L'Harmattan, 1996. 291–308.

———. "Place d'une littérature migrante en France: Matériaux pour une recherche." N.d. Accessed March 5, 2011. http://www.limag.com/Textes/Collimmigrations2/Christiane%20CHAULET.htm.

———. "Renaître et poursuivre, à propos de *N'zid* de Malika Mokeddem." *Algérie Littérature/Action* 49–50 (March–April 2001): 189–92.

Cheah, Pheng. "What Is a World? On World Literature as World-Making Activity." *Daedalus* 137.3 (2008): 26–38.

Chekroun, Mohammed. *Jeux et enjeux politiques au Maroc.* Rabat: Éditions Okrad, 1990.

Chems Nadir. *L'Astrolabe de la mer.* Paris: Stock, 1980.

Cheng, Anne Anlin. *The Melancholy of Race: Psychoanalysis, Assimilation, and Hidden Grief.* Oxford: Oxford University Press, 2001.

Choukri, Mohamed. *For Bread Alone.* Trans. Paul Bowles. New York: Saqi, 2012.

Chraïbi, Driss. *Birth at Dawn.* Trans. Ann Woollcombe. Boulder, CO: Lynne Rienner, 1990.

———. *Mother Spring.* Trans. Hugh Halter. Boulder, CO: Lynne Rienner, 1989.

Clancy-Smith, Julia. *Mediterraneans: North Africa and Europe in an Age of Migration c. 1800–1900.* Berkeley: University of California Press, 2011.

Cohen, Margaret. *The Novel and the Sea.* Princeton, NJ: Princeton University Press, 2010.

Cook, David. *Understanding Jihad.* Berkeley: University of California Press, 2005.

Copeland, Rita, and Peter T. Struck. *The Cambridge Companion to Allegory.* Cambridge, UK: Cambridge University Press, 2010.

Corpet, Olivier, Albert Dichy, and Mireille Djaider, eds. *Kateb Yacine: Éclats de mémoire.* Paris: IMEC, 1994.

Cowan, Bainard. "Walter Benjamin's Theory of Allegory."*New German Critique* 22 (1981): 109–22.

Crowley, Patrick. "Eugene Fromentin: Travel, Algeria, and the Pursuit of Aesthetic Form." In *Mediterranean Travels: Writing Self and Other from the Ancient World to Contemporary Society*. Oxford: Legenda, 2011. 146–61.

Cruz, Trino. "El bilingüismo gibraltareño: Aproximación a una literatura que se resiste a nacer." Congreso Internacional de la Lengua Española 2004. Instituto Cervantes. Accessed July 13, 2014. http://congresosdelalengua.es/rosario/ponencias/identidad/cruz_t.htm.

———. *Rihla (Poemas 1983–2002)*. San Roque, Spain: Luis Ortega Brú, 2003.

Çelik, Zeynep. *Urban Forms and Colonial Confrontations: Algiers under French Rule*. Berkeley: University of California Press, 1997.

Dakhlia, Jocelyne. *Lingua franca: Histoire d'une langue métisse en Méditerranée*. Arles: Actes Sud 2008.

———. *L'Oubli de la cité: La Mémoire collective à l'épreuve du lignage dans le Jérid tunisien*. Paris : La Découverte, 1994.

Daoud, Kamel. *Meursault contre-enquête*. Algiers: Barzakh, 2013.

Dash, J. Michael. *The Other America: Caribbean Literature in a New World Context*. Charlottesville: University Press of Virginia, 1998.

Déjeux, Jean. "Bibliographie méthodique et critique de la littérature algérienne d'expression française, 1945–1970." *Revue de l'Occident et de la Méditerranée* 10.10 (1971): 111–303.

———. *Maghreb littératures de langue française*. Paris: Arcantère, 1993.

Deleuze, Gilles. *Difference and Repetition*. Trans. Paul Patton. New York: Columbia University Press, 1994.

Deleuze, Gilles, and Félix Guattari. *A Thousand Plateaus: Capitalism and Schizophrenia*. Minneapolis: University of Minnesota Press, 1987.

De Man, Paul. "The Rhetoric of Temporality." In *Blindness and Insight*. 2nd edition. Minneapolis: University of Minnesota Press, 1983. 187–228.

Depierris, Jean-Louis. *Entretiens avec Emmanuel Roblès*. Paris: Seuil, 1967.

Derrida, Jacques. *Le Dernier des Juifs*. Paris: Galilée, 2014.

———. "Mnemosyne." In *Memoires for Paul De Man: The Wellek Library Lectures*. New York: Columbia University Press, 1989. 1–44.

De Toro, Alfonso, ed. "Dispositifs autobiographiques et épistémologies transversales." Special issue of *Expressions maghrébines* 10.1 (2011).

———. *Épistémologies "Le Maghreb."* Paris: L'Harmattan, 2009.

De Toro, Alfonso, Khalid Zekri, Réda Bensmaïa, and Hafid Gafaïti, eds. *Repenser le Maghreb et l'Europe: Hybridations-Métissages-Diasporisations*. Paris: L'Harmattan, 2010.

Dietz, Gunther. "Frontier Hybridization or Culture Clash? Transnational

Migrant Communities and Sub-National Identity Politics in Andalusia, Spain." *Journal of Ethnic and Migration Studies* 30.6 (2003): 1087–112.

Dine, Philip. "The French Colonial Myth of a Pan Mediterranean Civilization." In *Transnational Spaces and Identities in the Francophone World*. Ed. Hafid Gafaïti, Patricia M. E. Lorcin, and David G. Troyanksy. Lincoln: University of Nebraska Press, 2009. 3–23.

Djebar, Assia. *Le Blanc de l'Algérie*. Paris: Albin Michel, 1995.

Dobie, Madeleine. "For and Against the Mediterranean." *Comparative Studies of South Asia, Africa, and the Middle East* 34.2 (2014): 389–404.

Dodds, Jerrilynn Denise. *Al-Andalus: The Art of Islamic Spain*. New York: Metropolitan Museum of Art, 1992.

Donadey, Anne. "Introjection and Incorporation in Assia Djebar's *La Femme sans sépulture*." *L'Esprit Créateur* 48.4 (2008): 81–91.

———. "L'Expression littéraire du traumatisme dans *La Femme sans sépulture* d'Assia Djebar." In *Assia Djebar: Littérature et Transmission*. Ed. Wolfgang Asholt, Mireille Caille-Gruber, and Dominique Combe. Paris: Presses de la Sorbonne Nouvelle, 2010. 67–80.

———. *Recasting Postcolonialism: Women Writing between Worlds*. Portsmouth, NH: Heinemann, 2001.

Dugas, Guy. *Algérie, un rêve de fraternité*. Paris: Omnibus, 1999.

———. *Emmanuel Roblès*. Algiers: Éditions du Tell, 2007.

———. *La Méditerranée de Audisio à Roy*. Houilles, France: Manucius, 2008.

———. "Les Amitiés algériennes: Mohammed Dib et le rêve de fraternité." Institut Français, n.d. Accessed October 26, 2014. http://www.limag.refer.org/Textes/2013ColloqueDib/Dugas.pdf.

———. *Tunisie: Rêves de partages*. Paris: Omnibus, 2005.

Dunwoodie, Peter. "Colonizing Space: Louis Bertrand's Algeria in 'Le Sang des races' and 'Sur les routes du Sud.'" *Modern Language Review* 105.4 (2010): 997–1014.

———. *Francophone Writing in Transition: Algeria 1900–1945*. Bern: Peter Lang, 2005.

———. *Writing French Algeria*. Oxford: Oxford University Press, 1998.

Dussel, Enrique. "World–System and Trans-Modernity." *Nepantla: Views from the South* 3.2 (2002): 221–44.

Eickelman, Dale F., and James P. Piscatori. *Muslim Travelers: Pilgrimage, Migration, and the Religious Imagination*. Berkeley: University of California Press, 1990.

El-Ariss, Tarek. *Trials of Arab Modernity: Literary Affects and the New Political*. New York: Fordham University Press, 2013.

Elbaz, Robert. “N’zid ou la mémoire cutanée.” In *Malika Mokeddem*. Ed. Najib Redouane, Yvette Bénayoun-Szmidt, and Robert Elbaz. Paris: L’Harmattan, 2003. 251–71.

El Bouanani, Nerimane, and Dina Abdelouahab. “Entrevista a los Poetas Juan Gómez Macía y Trino Cruz.” *Kasbah: Revista del IES Severo Ochoa* 14 (2003): 2.

El Hachmi, Najat. *Jo també soc catalana*. Barcelona: Columna, 2004.

———. *L’ Últim Patriarca*. Barcelona: Planeta, 2008.

Elhariry, Yasser. “The Mediterranean Lyric.” In *Critically Mediterranean: Aesthetics, Theory, Hermeneutics, Culture*. Ed. Yasser Elhariry and Edwige Tamalet Talbayev. Forthcoming.

El-Harti, Larbi. *Después de Tánger*. Madrid: SIAL Ediciones, 2003.

Ellis-House, Marie-Therese. “Al-Andalus as a Metaphor of Collective Identity for 1940s Moroccan Intellectuals.” *Journal of Mediterranean Studies* 21.1 (2012): 101–26.

———. “Hybridity as Dissent from Imperialism in the Colonial Periodical *Forge*.” *Expressions maghrébines* 11.2 (2012): 107–24.

El-Nossery, Névine. “Malika Mokeddem: Une méduse nomade et sans tribu.” *Expressions maghrébines* 9.1. (2010): 199–209.

Eng, David L., and David Kazanjian, eds. *Loss: The Politics of Mourning*. Berkeley: University of California Press, 2003.

Esposito, Claudia. *The Narrative Mediterranean: Beyond France and the Maghreb*. Lanham, MD: Lexington Books, 2013.

Esposito, Claudia, Edwige Tamalet Talbayev, and Hakim Abderrezak, eds. “Le Maghreb méditerranéen: Littérature et plurilinguisme. ” Special issue of *Expressions maghrébines* 11.2 (2012).

Euben, Roxanne L. *Journeys to the Other Shore: Muslim and Western Travelers in Search of Knowledge*. Princeton, NJ: Princeton University Press, 2006.

Evans, Martin. *Algeria: France’s Undeclared War*. Oxford: Oxford University Press, 2012.

Fabre, Thierry. “La France et la Méditerranée. Généalogies et représentations.” In *La Méditerranée française*. Ed. Jean-Claude Izzo and Thierry Fabre. Paris: Maisonneuve & Larose, 2000. 13–152.

———. *L’Héritage andalou*. Tour-d’Aigues: Éditions de l’aube, 1995.

Fanon, Frantz. *A Dying Colonialism*. New York: Grove Press, 1967.

Farès, Nabile. *Le Miroir de Cordoue*. Paris: L’Harmattan, 1994.

———. *Un passager de l’Occident*. Paris: Seuil, 1971.

Fellous, Colette. *Avenue de France*. Paris: Gallimard, 2001.

Fernández Goma, Paloma. “Tres orillas desde la poesía de Abderraman El

Fathi y Trino Cruz." *Almoraima: Revista de estudios campogibraltareños* 30 (2003): 71–76.

Figeac, Jean-Louis. "La Géopolitique orientale des saint-simoniens." *Cahiers de la Méditerranée* 85 (2012): 251–68.

Finkielkraut, Alain. *Le Juif imaginaire*. Paris: Seuil 1980.

Flesler, Daniela. *The Return of the Moor: Spanish Responses to Contemporary Moroccan Immigration*. West Lafayette, IN: Purdue University Press, 2008.

Fogu, Claudio. "From *Mare Nostrum* to *Mare Aliorum*: Mediterranean Theory and Mediterraneism in Contemporary Italian Thought." *California Italian Studies* 1.1 (2010): 1–23.

Forsdick, Charles, and David Murphy. "Introduction: The Case for Francophone Postcolonial Studies." In *Francophone Postcolonial Studies: A Critical Introduction*. Ed. Charles Forsdick and David Murphy. London: Arnold, 2003. 1–16.

Foxlee, Neil. *Albert Camus's "The New Mediterranean Culture": A Text and Its Contexts*. Oxford: Peter Lang, 2010.

Gana, Nouri. "In Search of Andalusia: Reconfiguring Arabness in Diana Abu-Jaber's Crescent." *Comparative Literature Studies* 45.2 (2008): 228–46.

———. *Signifying Loss: Towards a Poetic of Narrative Mourning*. Lewisburg, PA: Bucknell University Press, 2011.

García-Arenal, Mercedes, and Gerard Wiegers, eds. *Los moriscos: Expulsión y diáspora. Una perspectiva internacional*. Valencia: Universitat de València, Granada y Zaragoza, 2013.

Genet, Jean. *The Thief's Journal*. Trans. Bernard Frechtman. New York: Grove Press, 1964.

Gerber, Jane. *The Jews of Spain: A History of the Sephardic Experience*. New York: Free Press, 1992.

Ghachem, Moncef. *Cap Africa*. Paris: L'Harmattan, 1989.

Giaccaria, Paolo, and Claudio Minca. "The Mediterranean Alternative." *Progress in Human Geography* 35.3 (2011): 345–65.

Glissant, Édouard. *Poetics of Relation*. Trans. Betsy Wing. Ann Arbor: University of Michigan Press, 1997.

Global Detention Project. "Morocco Immigration Detention." February 2014. Accessed April 17, 2014. http://www.globaldetentionproject.org/countries/africa/morocco/introduction.html#c354.

Gontard, Marc. *Nedjma de Kateb Yacine: Essai sur la structure formelle du roman*. Paris: L'Harmattan, 1985.

Gonzales, Jean-Jacques. "Une utopie méditerranéenne: Albert Camus et l'Algérie en guerre." In *La Guerre d'Algérie 1954–2004: La Fin de l'amnésie*. Ed. Mohammed Harbi and Benjamin Stora. Paris: Laffont, 2004. 597–620.

Goytisolo, Juan. *Cuaderno de Sarajevo*. Mexico City: Aguilar, 1994.

———. "El legado andalusí: Una perspectiva occidental." 1997. *La Insignia*, January 30, 2004. Accessed March 15, 2015. http://www.lainsignia.org/2004/enero/cul_081.htm.

Graebner, Seth. *History's Place: Nostalgia and the City in French Algerian Literature*. Lanham, MD: Lexington Books, 2007.

———. "Kateb Yacine and the Ruins of the Present." *SubStance* 112, 36.1 (2007): 139–63.

Granara, William. "Nostalgia, Arab Nationalism, and the Andalusian Chronotope in the Evolution of the Modern Arabic Novel." *Journal of Arabic Literature* 36.1 (2005): 57–73.

Grine, Hamid. *Camus dans le narguilé*. Paris: Après la lune, 2011.

Gsell, Stéphane. *Histoire ancienne de l'Afrique du Nord*. Paris: Hachette, 1913.

———. *L'Algérie dans l'Antiquité*. Paris: Adolphe Jourdan, 1903.

Gueydan-Turek, Alexandra. "'Homeland beyond Homelands': Reinventing Algeria through a Transnational Literary Community. Assia Djebar's *Le Blanc de l'Algérie*." *Cincinnati Romance Review* 31: 85–102.

Haddad de Paz, Charles. *Juifs et Arabes au pays de Bourguiba*. Aix-en-Provence: P. Roubaud, 1977.

Haddour, Azzedine. *Colonial Myths: History and Narrative*. Manchester, UK: Manchester University Press, 2000.

Hafez, Sabri. *The Genesis of Arabic Narrative Discourse: A Study in the Sociology of Modern Arabic Literature*. London: Saqi, 1993.

Hagège, Claude, and Bernard Zarca. "Les Juifs et la France en Tunisie: Les bénéfices d'une relation triangulaire." *Le Mouvement social* 197 (2001): 9–28.

Halevi-Wise, Yael. *Sephardism: Spanish Jewish History and the Modern Literary Imagination*. Stanford: Stanford University Press, 2012.

Halim, Hala. *Alexandrian Cosmopolitanism: An Archive*. New York: Fordham University Press, 2013.

Hallward, Peter. *Out of This World: Deleuze and the Philosophy of Creation*. London: Verso, 2006.

Hammoudi, Abdellah. *Master and Disciple: The Cultural Foundations of Moroccan Authoritarianism*. Chicago: University of Chicago Press, 1997.

Hargreaves, Alec. *Immigration, "Race," and Ethnicity in Contemporary France*. London: Routledge, 1995.

———. *Immigration and Identity in Beur Fiction: Voices from the North African Community in France.* Oxford: Berg, 1997.

———. *Multi-ethnic France: Immigration, Politics, Culture, and Society.* New York: Routledge, 2007.

Harris, W. V., ed. *Rethinking the Mediterranean.* Oxford: Oxford University Press, 2006.

Harrison, Olivia C. *Transcolonial Maghreb: Imagining Palestine in the Era of Decolonization.* Stanford: Stanford University Press, 2016.

Helm, Yolande. "La Méditerranée, espace transculturel dans *N'zid* de Malika Mokeddem." *Peuples & mondes*, December 22, 2003. Accessed January 5, 2009. http://www.peuplesmonde.com/spip.php?article16.

Hiddleston, Jane. *Assia Djebar: Out of Algeria.* Liverpool: Liverpool University Press, 2006.

———. *Understanding Postcolonialism.* Stocksfield, UK: Acumen, 2009.

Hochberg, Gil Z. "'The Mediterranean Option': On the Politics of Regional Affiliation in Current Israeli Cultural Imagination." *Journal of Levantine Studies* 1 (2011): 41–65.

Horden, Peregrine, and Nicholas Purcell. *The Corrupting Sea: A Study of Mediterranean History.* Oxford: Wiley Blackwell, 2000.

Horden, Peregrine, and Nicholas Purcell. "The Mediterranean and 'the New Thalassology.'" *American Historical Review* 111.3 (2006): 722–40.

Ibn Khaldun. *Muqqadimah.* Trans. F. Rosenthal. *Islamic Philosophy Online.* Accessed March 14, 2009. https://asadullahali.files.wordpress.com/2012/10/ibn_khaldun-al_muqaddimah.pdf.

Ilustre Ayuntamiento de San Roque. Accessed July 25, 2014. http://www.sanroque.es/content/rihla?language=es.

Jaffeux, Vincent. "Alger au temps des *Vraies Richesses*: L'ascension d'une génération littéraire nord-africaine autour d'Edmond Charlot (1936–1944)." *Cahiers d'histoire immédiate* 43 supp.: 19–29.

Jameson, Fredric. "Third World Literature in the Era of Multinational Capitalism." *Social Text* 15 (1986): 65–88.

Jay, Salim. *Tu ne traverseras pas le Détroit.* Paris: Mille et une nuits, 2001.

Karrouch, Leila. *De Nador a Vic.* Barcelona: Columna, 2004.

Kassab-Charfi, Samia. "Architecture et Histoire chez Colette Fellous." *Revue de Littérature Comparée* 327 (2008): 397–406.

———. "Entretien avec Colette Fellous." *Expressions maghrébines* 11.2 (2012): 145–57.

———. "Sémiologie du Lieu d'une migration: L'exemple de Testour, village morisque de Tunisie." In *La Rencontre, Actes du 12ème colloque international du CEREAP*. Ed. Dominique Berthet. Paris: L'Harmattan, 2011. 117–50.

Kateb, Yacine. "Djerba, l'île de l'Étrangère." *L'Action*, July 14, 1958.

———. "Le Lotos." In *L'Œuvre en fragments: Inédits littéraires et textes retrouvés, rassemblés et présentés par Jacqueline Arnaud*. Paris: Sinbad, 1986. 148–53.

———. "Le Papyrus, l'abeille et le serpent." In *L'Œuvre en fragments*. Ed. Jacqueline Arnaud. Paris: Sinbad, 1986. 256–57.

———. *Le Poète comme un boxeur*. Paris: Seuil, 1994.

———. *Le Polygone étoilé*. Paris: Seuil, 1997.

———. "Les Poissons sautent." In *L'Œuvre en fragments: Inédits littéraires et textes retrouvés, rassemblés et présentés par Jacqueline Arnaud*. Paris: Sinbad, 1986. 153–57.

———. *L'Œuvre en fragments: Inédits littéraires et textes retrouvés, rassemblés et présentés par Jacqueline Arnaud*. Paris: Sinbad, 1986.

———. "Nazim Hikmet ou le chant des exilés." In *Minuit passé de douze heures: Écrits journalistiques 1947–1989*. Paris: Seuil, 1999. 235–40.

———. *Nedjma*. 1956; Paris: Seuil, 1996.

———. *Nedjma*. Trans. Richard Howard. Charlottesville: University of Virginia Press, 1991.

———. "Une étoile de sang noir." In *Minuit passé de douze heures: Écrits journalistiques 1947–1989*. Paris: Seuil, 1999. 196–203.

Khaïr-Eddine, Mohammed. *Une odeur de mantèque*. Paris: Seuil, 1976.

Khanna, Ranjana. *Algeria Cuts: Women and Representation, 1830 to the Present*. Stanford: Stanford University Press, 2008.

Khatibi, Abdelkébir. *Amour bilingue*. Montpellier: Fata Morgana, 1993.

———. "Au-delà du trauma." In *Par-dessus l'épaule*. Paris: Aubier, 1988. 123–35.

———. "Diglossia." In *Algeria in Others' Languages*. Ed. Anne-Emmanuelle Berger. Ithaca, NY: Cornell University Press, 2002. 157–60.

———. *La Mémoire tatouée*. Paris: Les Lettres nouvelles, 1971.

———. *Maghreb Pluriel*. Paris: Denoël, 1983.

———. "Pensée-Autre." In *Œuvres de Abdelkébir Khatibi*. Vol. 3: *Essais*. Paris: Éditions de la Différence, 2008. 9–27.

Khatibi, Abdelkébir, and Jacques Hassoun. *Le Même Livre*. Paris: Éditions de l'éclat, 1985.

Khemir, Nacer, director. *El Haimoune/Les Baliseurs du désert*. SATPEC, Latif Productions, France média, 1984.

———. *Tawq al-Hamama al-Mafqud/Le Collier de la colombe*. Tarak Ben Amer, Carthago Films, 1991.

Khouri-Dager, Nadia. "Nouvelle Andalousie." Babelmed, February 13, 2009. Accessed February 12, 2015. http://www.babelmed.net/letteratura/256-spagna/4001-nouvelle-andalousie.html.

Khuri-Makdisi, Ilham. *The Eastern Mediterranean and the Making of Global Radicalism 1870–1914*. Berkeley: University of California Press, 2010.

Klinkenberg, Jean-Marie. *Des Langues romanes: Introduction aux études de linguistique romane*. Brussels: De Beock & Larcier, 1999.

Kinoshita, Sharon. "Mediterranean Literature." In *A Companion to Mediterranean History*. Ed. Peregrine Horden and Sharon Kinoshita. Oxford: Wiley Blackwell, 2014. 314–29.

Laâbi, Abdellatif. *La Poésie palestinienne de combat*. Honfleur: P. J. Oswald, 1970.

———. *L'Oeil et la nuit*. Casablanca: Atlantes, 1969.

———. "Méditations à Grenade." In *Sous le bâillon le poème*. Paris: L'Harmattan, 1981. 103–16.

LaCapra, Dominick. *History and Memory after Auschwitz*. Ithaca, NY: Cornell University Press, 1998.

Lacheraf, Mostefa. "L'Avenir de la culture algérienne." *Les Temps modernes* 19.209 (1963): 720–45.

Lakhous, Amara. *Divorzio all'islamica a Viale Marconi*. Rome: Edizioni e/o, 2010.

———. *Scontro di civiltà per un ascensore a Piazza Vittorio*. Rome: Edizioni e/o, 2006.

Lamrabet, Rachida. *Een kind van God*. Amsterdam: Meulenhoff, Manteau, 2008.

———. *Vrouwland*. Amsterdam: Meulenhoff, Manteau, 2007.

Laroui, Fouad. *Hollandse Woorden*. Amsterdam: Vassallucci, 2004.

———. *Verbannen Woorden*. Amsterdam: Vassallucci, 2002.

Laroussi, Farid, and Christopher L. Miller, eds. "French and Francophone: The Challenge of Expanding Horizons." *Yale French Studies* 103 (2003).

Lasnari, Ahmed. *La Littérature algérienne de l'entre-deux-guerres: Genèse et fonctionnement*. Paris: Publisud, 1995.

Latiri Carpenter, Dora. "'Née à Tunis virgule Tunisie': *Avenue de France* de Colette Fellous." *Expressions maghrébines* 5.1 (2006): 97–111.

Le Rider, Jacques. *Modernité viennoise et crises de l'identité*. Paris: Presses Universitaires de France, 1990.

LeSueur, James. *Algeria since 1989: Between Terror and Democracy*. London: Zed Books, 2010.

Liang, Yuen-Gen, Abigail Krasner Balbale, Andrew Devereux, and Camillo

Gomas-Rivas. "The Spain–North Africa Project and the Study of the Western Mediterranean." *Medieval Encounter* 19 (2013): 1–40.

Liauzu, Claude. *Histoire des Migrations en Méditerranée occidentale*. Brussels: Editions Complexe, 1996.

———. "La Mediterranée selon Fernand Braudel." *Confluences Méditerranée* 31 (1999): 179–87.

Linhard, Tabea. *Jewish Spain: A Mediterranean Memory*. Stanford: Stanford University Press, 2014.

Lionnet, Françoise. "Counterpoint and Double Critique in Edward Said and Abdelkebir Khatibi: A Transcolonial Comparison." In *Companion to Comparative Literature*. Ed. Ali Behdad and Dominic Thomas. Chichester, UK: Wiley-Blackwell, 2011. 387–407.

———. "Universalism and Francophonie." *International Journal of Francophone Studies* 12.2–3 (2009): 203–19.

Lionnet, Françoise, and Ronnie Scharfman, eds. "Post/colonial Conditions: Exiles, Migrations, and Nomadisms." Special issue of *Yale French Studies* 82–83 (1993).

Lionnet, Françoise, and Shu-Mei Shih. "Introduction: Thinking through the Minor, Transnationally." In *Minor Transnationalism*. Ed. Françoise Lionnet and Shu-Mei Shih. Durham, NC: Duke University Press, 2005. 1–26.

Lledo, Jean-Pierre, director. *Algérie: Histoires à ne pas dire*. Colifilms Diffusion, 2007.

Loichot, Valérie. *Orphan Narratives: The Postplantation Literature of Faulkner, Glissant, Morrison, and Saint-John Perse*. Charlottesville: University of Virginia Press, 2007.

Lorcin, Patricia M. E. "Decadence and Renascence: Louis Bertrand and the Concept of Rebarbarisation in Fin de Siècle Algeria." In *New Perspectives on the Fin de Siècle in Nineteenth-and Twentieth-Century France*. Ed. Kay Chadwick and Timothy Unwin. London: Edwin Mellen, 2000. 181–97.

———. *Historicizing Colonial Nostalgia: European Women's Narratives of Algeria and Kenya, 1900–Present*. New York: Palgrave Macmillan, 2012.

———. *Imperial Identities: Stereotyping, Prejudice and Race in Colonial Algeria*. London: I. B. Tauris, 1995.

Luzzati, Michele, ed. *Ebrei di Livorno tra due censimenti (1841–1938): Memoria familiare e identità*. Livorno: Belforte, 1990.

Mabrouk, Alia. *Les Blés de Dougga*. Tunis: Clairefontaine, 2004.

———. *Puissant par la Gloire: Genséric, roi des Vandales*. Paris: l'Entreligne, 1998.

MacDonald, Megan C. "The Trans-Mediterranean *navette*: Assia Djebar and the *Dictionnaire des mots français d'origine arabe*." *Contemporary French and Francophone Studies* 17.1 (2013): 58–68.

Macey, David. *The Penguin Dictionary of Critical Theory*. London: Penguin, 2001.

Machosky, Brenda. *Structures of Appearing: Allegory and the Work of Literature*. New York: Fordham University Press, 2013.

Maghraoui, Driss. *Revisiting the Colonial Past in Morocco*. London: Routledge, 2013.

Mahfuz, Najib. *The Journey of Ibn Fattouma*. Trans. Denys Johnson-Davies. New York: Anchor, 1993.

Majid, Anouar. *Freedom and Orthodoxy*. Stanford: Stanford University Press, 2004.

———. *We Are All Moors*. Minneapolis: University of Minnesota Press, 2009.

Malabou, Catherine. *Ontologie de l'accident*. Paris: Léo Scheer, 2009.

Mallette, Karla. *European Modernity and the Arab Mediterranean: Toward a New Philology and a Counter-Orientalism*. Philadelphia: University of Pennsylvania Press, 2010.

Marín, Manuela. "Arabistas en España: Un asunto de familia." *Al-Qantara* 13 (1992): 379–94.

Martin-Márquez, Susan. *Disorientations: Spanish Colonialism in Africa and the Performance of Identity*. New Haven, CT: Yale University Press, 2008.

Marzouki, Ahmed. *Tazmamart cellule 10*. Paris: Editions Paris-Méditerranée, Tarik Editions, 2000.

Masud, Muhammad Khalid. "The Obligation to Migrate: The Doctrine of *hijra* in Islamic Law." In *Muslim Travellers: Pilgrimage, Migration, and the Religious Imagination*. Ed. Dale F. Eickelman and James Piscatori. New York, Routledge, 1990. 29–49.

Mathieu-Job, Martine. *Kateb Yacine et l'étoilement de l'oeuvre*. Ed. A.-Y. Julien, C. Camelin, and F.-J. Authier. Rennes: Presses Universitaires de Rennes, 2010. 145–60.

McManus, Anne-Marie. "Unfinished Awakenings: Afterlives of the Nahda and Postcolonialism in Arabic Literature, 1894–2008." PhD diss., Yale University, 2013.

Mdidech, Jaouad. *La Chambre noire, ou Derb Moulay Cherif*. Casablanca: Eddif, 2000.

Meddeb, Abdelwahab. *The Malady of Islam*. New York: Basic Books, 2003.

———. *Pari de civilisation*. Paris: Seuil, 2009.

———. *Phantasia*. Paris: Sinbad, 1986.

Mehta, Brinda. *Dissident Writings of Arab Women: Voices against Violence*. London: Routledge, 2014.

———. "Geographies of Space: Spatial Impositions, Circularity, and Memory in Malika Mokeddem's *Les Hommes qui marchent* and *Le Siècle des Sauterelles*." *Meridians: Feminism, Race, Transnationalism* 4.1 (2003): 1–38.

Mellah, Fawzi. *Élissa, reine vagabonde*. Paris: Seuil, 1988.

Memmi, Albert. *La Statue de sel*. Preface by Albert Camus. Paris: Gallimard, 1980.

Menocal, María Rosa. *The Ornament of the World: How Muslims, Jews and Christians Created a Culture of Tolerance in Medieval Spain*. Boston: Little, Brown, 2002.

Merdaci, Abdellali. "Le Modèle littéraire colonial: Aspects socio-historiques." *Champs: Recherches en sciences humaines et sociales* 9.17 (2013): 7–28.

Mernissi, Fatima. *Dreams of Trespass: Tales of a Harem Girlhood*. Reading, MA: Addison-Wesley, 1994.

Mertz-Baumgartner, Birgit. "Identité et écriture rhizomiques au féminin." In *Malika Mokeddem: Envers et contre tout*. Ed. Yolande Helm. Paris: L'Harmattan, 2000. 121–36.

Michel, M. "Sur la parenté des Egyptiens, des Berbères et des Basques." *Bulletin de la Société d'Anthropologie de Paris* 4 (1863): 365–67.

Mieszkowski, Jan. "Art Forms." In *The Cambridge Companion to Walter Benjamin*. Ed. David S. Ferris. Cambridge, UK: Cambridge University Press, 2004. 35–53.

Mignolo, Walter. *Local Histories/Global Designs*. Princeton, NJ: Princeton University Press, 2000.

———. "The Many Faces of Cosmo-polis: Border Thinking and Critical Cosmopolitanism." *Public Culture* 12.3 (2000): 721–48.

Miller, Christopher L. *Nationalists and Nomads*. Chicago: University of Chicago Press, 1998.

———. "The Theory and Pedagogy of a World Literature in French." *Yale French Studies* 120 (2011): 33–48.

Miller, Susan Gilson. *A History of Modern Morocco*. New York: Cambridge University Press, 2013.

Mirbagheri, Farid. *War and Peace in Islam: A Critique of Islamic/ist Political Discourses*. Houndmills, UK: Palgrave Macmillan, 2012.

Melliti, Mohsen. *Pantanella: Canto lungo la strada*. Rome: Edizioni Lavoro/Iscos, 1992.

Mokeddem, Malika. *Des Rêves et des assassins*. Paris: Grasset, 1995.

———. *Je dois tout à ton oubli*. Paris: Grasset, 2008.

———. *Les Hommes qui marchent*. Paris: Grasset, 1997.

———. *L'Interdite*. Paris: Grasset, 1993.

———. *N'zid*. Paris: Seuil, 2001.

Morris, Ian. "Mediterraneanization." *Mediterranean Historical Review* 18.2 (2003): 30–55.

Mortimer, Mildred, ed. *Maghrebian Mosaic: A Literature in Transition*. Boulder, CO: Lynne Rienner, 2000.

Mostaghanemi, Ahlam. *Memory in the Flesh*. Cairo: American University in Cairo Press, 2003.

Musette [Auguste Robinet]. *Cagayous: Ses meilleures histoires*. Introduction, notes, and lexicon by Gabriel Audisio. Paris: Gallimard, 1931.

Nancy, Jean-Luc. *Being Singular Plural*. Trans. Robert D. Richardson and Anne E. O'Byrne. Stanford: Stanford University Press, 2000.

———. *The Inoperative Community*. Trans. Peter Connor et al. Minneapolis: University of Minnesota Press, 1991.

Netton, Ian Richard. *Seek Knowledge: Thought and Travel in the House of Islam*. Richmond, UK: Curzon Press, 1996.

Nocke, Alexandra. *The Place of the Mediterranean in Modern Israeli Identity*. Leiden: Brill, 2009.

O'Brien, Conor Cruise. *Albert Camus*. New York: Viking, 1970.

Ohana, David. Foreword to *The Place of the Mediterranean in Modern Israeli Identity*. Ed. Alexandra Nocke. Leiden: Brill, 2009. 1–3.

———. "Israel and the Mediterranean Option." Seminar on Israel. Palestinian Academic Society for the Study of International Affairs, April 10–14, 2000. Accessed January 25, 2012. http://www.passia.org/seminars/2000/israel/part11.html.

Orlando, Valerie K. "Écriture d'un autre lieu: La déterritorialisation des nouveaux rôles féminins dans L'Interdite." In *Malika Mokeddem: Envers et contre tout*. Ed. Yolande Helm. Paris: L'Harmattan, 2000. 105–16.

———. *Francophone Voices of the "New" Morocco in Film and Print: (Re) presenting a Society in Transition*. New York: Palgrave Macmillan, 2009.

———. *Nomadic Voices of Exile*. Athens: Ohio University Press, 1999.

———. *Screening Morocco: Contemporary Film in a Changing Society*. Columbus: Ohio University Press, 2011.

Ouerdane, Amar. *La Question berbère dans le mouvement national algérien 1926–1980*. Québec: Septentrion, 1990.

Oufkir, Malika, and Michèle Fitoussi. *La Prisonnière*. Paris: Grasset, 1999.

Parati, Graziella. *Mediterranean Crossroads: Migration Literature in Italy*. Madison, NJ: Fairleigh Dickinson University Press, Associated University Presses, 1999.

Peristiany, John George, and Julian Pitt-Rivers, eds. *Honor and Grace in Anthropology*. Cambridge, UK: Cambridge University Press, 1992.

Pieprzak, Katarzyna. "Bodies on the Beach: Youssef Elalamy and Moroccan Landscapes of the Clandestine." In *Land and Landscape in Francographic Literature: Remapping Uncertain Territories*. Ed. Katarzyna Pieprzak and Magali Compan. Newcastle, UK: Cambridge Scholars, 2007. 104–22.

Pomier, Jean. "L'Algérianisme: Sa théorie—ses applications." *Afrique* 1–5 (1924).

Pontecorvo, Gillo. *La Battaglia di Algieri*. Igor Films, Casbah Films, 1966.

Prochaska, David. "History as Literature, Literature as History: Cagayous of Algiers." *American Historical Review* 101.3 (1996): 670–711.

———. *Making Algeria French: Colonialism in Bône, 1870–1920*. Cambridge, UK: Cambridge University Press.

Puche, Michel. *Edmond Charlot, éditeur: Bibliographie commentée et illustrée*. Pézenas, France: Domens, 1995.

Qader, Nasrin. *Narratives of Catastrophe: Boris Diop, Ben Jelloun, Khatibi*. New York: Fordham University Press, 2009.

Raiss, Mohammed. *De Skhirat à Tazmamart: Retour du bout de l'enfer*. Casablanca: Afrique Orient, 2002.

Randau, Robert. *Cassard le Berbère*. Paris: J. Carbonel, 1926.

———. *Les Colons: Roman de la patrie algérienne*. Paris: Sansot, 1907.

Rastegar, Kamran. *Literary Modernity between the Middle East and Europe: Textual Transactions in Nineteenth-Century Arabic, English, and Persian Literatures*. New York: Routledge, 2007.

Raybaud, Antoine. "Nomadism between the Archaic and the Modern." *Yale French Studies* 82.1 (1993): 146–57.

Rencontres Méditerranéennes Albert Camus. *Audisio, Camus, Roblès, frères de soleil-leurs combats*. Paris: Edisud, 2003.

Rey-Mimoso-Ruiz, Bernadette. "Émergences fantasmatiques d'al-Andalus." In *Littérature et Espaces*. Ed. Juliette Vion-Dury, Jean-Marie Grassin, Bertrand Westphal. Limoges: Presses Universitaires de Limoges, 2003. 235–50.

Ricci, Cristián. *Hay moros en la costa: Literatura marroquí fronteriza en castellano y catalán*. Frankfurt am Main: Vervuert, 2014.

———. *Letras marruecas: Antología de escritores magrebíes en castellano*. Madrid: Ediciones del Orto, 2012.

———. *Literatura periférica en castellano y catalán: El caso marroquí*. Madrid: Ediciones del Orto, University of Minnesota Press, 2010.

Rice, Alison. *Polygraphies: Francophone Women Writing Algeria*. Charlottesville: University of Virginia Press, 2012.

———. *Times Signatures: Contextualizing Contemporary Francophone Autobiographical Writing from the Maghreb.* Lanham, MD: Lexington Books, 2006.

———."Translating Plurality: Abdelkébir Khatibi and Postcolonial Writing in French from the Maghreb." In *Postcolonial Thought from the French Speaking World.* Ed. Charles Forsdick and David Murphy. Liverpool, UK: Liverpool University Press, 2009. 115–25.

Rivas, Pierre. "La Quête d'identité dans l'autobiographie d'Emmanuel Roblès: Relations interethniques et problèmes d'acculturation." In *Espagne et Algérie au XXème siècle: Contacts culturels et création littéraire.* Ed. Jean Déjeux. Paris: L'Harmattan, 1985. 161–77.

Roblès, Emmanuel. *Camus, frère de soleil.* Paris: Seuil, 1995.

Rodríguez Mediano, Fernando. *Humanismo y progreso: Las ciencias humanas en España.* Madrid: Nívola, 2002.

Rogozen-Soltar, Mikaela. "Managing Muslim Visibility: Conversion, Immigration, and Spanish Imaginaries of Islam." *American Anthropologist* 114.4 (2012): 611–23.

Rosello, Mireille. "Becoming UnDutch: 'Wil je dat? Kun je dat.'" In *The Postcolonial Low-Countries: Literature, Postcolonialism, and Multiculturalism.* Ed. Elleke Boehmer and Sarah De Mul. Lanham, MD: Lexington Books, 2012. 203–20.

———. "Comment s'inventer un père écrivain: Albert Camus chez Maïssa Bey." *Expressions maghrébines* 14.1 (2015): 7–22.

———. *France and the Maghreb: Performative Encounters.* Gainesville: University of Florida Press, 2005.

———. *The Reparative in Narratives: Works of Mourning in Progress.* Liverpool, UK: Liverpool University Press, 2010.

Rothe, Arnold. "L'Espagne dans la littérature maghrébine." *Romanische Forschungen* 1 (1993): 67–93.

Rufat, Hélène. "À propos des dernières rencontre camusiennes: L'archipel méditerranéen d'Albert Camus." In *La Méditerranée de Audisio à Roy.* Ed. Guy Dugas. Houilles, France: Manucius, 2008. 35–45.

Said, Edward W. *Culture and Imperialism.* New York: Knopf, 1993.

Sansal, Boualem. *Alger, poste restante.* Paris: Gallimard, 2006.

Sayeh, Samira. *La Génération de 52: Conflits d'hégémonie et de dépendance. Reconsidération identitaire de la littérature algérienne en langue française d'avant l'indépendance.* Paris: Publisud, 2010.

Scharfman, Ronnie. "The Other's Other: The Moroccan Jewish Trajectory of Edmond Amran El Maleh." *Yale French Studies* 82.1 (1993): 135–45.

Sebag, Paul. *Histoire des Juifs de Tunisie: Des origines à nos jours.* Paris: L'Harmattan, 1991.

Sebai, Leila Ladjimi. *Elisha*. Tunis: L'Or du temps, 1993.

Segarra, Marta. *Leur pesant de poudre: Romancières francophones du Maghreb*. Paris: L'Harmattan, 1997.

———. "Migrant Literature: 'Jo tambè soc catalana' by Najat El Hachmi." *Mètode Science Studies Journal* 5 (2015): 75–79.

———. *Nouvelles romancières francophones*. Paris: Karthala, 2010.

Sellin, Eric. "The Algerian Novel of French Expression." *International Fiction Review* 1.1 (1974): 38–47.

Sellin, Eric, and Hédi A. Jaouad, eds. "North Africa: Literary Crossroads." Special issue, *Literary Review* 41.2 (1998).

Sénac, Jean. *Le Soleil sous les armes (Éléments d'une poésie de la résistance algérienne)*. Rodez, France: Subervie, 1957.

Serhane, Abdelhak. *Kazabal, les emmurés de Tazmamart: Mémoires de Salah et Aida Hachad*. Casablanca: Tarik, 2004.

Shannon, Jonathan. *Performing al-Andalus: Music and Nostalgia across the Mediterranean*. Bloomington: Indiana University Press, 2015.

Shavit, Yaakov. *The Hebrew Nation: A Study in Israeli Heresy and Fantasy*. London: Frank Cass, 1987.

———. "The Mediterranean World and Mediterraneanism: The Origins, Meanings and Application of a Geo-cultural Notion in Israel." *Mediterranean Historical Review* 3.2 (1988): 96–117.

Sibari, Mohamed. *Cuentos de Larache*. Larache, Morocco: AEMLE, 1998,

Siblot, Paul. "Cagayous anti-juif: Un discours colonial en prie à la racisation." *Mots* 15 (1987): 59–75.

———. "Pères spirituels et mythes fondateurs de l'Algérianisme." "Le roman colonial." Special issue, *Itinéraires et contacts de culture* 7 (1987): 29–60.

Silverstein, Paul. "France's Mare Nostrum: Colonial and Postcolonial Constructions of the French Mediterranean." *Journal of North African Studies* 7.4 (2002): 1–22.

Smith, Andrea L. *Colonial Memory and Postcolonial Europe: Maltese Settlers in Algeria and France*. Bloomington: Indiana University Press, 2006.

Smith, Kimberly. "Mere Nostalgia: Notes on a Progressive Paratheory." *Rhetoric and Public Affairs* 3.4 (2000): 505–27.

Spiquel, Agnès. "Camus: Amitiés et question(s) algériennes (1954–1960)." *French Review* 83.6 (2010): 1190–201.

Spivak, Gayatri Chakravorty. *A Critique of Postcolonial Reason: Toward a History of the Vanishing Present*. Cambridge, MA: Harvard University Press, 1999.

Stearns, Justin. "Representing and Remembering al-Andalus: Some Historical

Considerations regarding the End of Time and the Making of Nostalgia." *Medieval Encounter* 15 (2009): 355–74.

Stétié, Salah. "A Question upon a Very Old Shore." *Salahstetie*, April 10, 2014. Accessed March 23, 2015. http://salahstetie.net/?p=1007.

Stillman, Norman A. "Ghriba Synagogues." In *Encyclopaedia of Jews in the Islamic World.* Ed. Norman A. Stillman. Brill Online, 2014. Accessed December 7, 2014. http://referenceworks.brillonline.com/entries/encyclopedia-of-jews-in-the-islamic-world/ghriba-synagogies-COM_000508.

Stora, Benjamin. *La Guerre invisible: Algérie, années 90*. Paris: Presses de Sciences Po, 2001.

Suárez-Navaz, Liliana. *Rebordering the Mediterranean: Boundaries and Citizenship in Southern Europe.* New York: Berghahn Books, 2004.

Suleiman, Yasir. *The Arabic Language and National Identity: A Study in Ideology.* Edinburgh: Edinburgh University Press, 2003.

Tageldin, Shaden M. *Disarming Words: Empire and the Seductions of Translation in Egypt.* Berkeley: University of California Press, 2011.

Tahtah, M. *Entre pragmatisme, réformisme et modernisme: Le Rôle politico-religieux des Khattabi dans le Rif (Maroc) jusqu'en 1926*. Leuven: Peeters, 1999.

Talbayev, Edwige Tamalet. "Berber Poetry and the Issue of Derivation: Alternate Symbolist Trajectories." In *The Oxford Handbook of Global Modernisms.* Ed. Mark Wollaeger and Matt Eatough. Oxford: Oxford University Press, 2012. 81–108.

———. "Between Nostalgia and Desire: *L'Ecole d'Alger*'s Transnational Identifications and the Case for a Mediterranean Relation." *International Journal of Francophone Studies* 10.3 (2007): 359–76.

———. "The Languages of Translocality: What Plurilingualism Means in a Maghrebi Context." *Expressions maghrébines* 11.2 (2012): 9–26.

———."Mediterranean Criss-Crossings: Exile and Wandering in Tahar Bekri's Poetry." *Contemporary French and Francophone Studies* 17.1 (2013): 69–79.

Tambling, Jeremy. *Allegory.* New York: Routledge, 2010.

Temime, Émile. *Un Rêve méditerranéen: Des Saint-Simoniens aux intellectuels des années trente.* Arles: Actes Sud, 2002.

Thomas, Dominic. *Africa and France: Postcolonial Cultures, Migration, and Racism.* Indianapolis: Indiana University Press, 2013.

———, ed. *Afroeuropean Cartographies.* Newcastle upon Tyne, UK: Cambridge Scholars, 2014.

Tibi, Bassam. *Arab Nationalism: A Critical Enquiry.* London: Macmillan, 1990.

Tissières, Hélène Colette. *Transmigrational Writings between the Maghreb and Sub-Saharan Africa: Literature, Orality, Visual Arts.* Trans. Marjolijn de Jager. Charlottesville: University of Virginia Press, 2013.

Tlatli, Salah-Eddine. *Djerba, l'île des Lotophages.* Tunis: Cérès, 1967.

Tlatli, Soraya. "Les Ruines de l'Algérie chez Kateb Yacine." In *Hommage à Kateb Yacine.* Ed. Nabil Boudraa. Paris: L'Harmattan, 2006. 53–72.

Toumi, Alek. *Albert Camus, précurseur: Méditerranée d'hier et aujourd'hui.* New York: Peter Lang, 2009.

Udovitch, Abraham L., and Lucette Valensi. *The Last Arab Jews: The Communities of Jerba, Tunisia.* New York: Harwood Academic, 1984.

Valéry, Paul. "Inspirations méditerranéennes." In *Variétés III.* Paris: Gallimard, 1936. 243–66.

Vallejo, Ernest P. Tito. "In Pictures: The Story of the Gibraltar/Spanish Border." *New Statesman*, April 22, 2014. Accessed July 15, 2014. http://www.newstatesman.com/gibraltar/newstatesman-gibraltar/2014/04/pictures-story-gibraltarspanish-border.

Van der Poel, Ieme. "Le Drame des harragas vu de près et de loin: Youssef Amine Elalamy rencontre Hafid Bouazza." In *Littératures Africaines et Comparatisme.* Ed. Florence Paravy. Metz: Université Paul Verlaine, 2011. 155–70.

———. "Unlike(ly) Home(s): 'Self-Orientalisation' and Irony in Moroccan Diasporic Literature." In *The Postcolonial Low-Countries: Literature, Postcolonialism, and Multiculturalism.* Ed. Elleke Boehmer and Sarah De Mul. Lanham, MD: Lexington Books, 2012. 221–38.

Watson, Robert J. "Echoes of Mediterranean Plurilingualism in Contemporary Francophone Maghrebi Jewish Literature: Tunis, Alexandria, Casablanca." *Expressions maghrébines* 11.2 (2012): 125–44.

Welch, Edward, and Joseph McGonagle. *Contesting Views: The Visual Economy of France and Algeria.* Liverpool, UK: Liverpool University Press, 2013.

Wick, Alexis. "Sailing the Modern Episteme: Al-Tahtawi on the Mediterranean." *Comparative Studies of South Asia, Africa, and the Middle East* 34.2 (2014): 405–17.

Wolff, Sarah. "Border Management in the Mediterranean: Internal, External and Ethical Challenges." *Cambridge Review of International Affairs* 21.2 (2008): 253–71.

———. *The Mediterranean Dimension of the European Union's Internal Security.* Houndmills, UK: Palgrave Macmillan, 2012.

Woodhull, Winifred. "Postcolonial Thought and Culture in Francophone North Africa." In *Postcolonial Francophone Studies: A Critical*

Introduction. Ed. David Murphy and Charles Forsdick. London: Arnold, 2003. 211–20.

———. *Transfigurations of the Maghreb*. Minneapolis: University of Minnesota Press, 1993.

Xuereb, Jean-Claude. "Le Mythe al-Andalous et les écrivains algériens." Accessed July 4, 2016. http://moriscostunez.blogspot.fr/2011/06/le-mythe-al-andalous-et-les-ecrivains.html.

Yashin, Veli. "Beginning with the Mediterranean: An Introduction." *Comparative Studies of South Asia, Africa, and the Middle East* 34:2 (2014): 364–67.

Yborra Aznar, José Juan. "Espejos y espejismos: La poesía de Trino Cruz." *Eúphoros: Revista del Centro Asociado a la UNED del Campo de Gibraltar* 4 (2002): 23–37.

Zemmouri, Mohammed-Saâd. "*Le Miroir de Cordoue* de Nabile Farès, ou la quête du *lieu* inachevé." *Francofonía* 15 (2006): 239–56.

Zhiri, Oumelbanine. *L'Afrique au Miroir de l'Europe: Fortunes de Jean Léon l'Africain à la Renaissance*. Geneva: Droz, 1991.

———. "The Task of the Morisco Translator in the Early Modern Maghreb." *Expressions maghrébines* 15.1 (2016): 13–30.

Zohar, Zion. *Sephardic and Mizrahi Jewry: From the Golden Age of Spain to Modern Times*. New York: New York University Press, 2005.

INDEX